CW00751682

King Carol II

KING CAROL II

A life of my grandfather

Prince Paul of Hohenzollern-Roumania

Methuen

First published in Great Britain 1988
by Methuen London
Michelin House, 81 Fulham Road, London SW3 6RB

© Prince Paul of Hohenzollern-Roumania, 1988

Printed in Great Britain
by Richard Clay Ltd, Bungay, Suffolk

British Library Cataloguing in Publication Data

Paul, *Prince of Romania*
King Carol: a life of my grandfather.
1. Romania. Carol II, King of Romania
I. Title
949.8′02′0924

ISBN 0-413-16570-1

Contents

List of Illustrations

Acknowledgements

First and foremost I must thank my literary agent, Jeffrey Simmons, without whom this book might never have appeared. I have been given great help by members of my family, including my father, Prince Carol Mircea, and my great-aunts, Princess Nicolas and Princess Ileana (the Reverend Mother Alexandra). I am also particularly indebted to Mrs Monique Urdarianu, widow of King Carol II's Lord Chamberlain, and to the Academy of History of Portugal and its President Mr Verisimo Serraõ.

The following people in particular were helpful to me in matters of translation, genealogy and history: Mr Jean Burca, nephew of Roumania's famous statesman Titulescu; Miss Angela Clark, student in Roumanian history, London University; Mrs Lulu Miclescu; Mr Manuel Noronhe y Andrade; Mr Frederico Horta y Costa; Mme Synodino, daughter of Roumania's Vice Admiral Vasile Scodrea; Mrs Alexandra Dimancescu; Mrs Sanda Miller; Princess George zu Beitheim und Steinfurt; the Suddeutsche Zeitung Archives, Munich; the staff of the Public Record Office in Kew, notably Mr Howard Davies; Professor Aurelia Rauta in Madrid; and last but not least, Dr Dennis Deletant of the School of Slavonic and East European Studies at London University.

Preface

I have had it in mind for some time to write this biography of my grandfather, King Carol II of Roumania. I do not think that justice has been done to his memory. He was a man who cared deeply for his country and the welfare of its people, and who fought hard to maintain Roumania's independence. King Carol II's vitality made him live life at its fullest; he enjoyed driving racing-cars and piloting his own aircraft. Although the belief that he gave up his throne for his mistress is not totally correct, his love for Elena Lupescu, better known as Magda, is perhaps the royal romance of the century to rival that of Edward VIII and Mrs Simpson. Popular writers, including Barbara Cartland in England and Guy des Cars in France, have written about this love affair, which has helped to emphasize one side only of my grandfather's story.

His relationships with women are undoubtedly a very important part of his story. His earlier love for, and runaway marriage to my grandmother, Ioana Lambrino, usually called Zizi, is in its way equally as fascinating as his love for Magda Lupescu; and there is of course his marriage to Princess Helen of Greece, the mother of my uncle King Michael who succeeded Carol II as King of Roumania. In many ways, however, the woman who played the biggest part in his life, certainly during some critical times in his early career, was his very remarkable mother, Queen Marie – the English Princess who was the daughter of Queen Victoria's second son Alfred, Duke of Edinburgh. She published an autobiography in three volumes, and indeed Ioana Lambrino wrote a memoir of my grandfather, further stressing the female connection.

I am concerned that this understandable emphasis should not be allowed to detract from my grandfather's achievements in other fields. His playboy image has not been invented but it has succeeded

[handwritten marginalia: Affie]

[handwritten at bottom: ✷ Missy: Mother → Marie of Russia 1875–1938]

in obscuring his other activities. I want to show that he had a serious side, a political one.

At the end of this book, the reader will find a bibliography. It is not intended to be comprehensive, nor does the inclusion of a book imply that I approve of it. I have merely listed the books to which I have referred in the text and others that have proved very useful to me. They range from R. W. Seton-Watson's superb history of the Roumanians and Hannah Pakula's admirably researched life of Queen Marie, to works of an extremely ephemeral character. It will be seen that very few books indeed have been published which are specifically about King Carol II.

Ioana Lambrino's short biography appeared towards the end of my grandfather's life and was devoted almost exclusively to her limited personal knowledge of a man to whom she was married for a very short time. The only biography of my grandfather with claims to seriousness, that by Baroness von der Hoven, appeared thirteen years before his death and cannot therefore be regarded as in any way complete. It is a somewhat romantic work, supposedly based on personal knowledge but in fact heavily reliant on other sources. Various other books have dealt only with certain aspects of his life, and most were very poorly documented.

What finally prompted me to write the first complete biography of my grandfather is the vast quantity of documentary material that came into my possession in 1985. My grandfather's diaries were bequeathed to the Academy of History in Lisbon, in a special ceremony in which I had the honour to be involved, and I was thus one of the first to review and study them. They are perhaps more revealing than Queen Marie's diaries in the Casa Regala archives in Bucharest because she has already told her long story at length. I also have in my possession the seven notebooks in which my grandfather reflected on the political scene following the Treaty of Versailles. They were written in 1945 in his own hand while in Brazil, and they bear the title 'Orbit of Satan'. Among other sources I have used documents from my grandfather's library, as well as a large collection of photographs and many hundreds of personal letters and other communications with political and royal personalities of the time, including King George VI, Winston Churchill and Franklin Roosevelt.

Of particular interest are some letters from Queen Marie, among them the last letter she wrote to her son before her death; they show a different side to her character from that occasionally revealed in her published writings. Even since starting the book, my great-aunt Princess Nicolas, widow of King Carol's brother, has kindly provided me with many photographs, personal documents and diaries which were very revealing.

A problem for any biographer of a Roumanian is how to deal with proper names. Charles and Carol, for example, are interchangeable. The same person may in different countries be referred to as Elena, Helen, Helena or Helene. I have tried where possible to adopt a simple English usage or the version most commonly used.

There is also a problem with dates. Before 1900, the countries that used the Gregorian calendar were fourteen days ahead of those that used the Julian calendar; after 1900 this was reduced to thirteen days. Although the Russians adopted the Gregorian calendar in January 1918, it was not until June 1924, when the Orthodox Church in Roumania followed the Russian example, that Roumanian dates finally coincided with, for instance, British dates. The Julian calendar had been used in Moldavia and Wallachia at a time when the Gregorian calendar was in use in Transylvania, but when this latter province was finally incorporated into Roumania in December 1918, it became usual to give two dates thirteen days apart. When dealing with exclusively Roumanian affairs, I have usually adopted the calendar in use at the relevant time.

Roumania in 1893

Baltic Sea

Moscow

GERMANY

Berlin

Minsk

Warsaw

RUSSIAN EMPIRE

Prague

Kiev

Ukraine

AUSTRO - HUNGARIAN

Vienna

R. Danube

Budapest

Bistritza

R. Prut

Bessarabia

Jassy

Odessa

Cluj

Transylvania

Moldavia

EMPIRE

Timisoara

Alba
Julia

Tecouci

Jimbolia

Lugoj

Predeal

Sinaia

ROUMANIA

Curtea
de Arges

Ploesti

Bosnia-
Herzegovina

Belgrade

Turnu
Severin

Wallachia

Dobruja

Constantza

Sarajevo

SERBIA

Bucharest

Black Sea

MONTENEGRO

R. Danube

Adriatic

BULGARIA

Sea

Bicaj

Sofia

ITALY

OTTOMAN

Constantinople

O D

EMPIRE

Aegean

GREECE

Sea

Roumania
after the First
World War

Baltic Sea

Danzig

East
Prussia
(GERMANY)

GERMANY

•Berlin

•Warsaw

•Brest-Litovsk

Breslau•

P O L A N D

•Prague

C Z E C H O S L O V A K I A

Vienna•
AUSTRIA

R. Danube

Budapest•

H U N G A R Y

Transylvania
•Cluj

R O U M A N I A

Banat •Timişoara
•Jimbolia   Alba Julia•   Brasov•
Lugoj•   Transylvanian Alps
Predeal•
Belgrade•   Curtea   •Sinaia
de Arges
•Ploesti
Wallachia   •Bucharest

Sarajevo•

Y U G O S L A V I A

R. Danube

U S S R

•Kiev

Ukraine

R. Dniester

Bukovina

Moldavia   Jassy•
R. Prut
Bessarabia

Kishinev•

•Odessa

Dobruja

Constantza

Black

Sea

Adriatic

Sea

ITALY

ALBANIA

Sofia•

B U L G A R I A

Salonika•

GREECE

Constantinople
(Istanbul)

T U R K E Y

Dardanelles

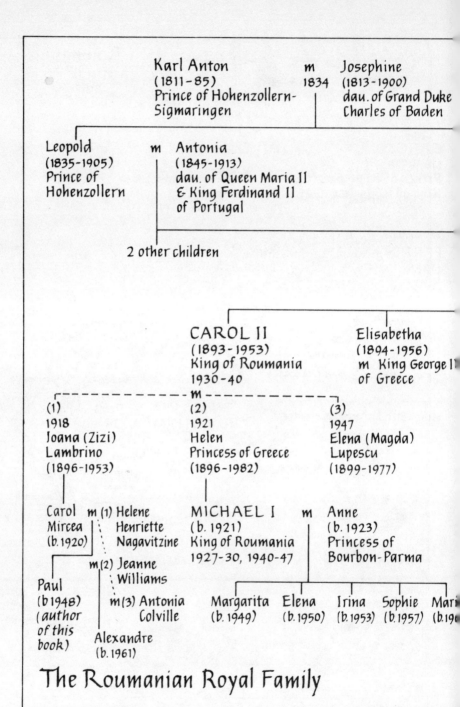

Karl Anton **m** Josephine
(1811-85) 1834 (1813-1900)
Prince of Hohenzollern- dau. of Grand Duke
Sigmaringen Charles of Baden

Leopold **m** Antonia
(1835-1905) (1845-1913)
Prince of dau. of Queen Maria II
Hohenzollern & King Ferdinand II
of Portugal

2 other children

CAROL II Elisabetha
(1893-1953) (1894-1956)
King of Roumania **m** King George II
1930-40 of Greece

---------------- **m** ----------------

(1) (2) (3)
1918 1921 1947
Joana (Zizi) Helen Elena (Magda)
Lambrino Princess of Greece Lupescu
(1896-1953) (1896-1982) (1899-1977)

Carol **m (1)** Helene MICHAEL I **m** Anne
Mircea Henriette (b. 1921) (b. 1923)
(b.1920) Nagavitzine King of Roumania Princess of
1927-30, 1940-47 Bourbon-Parma
m(2) Jeanne
Paul Williams
(b 1948)
(author **m(3)** Antonia Margarita Elena Irina Sophie Mari
of this Colville (b. 1949) (b.1950) (b.1953) (b.1957) (b.19
book) Alexandre
(b. 1961)

The Roumanian Royal Family

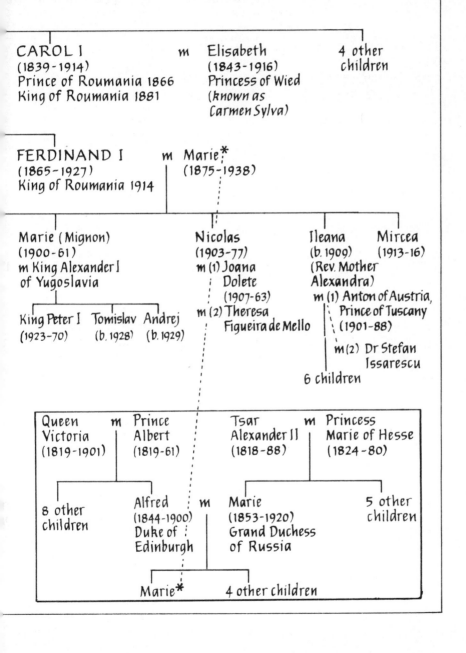

CAROL I   m   Elisabeth   4 other
(1839-1914)   (1843-1916)   children
Prince of Roumania 1866   Princess of Wied
King of Roumania 1881   (known as
                               Carmen Sylva)

FERDINAND I   m   Marie*
(1865-1927)   (1875-1938)
King of Roumania 1914

Marie (Mignon)   Nicolas   Ileana   Mircea
(1900-61)   (1903-77)   (b.1909)   (1913-16)
m King Alexander I   m (1) Joana   (Rev. Mother
of Yugoslavia   Dolete   Alexandra)
                                (1907-63)   m (1) Anton of Austria,
                            m (2) Theresa   Prince of Tuscany
King Peter I Tomislav Andrej   Figueira de Mello   (1901-88)
(1923-70)   (b.1928) (b.1929)
                                                     m (2) Dr Stefan
                                                           Issarescu
                                            6 children

Queen   m Prince   Tsar   m Princess
Victoria   Albert   Alexander II   Marie of Hesse
(1819-1901)   (1819-61)   (1818-88)   (1824-80)

8 other   Alfred   m Marie   5 other
children   (1844-1900)   (1853-1920)   children
                 Duke of   Grand Duchess
                 Edinburgh   of Russia

                 Marie*   4 other children

The Background

Before examining the life of my grandfather, it is necessary to give a very brief idea of the world into which he was born, and to explain how Roumania became a kingdom, in order to set King Carol's story in perspective. There are slightly differing theories about the origins of the Roumanian people but we need hardly go back further than the beginning of the second century AD when the Romans defeated the Dacians, who occupied the area from which modern Roumania arose. The Dacians sprang from the Getae, who in turn were almost certainly a Thracian tribe. The Romans occupied the country for 168 years before withdrawing, but they left a lasting legacy, having spread their civilization and language among the people, who adopted many Roman customs.

Modern Roumania is a political creation, but it is also a natural one in the sense that its people descend largely from an indigenous group that has lived in the area for over two thousand years, speaking the same neo-Latin language since the Roman occupation. This has helped maintain a strong nationalistic conscience that has kept alive the idea of a Roumanian identity even when the constituent parts of the country have been pawns in a game played by more powerful neighbouring countries.

For a thousand years after the departure of the Romans, the people kept their independence under the control of local chieftains, without any central organization, and in 1185 an alliance of Bulgarians and Roumanians who lived in the area that is now Bulgaria formed a short-lived and so-called Empire. But modern Roumania began with the establishment of the two provinces of Moldavia and Wallachia in the thirteenth and fourteenth centuries. Originally governed by lords or hospodars, they eventually became principalities, but, although they prospered, they could not avoid the attentions of the envious Turks.

Three great Roumanian champions of Christianity helped to keep the Ottoman Empire at bay – John Corvin, Duke of Transylvania, whose son became King of Hungary; Stephen the Great, Prince of Moldavia; and Michael the Brave, Prince of Wallachia. Michael actually succeeded in uniting the three main parts of modern Roumania for a short time in the sixteenth century; and although the union quickly broke up, Transylvania eventually being annexed by Austria in 1699, all three managed to resist the advance of Islam and escaped becoming Turkish provinces.

Moldavia and Wallachia were not strong enough, however, completely to thwart the Turks. They signed separate treaties with the Porte which, in return for the payment of tributes and an agreement to military service, left them with a large measure of self-rule and religious freedom. It was their proud boast that although they were virtually vassals of the Ottomans, there were no mosques or Turkish landlords on Roumanian soil.

As the power of the Ottoman Empire began to wane in the area, the Roumanian provinces were caught up in the struggles between the Turks on the one side and the Austrians and the Russians on the other. Having already annexed Transylvania, in 1775 Austria occupied that part of north-western Moldavia known as Bukovina. When in 1812 Russia took possession of Bessarabia, the eastern part of Moldavia, Roumania as a nation seemed doomed.

There were signs, however, of a revival of political and national sentiment towards the end of the eighteenth century. This led to a series of peasant revolts, beginning in 1784 in Transylvania, to protest at economic conditions. In 1821 the Wallachian peasants took action to rid themselves of the hated Greek administrators whom the Turks had installed.

The effect of events in Paris in 1848 was felt strongly in Bucharest and gave a fillip to the elite group of intellectuals who were struggling to revive a Roumanian culture that would lead eventually to the complete independence of the Roumanian territories. Almost immediately, an insurrection led to the formation of a provincial government in Bucharest which quickly produced a constitution that guaranteed the freedom of the press and abolished both serfdom and certain privileges of the nobility. Its success was temporary because neither Russia nor Turkey could tolerate such revolutionary concepts on their doorsteps and, in a joint action, they restored matters to an even worse state than previously. If however the Roumanian people had taken one step forward and two backward, they had at last been seized by the will to progress.

It was as a result of the Crimean War that the independence of Moldavia and Wallachia was at last guaranteed by the great European Powers, and in 1859 the two provinces chose Alexander Cuza as their joint ruler. He became the first Prince of the two united provinces, and was known as Alexander Jean I. He is best remembered in Roumanian history for uniting the two provinces, but his policies were a mixed bag and he was forced to abdicate in 1866 and leave the country permanently.

A short period of great uncertainty followed, during which Roumania's fate as a nation was again in the balance. The Russians and the Turks had acquiesced reluctantly, and with reservations, to the union, and they were not the only countries opposed to a united Roumania. Any apparent weakness or instability in Bucharest could well have resulted in intervention, and the Roumanian leaders knew that they had to appoint a new Prince without delay, thereby presenting the Great Powers with a situation that would cause more trouble to unscramble than to accept.

Their choice fell on the Count of Flanders, the younger brother of the King of Belgium, but he declined the position, under influence from Napoleon III. Finally they fixed on Prince Charles of Hohenzollern. A plebiscite was held in which the people approved the appointment, and a delegate was dispatched to Dusseldorf to offer Charles the slightly dubious honour of becoming Prince of Roumania. He was willing to accept but not without the blessing of the head of his family, the King of Prussia, who in turn was nervous about the response of the French. He was persuaded by Bismarck that the only way to force the other Powers to accept Charles was to present them with a *fait accompli*, which was exactly in line with the thinking of the Roumanian leaders.

So nervous were many of the people involved that Prince Charles travelled secretly to Roumania in the guise of a businessman. After a somewhat perilous journey, he crossed the Roumanian border, and news of his arrival brought together enormous and enthusiastic crowds in every town *en route* to the capital. On arrival in Bucharest, he was received at the cathedral by the Metropolitan, the head of the Roumanian Orthodox Church, and then proceeded to take the oath as ruler of the country on his twenty-seventh birthday, 20 April 1866, only two months after Alexander's forced abdication.

The Turks took immediate objection but were finally persuaded to accept Charles as hereditary Prince of the united provinces, which they agreed to recognize henceforth as Roumania, although they still claimed the territory, at least in name, as part of the Ottoman Empire. Thereafter Charles would be received in Constantinople as a Head of State, and the new Roumania would be entitled to maintain an army of 30,000 men.

Charles's most outstanding achievement was probably to organize the army on Prussian lines, with the latest German armament. By the time the inevitable war broke out between Russia and Turkey in 1877, Roumania had over 50,000 well-trained troops and a reserve force even larger. The Roumanians of course wanted to be entirely free from the Turkish yoke and would gladly have supported Russia, but the Russians sought only limited help until they became bogged down against the entrenched Turkish positions at Plevna. When now they called on Charles for real assistance, he proved an exceptionally tough negotiator and insisted on assuming personal command of the joint Russian-Roumanian force, with which he agreed to assault the Turkish troops under Osman Pasha. Charles's army suffered appalling losses but just when the situation seemed hopeless, the Roumanian contingent made a last-minute breakthrough. This was the turn of the tide. The Russians finally triumphed and Roumania won complete independence from the Ottoman Empire.

Prince Charles returned in triumph to Bucharest where, on 10 May 1881, he was crowned the first King of Roumania, becoming known as Carol I, to adopt the Roumanian equivalent of his name. His crown was fashioned of steel from a Turkish cannon captured at Plevna.

Carol's wife, Queen Elisabeth, was the daughter of the Prince of Wied. She was better known as Carmen Sylva, the *nom de plume* she adopted for her poetry and other writings, which were widely published throughout Europe. She surrounded herself with a group of intellectuals, artists and writers, and her gatherings became quite famous in Bucharest, helping to earn the capital city its reputation as '*le petit Paris*' of the Balkans.

She bore Charles a daughter, who died suddenly from scarlet fever when only six years old, and she never had another child. The King therefore brought his nephew Ferdinand to Roumania in 1886 to secure the succession, making him official heir to the throne. The son of Carol's eldest brother Leopold, he was named after his mother's father, King Ferdinand II of Portugal. Significantly, in view of what was to happen later to my grandfather, Ferdinand was forbidden by the King on political grounds to marry the woman he loved, Helena Vacarescu. She was a charming lady and a close friend of, and lady-in-waiting to, the Queen; but she was a Roumanian, and this was a fatal bar to her marrying the heir to the throne. Almost certainly to avoid friction internally, the King was determined that Ferdinand should seek a wife from among the available foreign princesses.

When Ferdinand fell in love with Helena Vacarescu, a liaison fostered by the romantic Queen, the King took severe action. He obliged the young man to choose between Helena and the throne, but in fact left him no alternative by sending him out of the country on an extended trip. Not content with this, he also sent the Queen to join her mother in Wied. She did not return to Roumania for two years, but Ferdinand was back much sooner. It is said that he wandered Europe broken-hearted, and perhaps he did for a time, but when he came back he surprised many people by bringing with him a bride; and even more people by his choice of bride, for she was none other than Princess Mary, granddaughter of Queen Victoria. Her father was Prince Alfred, Duke of Edinburgh, and her mother was Princess Marie Alexandrovna, only daughter of Tsar Alexander II of Russia.

We have no means of knowing Ferdinand's state of mind when he married Marie, as she became known in Roumania. She wrote about the three wedding ceremonies, religious and civil, in her memoirs, but she was not yet eighteen at the time of the marriage and can hardly have been aware of her husband's feelings for Helena Vacarescu. Perhaps he was no longer in love with Helena; in any case it would not have been difficult to fall in love with the beautiful young girl whom he married. The only thing that is certain is that he clearly put the throne ahead of any other consideration.

The meeting of the two young people had in fact been arranged secretly by King Carol, who of course was delighted with the outcome. Roumania's new Princess was a lovely, intelligent and highly romantic girl. She developed into a dominating figure whose character inevitably influenced her children. Ferdinand, who was just over ten years her senior, was on the other hand a quiet, easy-going man of shy temperament who used his wife to carry messages to the people. It was this that later helped to fuel the widespread belief that Ferdinand was weak and Marie was strong. In fact they complemented each other admirably.

The Beautiful Boy
with Golden Curls

There is no lack of information about the world in which my grandfather grew up, which is a matter of historical record. But there is no one living who can speak with personal experience of his childhood: a contemporary would today be over ninety years old. Of his brothers and sisters, only Princess Ileana is still alive. She resides in a monastery in the United States where she is known as the Reverend Mother Alexandra, but she was born in 1909 when her eldest brother was already a youth of fifteen, so even she cannot talk about his childhood except at second-hand.

From the limited sources at our disposal, what can we reliably say about his childhood? The facts are not of course in dispute. Prince Carol was born on 15 October 1893, only nine months and five days after his parent's marriage. If King Carol I was pleased with his nephew Ferdinand's choice of bride, he must have been doubly pleased that the couple had so quickly produced a son to secure the succession to the throne. The baby was born at the extraordinary Castle Peles, a fairy-tale peculiarity of a building constructed at enormous expense by King Carol so that his court could escape to the cooler Carpathian Mountains from the humidity of Bucharest in the summer. The castle was located at Sinaia, which was virtually the summer capital of Roumania, at least for those well enough placed or rich enough to enjoy its extensive facilities, including its famous casino.

Exactly two weeks later, on his mother's eighteenth birthday, the new Prince Carol was christened. His mother described him as her 'beautiful boy with golden curls'. 'From the very first,' she wrote, 'Carol was a big, healthy and exceedingly amiable baby.'

It was not long before he had a sister. Less than a week before his first birthday, his mother gave birth to her first daughter, who was later to become Queen of Greece and who died in 1956. The girl was named Elisabetha after the Queen, who was almost as well known by her *nom de plume* of Carmen Sylva, and who had returned home after almost two years' virtual exile just before Marie's confinement.

Marie was later to describe a world in which she and her husband, Crown Prince Ferdinand, very much played second fiddle to the autocratic King, especially in matters concerning the upbringing of their own children. 'The central figure of our world,' she wrote, 'was King Carol . . . dominating all those dependent on him. . . . We were entirely hemmed in, controlled, over-ruled.'

It was over five years before a third child was born, and both the King and Queen in their different ways sought to order the lives of young Carol and Elisabetha. 'My children were the central interest of my life,' Marie recorded, but she had to defer to others in many matters that she regarded as her proper concern. It was not altogether a happy time for her, a foreigner at the Roumanian court, and indeed it took her twenty years before she was fully accepted and loved by the Roumanian people. She had to contend with a stolid, scheming King, his feet very much on the ground, and a romantic, fantasizing Queen with her head in the clouds, who 'could never resign herself to a normal atmosphere'. She contrasted the royal couple rather poetically as like 'ice and fire', and this did not make for easy relationships.

Marie found that her husband was not strong enough, or did not have the will, to support her against the King in matters concerning their own children. In many respects Ferdinand was a typical army officer, trained to uphold authority, and not the type of man to encourage a rebellious streak, or even independence, in his wife. He had himself already submitted to the King's insistence that he give up his former lover Helena Vacarescu. A shy man, perhaps even unsure of himself except in military matters, his principal interest was botany, although as relations became more strained with his forceful young wife, he began to indulge in extra-marital affairs.

Fortunately Marie liked the first nanny chosen for the children by the King. She was Mary Green, an elderly and highly experienced Englishwoman who had 'served several royal families' in England and Russia. Marie described her as 'a figure worthy of Dickens . . . a motherly soul . . . broad of girth, loud-voiced and jovial, she did not mince her words'. What especially endeared her to the Crown Princess was that 'she feared no man. . . . I have seen old Green stand up fiercely before stern King Carol, arms akimbo, and give him, in atrocious French, a piece of her mind. . . .' Apparently both the King and the children's father were in awe of her, and she supported Marie at troublesome times.

In his biography of Queen Marie, Terence Elsberry referred to a postcard written by the younger Carol to Miss Green, thanking her for the present of an ink-bottle, which may well be the first communication ever penned by him (although no date is given), and Baroness von der Hoven told an amusing little story of how Miss Green threatened to box the ears of a coachman who was driving a carriage too fast for her liking. My grandfather, who was in the carriage with her at the time, later told the Baroness that this minor experience, presumably one of his first memories, had stayed with him into adult life. He had thought Miss Green meant somehow literally to imprison the coachman's ears in a box.

Even when, after three years of married life, Ferdinand and Marie moved into a home of their own, the palace of Cotroceni on the outskirts of the capital, they were still under the watchful eyes of the King and Queen, but this attempt at supervision was directed more at the children than at the parents. The King was primarily concerned with the fact that Prince Carol, in the natural order of things, would one day inherit the crown, and he regarded the boy's upbringing therefore as a matter of legitimate personal interest. Ferdinand himself had already assumed the mould that the King required of him and since being forced to give up his mistress, the Crown Prince had been no problem to the King. A much more likely source of trouble was the high-spirited and somewhat romantic young Marie, with her liberally foreign ideas about how to bring up a future heir to the throne.

Had the King been watchful of the parents, he would have observed the growing tension between them that could well have affected the young Prince's character more than the minor matters with which he did concern himself. Although they appeared very much in love at first, it was not long before Marie was complaining about her husband's attitude to her. His sexual indiscretions were probably less important to her than the fact that she found him inattentive and without sufficient thought for her. As a British diplomat in Bucharest was later to report to the Foreign Office in London, 'a taste for somewhat indiscriminate fornication' was a feature of life among the Roumanian upper classes, and Hannah Pakula, in her excellent biography of Queen Marie, wrote of Ferdinand having 'conquered one of Marie's best friends and one of her ladies-in-waiting'. The young wife can hardly have been unaware of this.

Perhaps it is not surprising that Marie was driven to seek consolation elsewhere, and in other ways. She loved dancing, but above all she loved riding. It was, in her own words, 'my greatest accomplishment . . . it was a sport at which few could beat me.' And in due course she came to love a man, who paradoxically was appointed by the King as an aide-de-camp during her husband's illness.

Ferdinand was struck down in May 1897 with typhoid fever and seemed at the point of death. Marie was summoned from bed to bid him farewell and the final rites were pronounced. Ferdinand, however, recovered and in August of that year, Lieutenant Zizi Cantacuzene was introduced into the household at the King's instigation, presumably to afford Marie some male support while her husband was desperately ill. Cantacuzene was not a particularly handsome man, but he had one accomplishment that endeared him to Marie: he was an excellent and attentive riding companion.

That winter, Ferdinand was sent to Nice to convalesce, on the advice of his doctors, and Marie went with him. They were both heavily chaperoned by people chosen by the King to accompany them. When Marie tried to include Cantacuzene in the party, the King vetoed the suggestion and accused her of being over-friendly with her aide. Strangely, however, on her return to Roumania she found that 'this absolutely insignificant person', as the King had described him, had now been appointed to teach her son gymnastics.

Whatever the relationship had been before the visit to Nice, there is no doubt that following the return it developed into a love affair. Gossip about it even reached the ears of Queen Victoria in England. Eventually Cantacuzene was sent abroad and the King reprimanded Marie with splendid honesty: 'We of course all know that Nando [as the family called Ferdinand] may not be so very entertaining but that does not mean that you may find your entertainment elsewhere.'

This was Marie's first extra-marital affair but not her last. She became reconciled with Nando and their third child was born in January 1900. This was Marie, known as Mignon, who later became Queen of Yugoslavia and who died in 1961.

But before then, Marie was faced with a great crisis in her life. Her romance with an army officer had made her even more vulnerable to those who wished to control her two children. Carmen

Sylva in particular sought to bring discredit on Marie to take the care of the children further out of their mother's hands, and she insisted on the appointment of a new governess to look after Prince Carol. The choice fell on the formidable Miss Winter, whom Marie identified in her memoirs as Miss W.

How much the young Carol knew about the relationships between the King and Queen and his parents, or about his parents' extra-marital activities, and how if at all this impinged on him, is a matter of speculation. He was just over five years old when his new governess took charge of him, and although he may have been ignorant of the reasons behind it, he is unlikely to have missed the antagonism between his mother and the woman she described as her 'arch enemy'.

Marie wrote complainingly of the governess's 'two years' reign'. In fact Miss Winter arrived in January 1899 and left in April 1900, so her rule of the nursery obviously seemed longer to Marie than it was. Miss Winter however kept in touch with the family, or at least her main charge, after her departure. Among my grandfather's books, there is a copy of *A Gordon Highlander* by E. Everett-Green, inscribed 'Xmas 1900. Prince Carol from his loving old friend, E Saxton Winter', which was presumably a Christmas present from her to my grandfather.

A loving old friend she may have been to the boy, but to his mother she was a poisonous and hostile spy imposed on her at the instigation of the Queen to alienate her from her son. Like so many royal governesses at the time, she was English, and had impeccable qualifications, but Marie took an instant dislike to her, describing her as 'thick set, heavy with staring, goggle-eyes' and a 'repulsive mouth'. In one of the put-downs of all time, she dismissed her as 'common, with a commonness that only one of her own nationality could rightly appreciate'. It has been alleged that Miss Winter instructed her charge to omit the words 'God bless Mamma' from his prayers and that she tried to turn the boy against his mother, making him deeply unhappy. If this is true, Marie had cause to see the governess as a monster.

When Marie became pregnant with Mignon, she went to stay with her mother in Gotha. While there, she received the dreadful news that her son had contracted typhoid fever, the illness that had almost killed her husband. She rushed back home. The child, just short of his sixth birthday, was near to death; but like his father, he, too, recovered. Marie's loathing of Miss Winter was increased when the governess evidently tried to stop her seeing her child immediately and, if Baroness von der Hoven is to be believed, cruelly implied to Marie that the doctors did not expect the boy to live.

It was Marie's mother who eventually took the initiative to get rid of Miss Winter. Not for nothing was the Duchess of Edinburgh, now the Duchess of Saxe-Coburg-Gotha, the daughter-in-law of Queen Victoria and the daughter of Tsar Alexander II. She insisted that Marie return to Gotha for her confinement, upbraided King Carol for allowing scandal about her daughter to have circulated so widely – while in no way condoning her behaviour – and finally demanded the dismissal of the offending governess.

When Marie returned to Roumania in the spring of 1900, she was at last rid of Miss Winter, who was replaced by someone much more to her liking. Although almost anyone would have been more to her liking than Miss Winter, Miss ffolliott (as her name was correctly spelt) was more acceptable in every way. Unlike her predecessor, this Irish woman treated the Crown Princess with the respect due to her position. Marie's household was suddenly a much happier place. Her mother's strictures were taken to heart, not only by Marie herself but to some extent by the King, especially when there was evidence that the Queen had encouraged Miss Winter to undermine Marie's authority and malign her reputation.

The young Carol's new governess seems to have encouraged his reading; in my grandfather's library are two books that she gave to him: *For the Colours: A Boy's Book of the Army* by Herbert Hayens, which bears the inscription 'Xmas 1901. Prince Carol, from A ffolliott'; and *From Tokyo through Manchuria with the Japanese* by Louis Livingston Seaman, inscribed 'Prince Carol, from A L ff Oct 1905'. In later years my grandfather became a voracious reader, particularly enjoying historical works and novels, including detective stories. It has been said that he could begin a book in the evening and finish it before going to bed, and that he started this practice in childhood. He signed all the books he read and kept, usually with the date and place, so I have a fascinating record of his reading habits.

It is instructive, at this early period of his life, to see what other people considered suitable reading for him. Miss Winter in 1900, when he was just seven, and Miss ffolliot the following year and in 1905 just before he was twelve, were offering him military books. He himself later wrote a short book, published in Jassy in 1917 and entitled *The Story of a Wounded Soldier*, confirming his interest in this subject.

His parents gave him different sorts of books, reflecting their different tastes. His father, who was something of a linguist and spoke Roumanian, English, German, French and Russian, gave his son books in German, Ferdinand's native language. As an adult, my grandfather inherited something of this linguistic ability but Marie reported that it was a long time before he mastered German. Perhaps that is why in 1910 Ferdinand gave his son a German encyclopedia, inscribed simply '*für Carol*'. A year earlier he had given him a two-volume edition of a book entitled *Transhimalaja*, in which he wrote '*für unserer lieben Carol*', and a German translation of Shackleton's account of his expedition to the South Pole.

If that says something about his father's tastes, what of the books his mother gave him? There was nothing military or adventurous in her choice of suitable reading. For Christmas 1913 she gave him *The Russian Ballet* by A. E. Johnson, illustrated by René Boll. In October 1916, with the inscription 'For Carol from Mama. War!', she gave him a truly *de luxe* edition of *La Nuit Venétienne* by Alfred de Musset, with marvellous illustrations by U. Brunelleschi. Although my grandfather was no longer a child at the time of these gifts, they indicate the influences that the markedly different tastes of his parents had on him.

In August 1903, when Prince Carol was nearly ten, his first brother was born. Nicolas, the fourth child, became something of a favourite in the family, especially with the King, while to my grandfather he remained very much the little brother. The relationship between the parents was now reasonably happy but there is no doubt that the year before Marie had been mightily smitten on a visit to England for the coronation of Edward VII. It was then that she met Pauline and Waldorf Astor, grandchildren of John Jacob Astor III from whom their father had inherited one of the very greatest American fortunes. Marie, Pauline and Waldorf became firm friends and there is little doubt that Marie fell in love with Waldorf, although most informed opinion is that their relationship remained platonic. Indeed, as Marie wrote to Pauline after Waldorf's marriage to the woman who would become famous as Nancy Astor, 'It was not as if he had been my lover'. The announcement of the marriage nevertheless deeply upset her and although she came to rely heavily on the friendship of brother and sister in later years, her relationship with Nancy was always rather uncomfortable.

The Astors played a big part in the life of Marie and were thus part of the background in which Carol grew up, but as a boy he was probably little aware of their existence. It was not for another five years after the meeting with Waldorf, and a year after his marriage, that Marie met the man with whom she would next fall in love. By then, Carol was thirteen and much more likely to have been aware of what was going on.

Meanwhile, some light on his life and character as a child in the palace is thrown by Baroness von der Hoven, who wrote of him listening excitedly to military bands and attending the Changing of the Guard, with his tiny sword drawn, issuing commands in a high-pitched voice to the soldiers and imagining that they were actually responding to him. She gave his age as eleven when he attended his first parade in uniform, which she said left a lasting impression on him. This ties in with Marie's account that he was receptive to learning about military matters and enthusiastic about uniforms, regulations and discipline. In fact Marie described him as 'a born soldier'.

'Carol was all order and precision,' his mother recorded, which reflects the Baroness's observation that he developed 'bureaucratic tendencies'. She gave as an example the story of my grandfather erecting a barrier in the palace corridor where the children played. He cut slips of paper which he used as receipts for the money that he obliged his brother and sisters to pay him to open the barrier and let them through. She did not say whether real or imaginary money passed hands but used this instance of the 'frontier toll', as she aptly called it, to illustrate my grandfather's attitude that 'things had to be done properly'. She also wrote that my grandfather invented a book of rules for a tennis club started for the royal children and their friends, but as he was the first child in age and rank, too much should not perhaps be made of this.

The year 1907 was a difficult one for Roumania, and Carol, at thirteen, was old enough to be at least superficially aware of what was happening. The two major Roumanian political parties, the Conservatives and the Liberals, were divided on traditional lines. The Conservatives were the party of the gentry and the agricultural population, while the Liberals represented largely industrial and urban interests. Because of effective Liberal opposition, the Conservative plan to establish an agrarian bank to help the farmers had collapsed; and although the Conservative government had been in power for three years, they had been able to do little for the agricultural community, who felt that nobody was effectively representing their interests. As Dr R. W. Seton-Watson put it, 'Roumania was one of the most fertile agricultural countries in Europe, and yet, as the more far-sighted of her sons recognised, the peasant was sunk in misery and neglect and had no say in the government of a country of which he was the real backbone.'

The dangerous outcome, although it had been foreseen by a number of intellectuals, took almost everybody by surprise. A serious peasant revolt, largely directed at the big tenant farmers and absentee landlords, started as if spontaneously on 15 March in Moldavia and quickly spread throughout the country. Even the army was unable to restore order, and there were occasions when troops were outnumbered by protestors. Within ten days the government resigned and the King called on the Liberals to form an administration.

The authorities were totally unprepared for this uprising, which took a very ugly turn. There were pitched battles between government troops and large rebel groups demanding the break-up of the great estates. There was also massive destruction of property. A number of concessions to the peasants failed to satisfy them, at which point the government reacted as governments usually do in circumstances where there is a serious threat to the established order: they sought to crush the rebellion ruthlessly.

In this they were supported by neighbouring countries looking anxiously over their shoulder at a situation that was in danger of getting out of hand and resulting in anarchy. Indeed anti-Semitic and anarchic elements attached themselves to the peasant cause, encouraging attacks on banks and Jewish establishments. More importantly, the middle classes rallied to the side of the authorities. Even those who may have supported the aims of the peasants could not condone their methods, or accept the results of their protest, even if this meant turning a blind eye to the brutal force that was applied to crush the rebellion. The new Liberal Prime Minister and the Conservative Leader of the Opposition shook hands and allowed General Averescu, the Minister of War, a free hand. As Dr Seton-Watson pointed out, the peasants were pursued by flying columns of troops and mounted artillery, villages were bombarded, destroyed and even burnt to the ground, and an estimated 10,000 peasants were killed in three days.

The official records of what was virtually a minor civil war were mysteriously and conveniently allowed to disappear, and although the King later published in Germany a four-volume account of his life, he did not even refer to the peasant issue. Neither did Queen Marie in her lengthy memoirs. She certainly had many things on her mind, but the peasant revolt was not one of them.

Force prevailed but Roumania was never quite the same again. Concessions were eventually made to the peasants, but the really significant reforms were delayed until after the death of the King and the accession of Ferdinand to the throne. In the meantime Roumania became more the focus of attention than it had been before to an outside world waiting – although who could have known it? – for the much more violent Russian Revolution and the Great War.

The old world was coming very rapidly to an end at the very time my grandfather was growing up, and the political events of the next few years undoubtedly influenced his thinking when he came to manhood. His education took place at home and he was not allowed to attend an outside school, so to some extent he was very isolated. The selection of a tutor for him became extremely important and after considerable investigation, the King's choice fell, rather oddly as it turned out, on a young Swiss.

When exactly this tutor took up his duties is unclear, but he was certainly in the palace in May 1907, according to a letter that Marie wrote to the British Queen, Alexandra. If indeed he was already installed at the time of the peasant revolt, his pronounced 'Socialist ideas', to quote Marie, may well have opened my grandfather's mind to the social injustices of the time. The tutor left his royal post in 1911, when his charge was a young man of seventeen, and he must therefore be regarded as Carol's single most influential teacher. It was he who encouraged Carol to start his stamp collection, a great passion of his life, and who also fostered his interest in Ferdinand's hobby of botany; under his tutor's influence, Carol collected plants in the mountains around Sinaia which he set in albums.

The tutor remains, however, something of a mystery. Even his name, which was in fact Mohrlen, has previously been unclear. Queen Marie called him Mr Z in the quaint way she had of using an initial, in this case a false one, to disguise the real name of someone she wanted to criticize, while not even attempting to disguise the identity! Much has been written about Mohrlen's strange character. Baroness von der Hoven spoke of his 'fits of depression and misanthropy'. Queen Marie described him as 'a pathological case' and a 'neuropathic'. She added that his influence on his pupil 'was not quite healthy or satisfactory' and went on to express the opinion that he 'ought never to have been left as sole companion of a young boy on the brink of life'. Hannah Pakula portrayed him as 'a Swiss homosexual devoted to botany, the Bible and the republican ideals of his homeland'.

He was an unusual choice in the circumstances as instructor to a royal Prince, and he may well have fallen into a sort of love with his pupil. He later supposedly confessed to Marie that he had been consumed with desire when he had seen the young boy kneeling by his bedside to say his prayers. This must have come as a terrible shock to her. She had suspected him of colouring her son's mind with 'disturbing doubts' of a political nature, but can hardly have thought seriously in terms of a homosexual influence. In fact she had described him as 'profoundly moral' and it is highly unlikely that his sexual interest was translated into action. Indeed Marie could hardly have thought so, because would she otherwise have sent Mohrlen money from time to time after he had left the royal employment?

If my grandfather was influenced in any way by his Swiss tutor, it was certainly not in the direction of homosexuality. Perhaps he himself should have the last word on the subject. 'With all his faults,' Baroness von der Hoven quoted Carol as saying, 'he did me a lot of good.'

1907, the year of the peasant revolt, was also the year that Marie was introduced to Barbo Stirbey, a Roumanian aristocrat, who fell in love with her. Prince Stirbey was a married man and at first Marie tried to keep aloof, perhaps still recovering from Waldorf Astor's marriage; but she soon fell in love with him. The following year Ion Bratianu (not to be confused with his father of the same name who had brought Carol from Germany to become King) became Prime Minister and in turn leader of the Liberal Party. He was Stirbey's brother-in-law, being married to Stirbey's sister Elise.

There thus was formed an extraordinary political liaison, which was to have a profound effect on Roumanian politics, between the Prime Minister, his brother-in-law and his brother-in-law's mistress, the Crown Princess. Bratianu realized that the old King, who had been intermittently ill, had not long to live, and he needed Marie's support to influence her husband and perhaps control the next King. He regarded Ferdinand as weak and pliable, and could see the day when Marie's help might be vital to his interests. He was not above using his brother-in-law's relationship with Marie for his own purposes. The King, meanwhile, was pleased to have the son of his old friend as Prime Minister and when later, in 1913, he appointed Stirbey to head the royal household, he was virtually condoning the

Crown Princess's affair with Stirbey and giving his blessing to Bratianu's machinations.

The effect on my grandfather was devastating. He was a boy of thirteen when his mother met Stirbey and a young man of nineteen when Stirbey was appointed Superintendent of the Crown Estates, to give him his official title. He had seen the relationship grow and he objected to his mother's closeness to her lover and to the fact that, as he believed, she was being manipulated for political purposes. This alone did more to alienate him from his mother and colour his future conduct towards her than all the influence of nannies, governesses and tutors on whom she put the blame and about whom she constantly complained.

Marie had given birth to her fifth child, Ileana, at the start of 1909. 'The child of my soul', she called her. Her last baby, Mircea, was born almost exactly four years later. Sadly he succumbed to typhoid fever, which had so nearly killed his father and eldest brother, in November 1916, before he was four years old. Baroness von der Hoven wrote of my grandfather, whom she said adored children, carrying his little brother up and down his mother's room while she was ill in bed, recovering from the birth. There were inevitable rumours that Prince Stirbey was the children's father. Hannah Pakula, who was able to study Stirbey's letters to Marie, dismissed the gossip where Ileana was concerned but left open the possibility that Ferdinand may not have been the father of the youngest child.

Forming a wider background to this early story of Prince Carol's life were the complex events of the Balkan Wars. They arose out of the gradual disintegration of the Turkish Empire, following which every country in the area was out to grab whatever Turkish territory it could lay claim to secure. In 1912, Bulgaria, Greece and Serbia took advantage of Turkish weakness, following a defeat at the hands of the Italians, to declare war on the Turks, who were forced to sue for peace. Roumania, itself not long freed from Turkish hegemony, supported its Balkan friends, without actually entering the war. When later the Bulgarians fell out with their former allies, the Greeks and Serbs, Roumania, angry at Bulgarian territorial demands that included land coveted by Roumania, joined in a new war against the greedy Bulgarians. This war was of very short duration and ended in a humiliating Bulgarian rout. It was as a result of this venture that Roumania completed her possession of the Black Sea coast area of Dobruja.

Another legacy of the war was an epidemic of cholera, which fell heavily on the Roumanian troops in Bulgaria. Marie broke protocol by crossing the border without permission to inspect the situation for herself. She was so shocked at the appalling conditions she encountered, in which men were dying for lack of adequate medical and nursing attention, that she decided personally to do something about it. She was not the only Roumanian woman, nor the first, who rose to the occasion but she was the most important, and her position enabled her to get things done that no other woman could have managed. She described this episode as 'a turning point in my life'. 'I am a changed woman,' she wrote to her mother.

She was given permission to take charge of a cholera camp at Zimnitsa in Bulgaria, where her work at last earned her the love and respect of the Roumanian people and made her a heroine throughout Europe. If the King had retained any doubts about her, he now saw her as a key figure in Roumania after his death. Almost equally important, she regained considerable respect from her eldest son, who had entered Bulgaria with his father and who actually asked to be permitted to join his mother at the camp, where he proved an excellent and protective assistant. This also brought him for the first time in close touch with the army, which seemed genuinely to love him for his efforts on their behalf.

The following January, 1913, he was sent to the military academy at Potsdam in Germany to join his father's old regiment, indeed the King's old regiment also. The idea surprisingly came not from his father or the King but from his mother. He was accompanied by one of the King's former aides-de-camp and his wife, who were to look after him, and he seemed very happy in his new surroundings. He became friendly with a German cousin who was serving in the same regiment.

Baroness von der Hoven related that he was permitted at this time to redecorate his rooms at Cotroceni to his own taste. Apparently he removed all the wallpaper and had the walls whitewashed as in a peasant house; he installed Roumanian furniture, Roumanian rugs and a Roumanian open fireplace, all of which reflected a special interest in local art and culture. There was a great flourishing of Roumanian art in the twenties, and my grandfather's early interest is a significant indication of what was to come. The Baroness, who reported elsewhere that my grandfather developed a love of music in Germany, wrote that 'beauty in art, or theatre, or music, gave him an almost physical sensation akin to pain'.

She also referred to a 'a wealth of repressed affection' in my grandfather, but said that he was shy. She stated categorically that he 'was not a ladies' man', which is interesting in view of the reputation he was to gain, and insisted that he 'felt more at home among the soldiers'. Whatever the truth of her observations, he certainly showed no interest in Grand Duchess Olga, daughter of Tsar Nicholas II, nor she in him, when they were introduced with a view to possible matrimony, which it was considered might have favourable political consequences.

The first encounter took place in February 1914, when Carol was twenty years old. His parents collected him from Potsdam *en route* to St Petersburg in the hope that he might fall for Olga while stopping at the Russian court. There was a return visit by the Russian royal family to the Roumanian Black Sea port of Constantza in June, but although it was regarded as a feather in King Carol's cap to receive so distinguished a visitor as the Tsar, no romance developed between the children. Olga is said by Baroness von der Hoven (who claimed to have been on the spot during the visit to Russia) to have been so determined not to leave her native country that she deliberately uglified herself for the first meeting. Whether or not my grandfather was a ladies' man, his three wives were all beautiful and, in his mother's words, Olga was 'not pretty'. Perhaps that explains it all. Of course, as has been pointed out, if only Olga had married my grandfather, she would have escaped the terrible fate that was to befall the Russian royal family at the hands of the Revolution. For his part, Prince Carol at this age was considered handsome. Marie's beautiful boy with golden curls had grown into a tall, strong, slim figure with clear blue eyes and a mop of golden hair, which he wore swept back and which would gradually grow darker.

Exactly fifteen days after my grandfather and Olga had sat down unwillingly to dinner next to each other in Constantza, the Archduke Franz Ferdinand and his wife were assassinated at Sarajevo. One month later to the day, on 28 July, Austria declared war on Serbia, precipitating the First World War.

On 10 October King Carol I died and Ferdinand I became the new King of Roumania. Five days later the new Crown Prince came of age. It is not too fanciful to think that he achieved his manhood as the Great War gave birth to an entirely new world.

2

Sound of Battle

Those who so blindly, and often enthusiastically, threw themselves headlong into war in 1914 did not realize that they were orchestrating the death-rattle of the old order. They were like distinguished actors who had occupied the centre-stage of world affairs so long that they did not see that there were others, brought up in a different school, waiting in the wings for them to falter in order to take their place. Within three years, there was a different play that required a new style of acting. The United States had entered the war, laying down its claim as a great world power, and the Bolsheviks had replaced the Tsar in Russia, creating an entirely new situation and a new balance of power.

The war seriously tested loyalties, not least among the royal families of Europe, all so closely and almost incestuously related, who now found themselves in danger of being on opposite sides. Even inside sovereign states, there were minorities with conflicting allegiances. Each country sought whatever advantage it could, hoping to benefit from the spoils of war and allowing considerations of greed to determine policies that affected the lives of millions.

Roumania, like every other country in Europe, had to decide whether to throw in its lot with the Central Powers led by Germany and the Austro-Hungarian Empire or the Entente led by Britain, France and Russia, or, if it were a practical possibility, to remain more or less neutral. There was no doubt about the natural allegiance of the elderly King and Queen. Both were of German origin and, as someone who had received his military training in Germany, the King believed that the superiority of the German army made it impossible for Germany not to succeed, and he believed also in being on the winning side. Moreover, a secret treaty had been signed as long ago as 1883 which bound Austria-Hungary and Roumania not to enter into any alliance against each other and which guaranteed assistance for Roumania if it were attacked from whatever quarter. The Germans simultaneously endorsed this treaty, putting them in the same relationship to the Roumanians as the Austrians. The treaty was valid for five years initially or for eight years if neither side gave notice to determine it, and in fact five years later Italy too became a party to the arrangement, which was renewed in 1892, 1896, 1902 and February 1913.

Crown Princess Marie, being of British and Russian extraction, not unnaturally favoured the Entente and had good reason to think that her views coincided more closely with the feelings of the country than did those of the King. Crown Prince Ferdinand, as Marie herself wrote in her memoirs, was 'exceptionally silent'. She described him as 'a closed book to his people: no one knew what he felt . . . he never expressed himself'. His instinct was probably pro-German, but his influence was less than that of his wife.

The Central Powers at once brought great pressure on Roumania to side with them, offering Bessarabia and certain other territories as a bribe if Roumania would mobilize against Russia. On 3 August a crucial council was held at Sinaia, attended by the King, the Crown Prince, government ministers and opposition leaders. The King strongly argued the cause of the Central Powers but found little support. When he called into issue the treaty of 1883, so recently renewed, its semi-secret nature cut the ground from under his feet. When it had been renewed in 1892, only four ministers had been informed, and the fact was even kept from the Roumanian representatives in Berlin and Vienna. The most recent renewal had not been notified, in accordance with custom, to the opposition leaders, and the Foreign Minister had not even seen the text. It was too late now to seek parliamentary approval.

In return for the help that the treaty provided for Roumania, the latter was obliged to assist the Central Powers if they were attacked in any part of their territories bordering Roumania, although that did not in any case appear to be the position. Even the Italians took this view when, on the very day that the Roumanian council met, they declared their neutrality for the time being.

In the event Roumania also decided to remain neutral, at least for the moment. The decision was a terrible blow to the old King, who sought unsuccessfully to solicit the support of the army, and it may indeed have hastened his death two months later. His wife survived him only seventeen months. In more than one sense, the war drew a curtain on Roumania's past. 'Legend will have it,' wrote Marie, 'that Uncle died of a broken heart.'

For two years Roumania walked a tightrope, awaiting events. There is no doubt which camp popular opinion supported. Anguish at the treatment of the Roumanians in Transylvania and anger at German support for rival Bulgaria had been effective in creating sympathy for the Entente. Roumania's geographical position, however, left it vulnerable to pressure from the Central Powers. It was only when the Russians appeared to be carrying all before them, having achieved victories over the Austrians that had brought Russian forces to the Carpathians, that Roumania at last felt safe enough to take the plunge. On 17 August 1916, a secret arrangement was signed with the Entente nations which promised Roumania large territories, including the whole of Transylvania, in return for entering the war. Ten days later Roumania declared war on the Austro-Hungarian Empire, and Roumanian troops immediately entered Transylvania.

The thinking behind the action was that the Austrians were in retreat and had been so seriously weakened that they would be unable seriously to defend the province. It was also considered that Germany, which was not included in Roumania's declaration of war, would be too heavily committed elsewhere to be able to intervene. Whereas there was truth in the first premise, and Roumanian troops met little opposition, no consideration was given to the thought that the Russians might prove unreliable allies. In fact at critical times the Tsar, beset by economic collapse in a country on the verge of revolution, was unable to deliver the military support that Roumania expected.

An even more serious miscalculation concerned the German response. German troops under the command of Field Marshal von Mackensen and General von Falkenhayn attacked Roumania, notably on the Dobruja front, with such strength and skill that Roumanian troops had to be withdrawn speedily from Transylvania. The old King had been convinced of German military invincibility, and had the German forces not been so over-extended and committed to many different campaigns, he might have been proved right. As it was, the Germans almost literally swept through Roumania and menaced the capital itself, bombarding it also from the air. So serious was the situation that the British arranged to blow up Roumania's greatest asset, the oilfields at Ploesti, to prevent the Germans from benefiting by their capture.

Apart from its pro-German element, Bucharest was evacuated by everyone who could afford to leave. The royal family moved to Jassy, near the Russian border in Moldavia, and suddenly a town of 50,000 people found itself housing 200,000 refugees, with remnants of the Russian army encamped on the outskirts; Prince Carol described it as 'a sardine tin'. On 6 December the Germans entered the capital. The position of the monarchy was precarious, especially since the Kaiser regarded the Roumanian King as a traitor Hohenzollern. Fortunately for Roumania, the Central Powers had so much else to preoccupy them that, having achieved their main objective in the country, they left it alone.

1917 looked to be a bleak year for Roumania but it turned out to be a year of extraordinary vicissitude. In March in neighbouring Russia, the Tsar was forced to abdicate, although the Provisional Government that took control was still committed to the war, and in July the Russians began what was to be their final offensive, assisted by a small Roumanian army equipped with new arms by a French mission to Jassy under the leadership of General Berthelot. The Central Powers forces were first checked and later badly defeated at the week-long battle of Marasesti in August.

Credit for this victory was due almost entirely to the Roumanian troops led by Generals Averescu and Prezan. Although the Russians played their part, Bolshevik propaganda was already having its effect and thousands of Russians deserted their posts, making the Roumanian contribution even more remarkable. In one short campaign, Roumanian honour was restored and the nation appeared to have a new future. However, developments beyond its borders over which Roumania had no control meant that three months later Lenin had replaced Kerensky in Russia, and it was not long before he was suing for peace, leaving Roumania totally exposed. In face of the Russian defection, Roumania could not possibly hold out alone in the area against the Germans. Victory had been turned dramatically into defeat.

Worse still, some Russian troops were inflamed by revolutionary fervour and murdered their own officers; a Bolshevik attempt to capture the Roumanian royal family was thwarted, and an assassination plot was discovered against King Ferdinand and his sons. In these threatening days for the family, George V offered Queen Marie and her children asylum in England. She thanked her cousin warmly but did not take up the offer. The Roumanian peasantry remained substantially loyal, despite the efforts of the Bolsheviks to seduce them from their allegiance. The royal promise to break up the big estates and give land to the peasants no doubt helped.

The Central Powers now threatened Roumania with annihilation if it did a it follow the Russians and make peace. This brought about the resignation of Prime Minister Bratianu in February 1918 and his replacement by Averescu, the hero of Marasesti. The proposed conditions were appalling, depriving Roumania of the Dobruja and large tracts of Transylvania, among other territories; an army of occupation was to be set up in Wallachia at Roumanian expense; and Roumanian oil and certain agricultural produce were to be controlled by a company representing German and Austrian interests. The only consolations were that Roumania would be permitted to maintain its monarchy and to annex Bessarabia, if the people of the province agreed. The Bessarabian National Assembly in fact voted for union with Roumania on 8 April.

The final terms, incorporated in a treaty signed on 7 May, were slightly less harsh than originally suggested, but Roumania lost all the territories it had won from Bulgaria in 1913. Averescu, having refused to sign the armistice, had by then been replaced by a Conservative politician whose earlier recommendation in favour of a German alliance made him more acceptable to the Central Powers and gave his country, through him, more influence with its former enemies. This was Alexandru Marghiloman.

At the start of these momentous events, which in turn were part of an even larger scenario that would shortly again restore Roumania's fortunes with the final defeat of the Central Powers, Prince Carol was not quite twenty-one, and he was twenty-four when Roumania signed the humiliating peace treaty. There is little doubt as to where the young man's sympathies lay. Although he had received some military training at Potsdam and had numerous German friends and relations, his loyalties were first and foremost to Roumania. He had not been born abroad like his great-uncle and his father, and he was personally committed to a Roumanian entity and culture. In particular, his consideration for the Roumanian people in Transylvania who were under the whip of the Austro-Hungarian Empire made him a natural ally of his mother's cause. At a time when Roumanian fortunes were at their lowest, he embraced his mother effusively after she complained bitterly that there were 'no men in this country' and that she was 'ashamed of being the Queen of nothing but cowards'.

When Roumania entered the war, he was leading the happy-go-lucky life of a young man in a privileged position. He had his duties as an army officer but these were not exacting. In a letter written in November, less than three months later, his mother complained about what she regarded as his frivolous behaviour, accusing him of 'leading a comfortable life, poring over maps and plans for perhaps two hours in the day, and all the rest of the time reading interesting books, driving in a superlative motor . . .' (he had a Rolls) '. . . eating good food, sleeping in a good bed, going into town to *amuse* yourself . . .' (the word amuse was underlined for emphasis) '. . . to visit your ladyfriends like in time of peace, to drink tea and chatter about those that are fallen while you sit in a comfortable chair'. (She invariably wrote to her son in a slightly foreign English, and I have only occasionally corrected her spelling and punctuation.)

She wanted him to go to the front, and in vain did he point out that, as Crown Prince, the authorities refused to allow him to put his life at risk. It was not, he protested, his fault that he was in his 'comfortable corner, far away from the sound of battle', as his mother put it in the same letter, 'far from your comrades . . . far from those that are suffering and enduring mortal pain and privation'. But Marie did not see it that way. He might not have the right to share their dangers, she averred, but he should be prepared to share what he could of their hardships. There was a difference.

'Why are you not moving from place to place,' she continued, 'from regiment to regiment, encouraging them, showing them your sympathy, your interest, your belief in their courage and tenacity? . . . You do not even go occasionally to a hospital where the mutilated men would be happy to see you, to receive a word of praise or encouragement from their Crown Prince. A small word suffices them. I am quite ashamed of how grateful they are for the smallest kindness, those simple stoic men who have been torn away from their starving families, understanding nothing of the higher reasons for war, and yet patiently allowing themselves to be hacked to pieces because "their country called them". . . .

'Till now when I heard people murmuring against you, I have tried to find excuses for you. Each time I saw you, I asked you when you were going, always to receive the same answer – that you did not know.

'Tonight it is three weeks since my Mircea was torn from me . . . I do not ask of others to continue to mourn with me. The tears that I weep, I weep at the dead of night when they need be a burden to no one, but the weight I carry with me does not prevent me trying to do all I can to help others to lighten the intolerable suffering that is spread all over our country. Why do you not help me by doing your share?

'How can you bear to sit still whilst your country is being invaded, when each day brings more desperate news? Do you not understand the beautiful part that might be yours to play? They love you! You are their future. It is for you that they are fighting, shedding their blood, and you never go with them, never try to get near them, never tear yourself away from your every day's selfish comforts and habits to bring them a word of hope or encouragement, a pack of cigarettes or a glass of wine.

'Oh! if I were a man at this moment, and above all the man that they are fighting for, I would always be near them – somewhere, anywhere, everywhere, like a flag that all hearts would believe in, to which all eyes would turn. . . . You little realise the glorious chance you are wasting. You might be the army's idol, their faith, their hope; instead of that you are nothing, nothing but a big boy wasting his time at home. . . . You were their friend in time of pleasures, ought you not to be doubly their friend in time of woe?'

Queen Marie admitted that these were 'hard words' and she called on her son to do his duty and to cease living a selfish life. 'Be the son that I would like you to be,' she pleaded, 'the son that I really believe that you are.'

Her eloquence was not reserved for him alone. She accused her husband of playing with their son's future by keeping him away from the front, where he would have the opportunity to endear himself to the army. These representations were, however, ineffectual, at least until July 1917. Even then, as the offensive started that was to result in the victory at Marasesti, Carol was not allowed to engage in fighting and had to be satisfied with driving from regiment to regiment for brief visits with the troops.

There was some talk of his being given a command at this time but his mother somewhat surprisingly opposed this, fearing that he was too inexperienced. He was eventually permitted to set up his own military group, the Vanatori de Munte or Chasseurs Alpins. He was in command of this battalion in July and August 1918, but this was after the signature of the treaty that had effectively ended the war, when it was no longer possible for him to lead them into battle.

Whatever the justification for his mother's strictures, in one significant respect her instinct was absolutely right. The most important matter on my grandfather's mind during much of this time was a woman.

3

The Dream
Comes True

Ioana Marie Valentine Lambrino, known since childhood as Zizi,
came from an old aristocratic family of Greek-Byzantine origins,
descended from the princely Brancovans and related by marriage to
Prince Alexander Cuza. Her father, Constantin Lambrino, was a
kinsman of General Alexander Lambrino and a good friend of Prime
Minister Alexandru Marghiloman. Her brother Ion was one of Prince
Carol's friends and the Lambrinos were often seen at court.

In an unpublished typescript about her life, Ioana stated that she
was five years old when she met Carol, and in her published account
of their relationship, she referred to a charity gala given under Crown
Princess Marie's patronage at Cotroceni, when she was among a
number of children who took part in theatricals; Carol, three years
older than her, was aged ten or twelve at the time. 'The Prince made
a deep impression on me,' she recalled, 'because he wore big boots
like those of an officer, and they creaked at every step. I thought this
was the highest possible form of elegance.'

They first seem to have begun to notice each other in more than
an ordinarily friendly way when Carol was about nineteen and Ioana
sixteen. She referred to a party given by Marghiloman, probably in
early 1913, which may well have marked the occasion when they first
became strongly attracted to each other. According to the unpublished diaries of Carol's brother Nicolas, Carol had first fallen in love
with a girl named Ella Filitti, who was sent out of the country. Ioana
appears to have been his second love.

She reported that she and Carol met every day, but whatever their
romantic attraction, she was by no means uncritical of him. He was a
very bad dancer (as also stated by Baroness von der Hoven) and an
even worse skater; he was a poor tennis player and disliked horse-
riding, his mother's favourite occupation. On the other hand, he was
a skilled driver and mechanic, and she shared with him, and indeed

with most young Roumanians at that time, a passion for aircraft and flying. Their closeness was interrupted by Carol's time in Potsdam, but he corresponded regularly with Ioana's brother Ion, and he never failed to enquire after her. By 1914, his interest in Ioana no doubt explains his unreceptive response to the Tsar's daughter.

For about two years after the beginning of the war, while Roumania remained neutral, Carol and Ioana were together in Bucharest for much of the time. She wrote about a group of young people who boated on a lake in the capital every day, when 'unconcerned with princely protocol, Carol rowed the lady of his thoughts across the lagoon with the ardour of a Venetian gondolier'. He had become 'a very good-looking young man,' she said. 'Tall, slim . . . with golden hair, an extremely lively eye. . . .' She was short and dark, with an animated, attractive face.

Her father died just before Roumania's entry into the war in 1916, which may have made her even more dependent on Carol for a male shoulder on which to lean, particularly in the difficult days ahead. She described an aerial attack on Bucharest on 25 September that year, when she was having tea with Carol, and wrote about a little clock he gave her 'to mark the time of our affection,' as she put it, 'I dare not yet say of our love.'

Five days later he came to tea again before leaving Bucharest for his regiment, when she gave him a letter to her brother, who was fighting at the front. It was no longer safe to stay in Bucharest which was soon to fall to the Germans, and Ioana and her mother left on one of the overcrowded trains for Tecouci in Moldavia, where they had friends. They were refugees, along with thousands of others. On both sides of the tracks, the young girl could see the exodus of people, carrying whatever they could with them, some on foot, some with horses and carts, others more fortunate in automobiles.

Once in Tecouci, Ioana helped the wounded who crammed the hospital but her mind was far away, and when the German advance made it prudent to leave Tecouci for Jassy, she was overjoyed that she would be near Carol again whenever he was at home from his military duties. Since he was not permitted to risk his life in battle, he was able to spend a great deal of his time with his family. The Lambrinos' meagre accommodation in Jassy consisted of a living room and bedroom, and the winter was the worst in living memory, but there was compensation for Ioana in seeing Carol. He took her on excursions in the car, played cards with her and decided to teach her Roumanian history, about which he did not judge her sufficiently knowledgeable.

At least from the time that Ioana left Bucharest, the two young people maintained a lively correspondence. She was Zizi at first, and later Baby or Zoucky. He was Carol or sometimes Child or Childy, and later Boy or Boyky or Boysky. It is perhaps unfair to expose youthful love-letters to historical scrutiny but Ioana kept most, if not all, of Carol's letters and they do reveal the growing bond between them. In February 1918, he was writing (in French): '. . . the hours I spend near to you always seem to me so good, so sweet. That is what sustains me. . . .' Then, in English, 'Baby dear, you are so sweet and I love you so.' On one occasion when Carol contracted jaundice and was confined to bed in the palace at Jassy for six weeks, he wrote to Ioana every day.

They were obviously in love, although the King and Queen, preoccupied with the war, may not have realized how far the affair had gone. According to my grandmother's unpublished script, Carol actually announced his intention to marry Ioana at a family dinner party. 'A great silence followed,' she wrote. 'The Queen continued to smoke her cigarette. King Ferdinand calmly stroked his beard. Princess Elisabetha bit her smiling lip, Princess Mignon opened her eyes wide for a moment and Prince Nicolas remained uninterested.' Princess Ileana was probably asleep upstairs.

In her book, Ioana described the scene shortly afterwards, one evening towards six o'clock in June 1918, when she was with two friends and Carol arrived unannounced in his car. After dinner, he took her aside and asked her to marry him. 'I have only one dream,' he declared, 'one wish: to be joined to you for life.' In accordance with custom, they exchanged rings.

What was in his mind at the time? He was not far short of his twenty-fifth brithday, so this proposal cannot be dismissed as a youthful whim. Did he seriously think that there would be no opposition to his wish to marry a Roumanian girl? He must surely have been aware that his own father, when faced with a similar choice, had abandoned the woman he loved because, as a Roumanian national, she was not considered a suitable wife for the heir to the throne. Did he wish deliberately to challenge this practice? Perhaps he consciously want to start a truly Roumanian dynasty, or thought that after a world war, his parents and the country's leading politicians would have very little interest in the actions of two young people in the light of the momentous events that they had all experienced and the major post-war issues that needed to be faced.

Although he may have been motivated to some extent by his nationalistic feelings, he probably at first did not really think about the problems he was creating for himself. There is no evidence that he sought seriously to discuss the matter with his parents, or indeed with anyone, perhaps because he realized that they would try to thwart him. The obvious conclusion is that he had fallen madly in love with Ioana and was borne along on a wave of romanticism. Certainly his subsequent actions were less those of a calculating mind than of one confused by passion.

He was not, however, unaware of the problems. On 21 June he wrote to Ioana: 'The great difficulty is the legal question; I must study it in all its forms.' He seems to have taken the view that he could not legally be prevented from marrying Ioana Lambrino and that if and when in due course he became King, she would become Queen of Roumania. Anticipating the objections that would be made if he declared his hand openly, he probably decided that his best course of action was to present the world with a *fait accompli*. In any case he was in a hurry; if he allowed the question of his marriage to become the subject of public or even family debate, it could drag on for months.

Having made the decision to marry Ioana, it was for Carol a matter now of deciding how and where to do so. The plan was to marry in secret, to avoid opposition, but since the marriage ceremony could not be performed inside the country without risk of discovery, Carol decided they should cross the border into Russia, and marry there. If his parents refused to accept him back home as a married man, he and his wife would proceed to France and there take up the Roumanian cause in exile. If it occurred to him that for an army officer to leave his post to travel abroad without permission was technically desertion, amounting even to treason, his defence (as recorded in a subsequent letter to his father) was that he had never been required to take an oath of allegiance and that he was breaking no vows.

Since the end of hostilities in Roumania, a number of anti-Bolshevik army officers had been crossing the Russian border to assist the forces opposed to the Revolution, and Carol conceived the idea of joining the next group; but in the end he chose to use the services of an officer named Henri Serdici de Golobardo, who was planning to cross the frontier to marry his Russian girlfriend. Carol proposed in the strictest confidence that he and Ioana should accompany Serdici, ostensibly as his brother and sister and as marriage witnesses.

When Serdici chivalrously fell in with this plan, Carol wrote excitedly to Ioana: 'You must have received a quick word from me this morning, announcing the good news that must fill our hearts with happiness. Now, Baby, the dream comes true. What a mad dream it has been, and what an enchanted life lies ahead. . . . These last days have been terrifying for me, nerve-racking in a way you cannot easily imagine. For two or three nights I could hardly sleep, so much did my thoughts worry me, and a foolish fear grabbed my heart. Oh, I was frightened, afraid as never before in my life, when I asked the fatal question.' (He was referring to his request to Serdici.) 'My God, I was so fearful that the reply would be "NO", a pitiless and irrevocable no; instead of which, all was agreed, without discussion and even perhaps with pleasure. . . .

'You can easily imagine what an impression this made on me and how surprised I was to have a reply that I hardly hoped for. This has been a relief to me, a weight that has hung on my heart for two months and that seriously weakened me physically and above all morally. But now I no longer have regrets, the dreadful sufferings of the month of June are gone forever, the golden dream begins and the life of happiness is born. You, my adored darling, will be mine for life. . . .'

Serdici was friendly with an official in the passport office and obtained passports for himself, as well as his supposed brother and sister. Carol spent the evening of 19 August in Ioana's house and although she hated the deception, Carol and she played an elaborate charade for the benefit of her mother. She asked him to lend her his car at eight o'clock in the morning to visit friends in the country, to which he replied that he would need the car the day afterwards to join his regiment. She promised that she would return by the evening, and he therefore agreed to her request.

Thus it was that Carol's chauffeur called to collect Ioana early the next morning. It was raining heavily, 'but not in our loving hearts', she wrote. They collected Serdici first, then proceeded to the palace to pick up Carol. Fifteen minutes later, they were on their way, with Carol in the driving-seat, Ioana at his side, and Serdici and the chauffeur in the back, surrounded by luggage.

There was something wonderfully amateur about the whole venture. The bad weather made the roads impassable and the car became stuck in the mud. Time was of the essence because the Crown Prince's unannounced departure might be discovered at any time. They came to an inn where Serdici, not without great difficulty, persuaded the innkeeper to lend them a horse and carriage, in which they drove to the nearest railway station at Parlitzi. The chauffeur was detailed to meet them later with the car, at a point on the Russian border, assuming the weather improved sufficiently for him to get the car out of the mud. But although he managed his part in the affair, things did not go exactly according to plan for the others.

They took the night train to the frontier station at Bender, where Serdici left his companions in the carriage while he obtained the necessary visas to allow them into Russia. There was no problem, but they now had to get out of the train to leave the station and cross the bridge that straddled the border. There were guard dogs and sentries at both ends. Their passports and luggage were examined cursorily on the Roumanian side and they crossed over, Serdici walking slightly ahead with the passports, which he presented to the Russian customs officer. At the time this part of Russia was under German occupation and the German guards had been ordered to keep a watchful eye on visitors. The worst part of the ordeal seemed to be over when a particularly vigilant German officer, who had been looking on, suddenly interrupted. 'One moment,' he said. 'This is Prince Carol of Roumania!'

It is perhaps astonishing that Carol should have been recognized not by one of the Roumanian guards but by a German. This was the last thing he had expected. According to Ioana, he turned pale and there was a hum of amazement among the officers. The three young people had a quick discussion among themselves. Serdici was for bluffing it out, but Ioana pointed out that a search of their luggage would inevitably reveal their true identities to anyone who was suspicious.

Carol rose to the occasion, and asked to speak to the commanding officer. 'I shall not hide,' he said, 'that I am the Crown Prince of Roumania but I am travelling incognito and I appeal to your sense of propriety. I am going to Russia to act as a witness in the marriage of my friend Serdici, but because of the war and the very recent end of hostilities, I have to travel abroad anonymously. I ask you to keep it secret.'

It was fortunate, Ioana recorded, that the German officer was an aristocrat of the old school for whom respect to princes was part of his code of honour, especially a prince of partly German blood who had been at Potsdam. He clicked his heels, and said that as far as he was concerned they could proceed but that he had to seek higher authority. Orders were given that Carol and his party were to be taken to the headquarters of General Zeidler in Akermann, inside Russia.

Zeidler, who commanded the region, invited his visitors to lunch. He was so polite, Ioana wrote, that 'we did not know if we were his guests or his prisoners'. Not only did he permit them to proceed to Odessa but he actually booked rooms for them at the Bristol Hotel, one for the two men, the other for Ioana. However, he also appointed a German aide-de-camp to accompany them, who was obviously a spy, and everywhere they went, they were closely watched. In such circumstances it was obviously not going to be easy for Carol and Ioana to marry in secret. Since Serdici had, however, come to Russia with the declared purpose of getting married, it caused no surprise that he should visit a local church, ostensibly to make arrangements for himself. In fact he persuaded a priest named Charoffsky at the Pokrowska Church to marry Carol and Ioana, and a date was set for 31 August.

There was a last-minute drama when, towards midnight on the eve of the wedding, Ioana was taken ill. She was suffering from food-poisoning, probably from crayfish that she and Carol had eaten to excess. She did not tell Carol at first but confided in Serdici. He called a doctor who said that the illness was not serious but wrapped her in cold sheets, prescribed an emetic and recommended several days' rest.

When Carol found out, he was desperate, but Ioana was determined not to fall at the last fence. At nine o'clock, despite her fever and exhaustion, she got up and dressed. She had herself made a white dress with three metres of crêpe-de-chine that she had bought locally. It was not the grand work of art that she would have worn had she married the Crown Prince in the cathedral in Bucharest in the presence of the royal family, but, as she described it, 'the poor and honest dress of a love marriage'. When they left the hotel, the wedding dress was carefully hidden beneath a raincoat, and she wore ordinary shoes and stockings as if just going out for a walk. In his coat pocket, however, Carol concealed another pair of stockings and her white dancing-shoes.

She was so weak, she said, that had Carol not supported her, she would have collapsed in the street, but they reached the church where they were greeted by Charoffsky, who was attended by three army officers, one of whom was his son, who were to act as witnesses or in some other supporting function. There were only a few casual worshippers in the church, one of whom happened to be Princess Kropotkine.

Ioana was escorted to a small room where she dressed her hair with the traditional orange-blossom crown and changed her shoes and stockings. Despite the fact that this was a wedding without family, attendants and friends, she was acutely conscious that she was about to marry the Crown Prince of Roumania, whose Queen she expected one day to become. Her highly emotional state, combined with the heat and her fever, almost caused her to faint and one of the witnesses twice had to offer her a sip of wine. She made a point in her book of declaring that at the time of the marriage she was not the ambitious girl that Queen Marie later alleged. Aware though she was of Carol's status, she was above all in love, and if anyone was unrealistic, it was surely Carol and not she. To say that she set out to trap him is belied by the fact that Carol had made practically all the running.

The part of the ceremony that most impressed her was when the priest held the two magnificent golden crowns, studded with precious stones, above the two young people's heads. When it was all over, she was dazed and overcome with happiness. The priest provided champagne and gave her a Russian Bible and a beautiful bunch of white roses. Carol kissed her and told her that he was the happiest man in the world and that they were united until death.

The Roumanian consul in Odessa, Sebastian Greciano, who had been alerted by Serdici, sent an emissary to convey his greetings and good wishes. He was himself confined to bed with some minor ailment, which may well have been of the diplomatic variety. Notification of the marriage to his country's representative was important to Carol because it confirmed the consul's knowledge of the wedding. The Crown Prince had married a girl of the same religion in accordance with the rites of the Orthodox Church and by a priest of that faith. Roumanian law must uphold the validity of such a marriage, which had taken place with the knowledge of Roumania's representative on the spot.

The position of the consul is ambiguous. He did nothing to frustrate the ceremony; indeed he seems to have acquiesced in it, although he personally kept aloof. It is probable that Carol, through Serdici, asked him to keep the matter secret, and there is no evidence that he communicated with Bucharest, assuming he had time to do so. In fact the whole question of how much the royal family knew is extremely difficult to resolve. There is no record of what steps they took to trace the Crown Prince when his absence from the palace was discovered, or if indeed they took any steps at all. They may simply have assumed that he had rejoined his regiment and had omitted to notify them. In any case he was a grown man whose temporary absence might not have been remarkable. There is certainly no indication that they made any connection with the similar disappearance of Ioana Lambrino or that they were aware that Carol had left the country. When they learnt of the marriage, they were evidently taken completely by surprise.

Although Carol had left behind three letters, it was only in his letter to Ioana's brother Ion that he revealed his true intentions. He was more devious in a letter to his sister Elisabetha, in which he actually mentioned his first girlfriend without referring to Ioana! He instructed his sister on how to deal with his belongings in the event that he did not return to Roumania, proving that he had this eventuality in mind and that, at the time, his love for Ioana was more important than the possibility of having to sacrifice the crown, although he probably never thought it would really come to that.

The third letter, to his father, also strongly suggests that he was by no means sure that he would be allowed back into the country, at least until time had passed, when he would probably be forgiven if he could restore Roumania's prestige in exile. The letter seems further to confirm that the French option was the one strongest in his mind. Once again there was a deliberate deception in that there was no mention of Ioana or marriage. Carol told his father that the humiliating conditions in defeated Roumania made it impossible for him to continue serving as a soldier and he was therefore leaving the country for political reasons. This letter was later regarded by many people as testament to a renunciation of the succession.

Exactly what arrangements Carol made for the delivery of these letters is uncertain, but whether by design or accident – almost certainly the former – they did not reach the royal family until after the marriage had taken place. According to Ioana, on the day after the wedding Carol also sent his father a telegram which read: 'I am married to Zizi Lambrino. Reply if I may return with her or if I must continue my journey to France.' The marriage was also reported to Bucharest in a telegram from the authorities in Berlin. The news was received with consternation.

4
Crack of
the Whip

After the dream came the reality. 'Our happiness', wrote Ioana, 'lasted ten days, ten poor little days which were my entire life and after which there were for me only anguish and disappointments.' Carol at first merely waited on events at home while he enjoyed his honeymoon in Odessa. When put to the test, he was curiously indecisive. Had he been determined to direct events, he might well have proceeded at once to Paris or some other European capital that would have received him and his bride. That way at least he might have retained his wife, even if he lost his throne, although he clearly still hoped to keep both, with his father's consent.

His problem was that he had no real power base in Roumania on which to draw support for his action. His influential mother was extremely upset by the news of his marrige to Ioana, whom she would always consider an adventuress who had trapped her son. The circumstances of the marriage have been compared to those of King Edward VIII and Wallis Simpson, who was similarly vilified; but of course there were many differences, although both women were rejected as unsuitable because of their birth and background. Mrs Simpson, unlike Ioana, was a divorcee; nor did she have Ioana Lambrino's distinguished pedigree. Edward was King whereas Carol was Crown Prince, and the British monarch and his bride were much older and more experienced. Paradoxically, too, one of the arguments used against Ioana was that she was not a foreigner, an argument used in reverse against the American Mrs Simpson.

Queen Marie was also deeply wounded that her son had not confided in her. Although he had written to his father, his sister Elisabetha and his new brother-in-law, there was no letter for her – 'not a word, not a sign, not a greeting, not a thought, and I am his mother, I have always been his defender. . . .' He later told her that he had to keep the marriage secret and he had not wanted to lie to

her. Perhaps he knew that she would never have agreed to the
marriage, and would undoubtedly have tried to stop it. She was a
more determined person than his father, and in fact it was the King
who sought to find excuse for him.

Marghiloman, in his political diary, reported a meeting with
Ferdinand on 7 September, at which the Prime Minister told him
that he had consulted government ministers, though not the opposition leaders, and that public opinion was against the Crown Prince.
'The Prince is not loved,' he declared, and accused him of a lack of
judgement that boded ill for the future. He went further and
suggested that young Prince Nicolas should be made heir to the
throne. This suggestion came from a man who realized that Carol's
behaviour was a serious blow to the dynasty at a time when the
country was at its weakest, following its humiliation by Germany –
and a man incidentally who had been a good friend of Ioana's father
and who was in no way prejudiced against her personally, but only
politically.

Marghiloman recorded that the King's eyes were red with tears at
this meeting. He pleaded for his son, saying that the boy had his
good points. 'What makes me so hesitant,' he said, 'is that I too gave
way to sentiment.' The Prime Minister was quick to respond that
'Your Majesty did not commit the act, did not desert. . . .' The young
Ferdinand may have loved Helena Vacarescu, he was implying, but
he did not marry her; he put duty before personal happiness.

The King wanted if possible to meet his son face to face, but
Marghiloman begged him not to do so until a definite decision had
been taken about Carol's future. There followed frantic discussions
with political and military leaders, who offered conflicting advice. It
was argued that the marriage was void because it was unauthorized,
though on what legal basis is unclear; and that it was not valid
because it had been conducted in a Bolshevik form, although there
had of course been a proper religious ceremony. There was considerable support for substituting Nicolas as Crown Prince, but objections were raised both that he was untrained for the task and also on
legal grounds. It was wisely pointed out that if it appeared easy to
disinherit the Crown Prince, might this not open the door to the
anti-royalists who wanted to get rid of the monarchy itself?

Carol found more support among his fellow army officers than his
mother might have expected. Indeed General Herjeu told Marghiloman that there would be a revolt in the army if there were an attempt
to deprive the Crown Prince of the succession, and this factor may

have outweighed the influence of those who sought to put his younger brother in Carol's place. Herjeu also posed the Prime Minister an interesting question: what would happen if a child had already been conceived?

The King had the idea that if he could separate the two young people temporarily, it might be possible to persuade Carol, or perhaps both of them, to abandon the marriage. He thought therefore of sentencing his son to sixty days' imprisonment for desertion, hoping presumably that Carol would consider it worth accepting this minor deprivation of liberty in order to return to Roumania with his bride. Although a specious argument was raised that there had been no desertion because the Crown Prince had notified his father by telegram of his absence within a week or so of departure, this course found favour with the generals. The final sentence was one of seventy-five days' imprisonment at Horaitza, a monastery near Bicaz in the mountains; but of course Carol had first to be persuaded to return home and submit to royal authority.

Emissaries were sent to Odessa and Carol was somehow persuaded that he and his bride should join the royal train at the frontier to discuss the situation. He was assured that 'His Majesty will take all the measures he believes are favourable to his son'. There is no doubt that, as Marghiloman had said, Carol's judgement at the time was unsound. Just when he needed to be decisive in his own interests, he was irresolute and unable to withstand the enormous pressure. Clearly he had not foreseen with any accuracy what would happen, although he had had plenty of time to consider the possibilities.

We can only speculate as to Carol's reasons for agreeing to return to Roumania before his position had been clarified. He must have realized that he had only two real options, to continue to live in exile even if this meant giving up the crown in due course, or to return home and face the uncertain consequences. Probably he had a rosy, romantic optimism that, in the last resort, something would be worked out. It is doubtful that he seriously considered the possibility that the validity of his marriage would successfully be challenged.

There was almost certainly a degree of deception to persuade him to join the royal train, but he doubtless thought it in his interest to seek a settlement that would secure his position in the country and gain recognition for his wife. The alternative of remaining in exile was not really an option while there was a chance that he could have his cake and eat it. His naivety lay in his apparent failure to understand that he could easily achieve one of his aims, but not both.

The most powerful figures in the land would support his position as heir apparent but there was nobody to support the marriage.

No sooner had Carol and Ioana boarded the special train than they realized that they were virtually prisoners. For three days, while discussions were continuing in high places, the train travelled aimlessly from place to place and back again. At one stop Queen Marie arrived in an attempt to influence her son. He had no sense of duty, she complained, and no respect for the fundamental laws of the Roumanian monarchy. He protested that the introduction of Roumanian blood into the royal family was the best way to found a truly national dynasty. As someone descended from two of the great royal dynasties of Europe, his mother found his suggestion totally unacceptable, and begged her son to give up Ioana, at least until the country had returned to normal; after which, she offered lamely, he could go away with his wife. She urged him to reflect on the matter while there was still time.

She was in fact warning him that if he did not concur voluntarily, he would be forced to submit. Carol, however, remained secure in the belief that his marriage was legal and could not be set aside. Once again his sense of political reality let him down. Ioana reported that neither of them guessed what was in store; and the sentence of seventy-five days' imprisonment came as a total shock. The punishment, which was to be effective immediately, was for leaving his command and crossing the frontier without permission. When Carol protested to his mother that imprisonment would completely destroy his prestige, her reply was interesting: 'Faults can be lived down. I know it myself. Once, when I was young, the world wanted to cast me adrift, but I lived it down.'

Carol finally agreed to accept his punishment, but in fact he had no option. The following day he was escorted to the mountain monastery and Ioana was taken to her family in Jassy. At a meeting on 10 September between the King and the Prime Minister, Marghiloman recorded that Ferdinand had 'grown thin and very sad – he frequently stops when choked with tears'. The King told him that Prince Carol was already in prison and that he would ensure that 'the lady could in no way make contact with him'. The King's plan was to provide time to persuade his son to accept an annulment of the marriage. 'Perhaps this crack of the whip will reawaken his conscience,' Ferdinand said. Marghiloman added ominously: 'The King has said formally and very decidedly that if the marriage is maintained, the Prince will be deprived of the throne.'

Carol's resolution was not very strong, possibly because he had been deceived into thinking that he would be free to save the marriage once his sentence had been served. Even at this same meeting, the King told Marghiloman that his son 'submits to everything', but that was perhaps wishful thinking, unless Carol was being extremely devious. More likely he was confused, and his attitude wavered considerably.

Ioana for her part did not make due allowance for her husband's difficult position. She believed that he did not have to capitulate to his father. 'If love and distress had not blinded me,' she wrote, 'then I must have understood that this first weakness in his character betokened further submissions and cowardly actions.'

The news of the marriage was kept completely out of the newspapers. Ioana took to her bed in her grandmother's house, only getting up sometimes for meals. She wrote several letters to her husband but did not know where to address them until, towards the end of the month, an old family friend revealed Carol's whereabouts and offered to relay a message from her. She put all the unposted letters in one large envelope, asked him to deliver it and eagerly awaited a response.

Three days later the friend returned with a packet of letters from Carol which had been smuggled out of Horaitza by a monk and a village peasant. She read them excitedly but with growing concern. The first, dated 9 September and written *en route* to the monastery, was effusive: 'I can only repeat your name and tell you over and over again: I love you, I love you, my little wife, my only happiness.' The letter of 26 September was just as loving: 'This evening I am crazy with excitement. I have just been told that tomorrow I shall have news of you. . . . Dear, dear darling, above all trust me. Remember the words that must be our motto: faith and hope.'

After the sentiments of these letters, the third, written only three days later, was very disturbing. As she herself put it, it 'ought to have been bordered in black'. 'Baby,' it read, 'I would so much have liked to talk to you and to explain everything face to face. . . . Yes, darling, it is an official separation until the end of the war with no possibility of seeing each other. I did not want this, but I had to accept it, having no alternative. . . . After a general peace, I shall have back my freedom. My idol, my life, do not cry that I have betrayed you, I have not. Baby, my adored treasure, it is you alone who are and will be my wife. These are not just words that I write, but the most solemn oath that can be made. I swear to you that as soon as we have peace, I shall find you again and we shall live together happily. I swear it before God. . . .'

Carol was still declaring his love but from the tone Ioana realized that he was being influenced against her best interests. She detected a weakening in his resolve and foresaw that he would proceed from one capitulation to another. He was not subtle enough to defeat their powerful adversaries. Her doubts were confirmed when she read on; the passage hit her like a sledgehammer: 'Trust me completely,' Carol wrote. 'Even when you see that the marriage has been annulled, trust me, for it will only be to calm the situation. . . . Separation does not mean surrender.'

Although Roumania was no longer actually at war at this time, large areas of the country were still occupied by foreign troops and there was no knowing when the 'general peace' referred to by Carol would be established. Ioana had no firm idea therefore how long she and Carol would be separated, assuming there were no further weakening of their position. Even if Carol were pretending to acquiesce in the annulment to regain his freedom and escape with her, he was beginning to seem unreliable, despite his protestations of love. In fairness to Carol, he hated himself for appearing to let her down, and in what she described as a fearful postscript to his letter of 29 September, he begged her to 'let no one know the true settlement, in the name of heaven; I shall never be forgiven'.

The outcome was probably inevitable. Horaitza was a prison only in name and Carol's quarters were very comfortable, but he was isolated (except for his dog) and unable to seek legal or other advice, apart perhaps from spiritual. The pressures on him were enormous, not least from his mother, who very honestly described her own efforts as 'a cruel and sickening victory'. We know the nature of the pressures applied, but not all the details.

The King sent at least two experienced negotiators to see his son, one of whom was no less a personality than General Averescu, while the Queen sent her extraordinary Canadian friend, Colonel Joe Boyle. She also made several visits herself. Marghiloman reported a meeting with the King on 16 September at which Ferdinand told him that Carol would not hear of divorce but was considering the possibility of an annulment. Four days later the King told the Prime Minister that he had seen his son in person. 'I spoke to him as a father,' he said. Carol apparently acknowledged his wrongdoing in leaving his command and crossing the border without permission and was disposed to accept the dissolution of his marriage, but he was unsure whether divorce or annulment was the better course.

With such constant pressure from such high places, it is little wonder that a young man alone should have been confused, and wavered in his intentions. There is absolutely no evidence, however, that the pressure went as far as threats that some harm might befall Ioana if he did not agree to at least a temporary annulment. There was indeed some sympathy for a girl who may have lost her virginity as a result of the Crown Prince's passion for her; and no attempt was made to restrict the liberty of her brother or even of Serdici.

One curious fact is that at the meeting on 20 September between the King and the Prime Minister, Ferdinand revealed that Carol had given him a letter for 'Miss Lambrino', announcing his decision to agree to an annulment. She made no reference to such a letter in her memoirs, and presumably cannot have received it, because otherwise the letter dated the 29th would not have come as a shock. The King for some reason must have decided not to deliver it at that time.

In addition to the pressures on Carol to forsake his marriage, attempts were made to persuade Ioana likewise. She refused to receive General Petala but she did meet Colonel Boyle. Joseph Whiteside Boyle was a devoted admirer of Queen Marie, who described him as 'a curiously fascinating man who is afraid of nothing' and as 'a real Jack London type'. This was an accurate observation, for he was a tough adventurer and the sort of character that a writer like London could well have created, a larger-than-life figure who had tried his hand at many different activities before making his fortune in the Klondike gold rush. Marie spoke of his 'relentless energy' and of a 'quiet force' that emanated from him.

In 1916 he had joined a transport mission that the American Society of Engineers sent to Russia and, ever the showman, he designed for himself the uniform of a British colonel, with lapel badges of real gold, allegedly mined in the Klondike. He was referred to in the British press as the Duke of Bucharest, and at other times as the Duke of Jassy. (The story of his fantastic life was written by Captain George Hill, a British secret-service agent who came to know him well.)

He and Queen Marie met early in 1918, and there is little doubt that he was in love with her, although he was married at the time to his second wife. Marie may have been in love with him, although she was no longer the young girl who would give way to her feelings, especially at a time when she was urging her own son to put duty before love. Hannah Pakula described Marie at the time as 'a desperate queen looking for a twentieth-century Lancelot', and that is probably exactly how she regarded Boyle: as a story-book hero. There was nothing he was not prepared to do for her, even rescuing her relations from the grip of the Russian Revolution, and the more challenging the task, the more enthusiastically he embraced it.

A letter from him to Marie on the occasion of her birthday, 29 October (no year given), speaks for itself: 'God love you My Queen and bless and protect you through many happy years. May each succeeding return of today be the recording mark of the close of a year happier than its predecessor and the herald of a happier one still. I feel that my little token of remembrance will convey to you the knowledge that though absent and serving in a foreign land, my devotion is unalterable and on this day my one regret is that I am not allowed to devote all of my time and energy in the service of My Queen.' It was signed 'Your Colonel'.

It was not therefore surprising that Marie should have sought his help to intervene with her son and Ioana. Boyle, however, did not affect Ioana in the way that he did the Queen. To quote Captain Hill, 'Etiquette and procedure meant nothing to him, especially if a job had to be done.' Perhaps that is why he failed so badly with Ioana, who was scathing about the tricky Canadian, completely lacking in finesse, who called her 'little girl' and referred to Carol as 'the boy'. He tried to persuade her that an annulment was necessary because a valid marriage was legally impossible between the Crown Prince and a Roumanian subject, but he presented annulment as a legal expedient, an arrangement for the sake of appearances only. There was also an attempt to buy her consent.

Ioana consulted two distinguished lawyers, who both gave their opinion that the marriage was valid in law, although one of them told her that in practice she should not expect justice. 'The King,' he said, 'will obtain whatever verdict pleases him.'

This personal drama, although of absorbing importance to its participants, might seem insignificant in the context of the war in Europe, which was finally coming to a close, and when a beaten Roumania had only to sit back and await events as they moved in its favour. The question of Carol's marriage had, however, an importance beyond the legal and private issues. In a volatile situation, with almost every country bordering Roumania on the brink of defeat or in the hands of revolutionaries, the Roumanian monarchy was insecure, and the action of the heir apparent, if publicly known, seemed likely to weaken its cause. It was politically expedient that no shadow should mar the country's joy in the defeat of the Central Powers and the victory of the Entente and its new American allies.

The rejoicing at the end of the Great War provided an excuse for Carol's early release from Horaitza. On armistice day, 11 November (29 October in the old calendar), the Crown Prince was allowed to lead his battalion into Jassy, although it was made a condition of his release that he must not contact his wife. She anxiously took up a position on the route where he could not fail to notice her, but she was shattered when she saw him look at her with what she described as tragic bewilderment. He passed without a word or a sign and although he later tried to see her, it was always done stealthily and never openly.

A few days later, the new Prime Minister, General Coanda, an old friend of the Queen who had replaced the Germanophile Marghiloman, personally met Ioana and told her that annulment was for her a patriotic duty, a sacrifice she should make for her country, and, like Joe Boyle before him, he offered her a liberal financial settlement. She replied that neither money nor honours could make her give up her husband.

Less than three weeks later, Bucharest welcomed back the royal family and government. A triumphal parade was headed by the King and Queen, and their eldest son again rode at the head of his troops. Roumania was announcing its freedom to the nation and the world, but as Marghiloman recorded a fortnight later, 'The mother-in-law and wife of Prince Carol are watched by police in Jassy and are not allowed to leave their home or return to Bucharest.' He made his feelings clear with the addition of the words: 'Land of liberty!'

Although still separated, Carol and Ioana kept in touch. He sent her two books for Christmas and again declared his love, but it is almost certain that, deprived of access to his wife, he had started an affair with an ambitious milliner. The possibility of this latest escapade getting out of hand had a dramatic effect. Scared that this new liaison would cause even further problems for the royal family, particularly when it seemed that it might be exploited for personal advantage, the decision was taken to relax the restriction on Ioana. She was allowed to return to the captial and to Carol, on the principle that it was better to stick to the devil they knew, who was after all of noble birth.

About this time it was also first contemplated to find an excuse to send the Crown Prince abroad on some official or semi-official journey. The Queen was genuinely concerned about her son's unhappiness and actually started a transport business for him to run, hoping that his love of cars would give him an absorbing interest. In the meantime it was hoped that the return of Ioana would keep him out of the clutches of a more dangerous relationship. That his reunion with Ioana was only regarded as temporary is absolutely clear. Steps had already been taken to dissolve the marriage, and as far as the King was concerned, dissolution had already been effected or was in any case a formality.

For a short time, the young couple enjoyed a second honeymoon. Carol left each morning to attend to his military duties, which were not onerous, and he usually returned in the afternoon to go for a walk with Ioana or make some short excursion with her into the countryside. In the evenings, they might play bridge with friends – he always lost, Ioana reported – or listen to gramophone records. Ferdinand and Marie may or may not have given thought to the potentially greater problem that might result from allowing this return to family life, even temporarily, but it was not long before Ioana realized that she was pregnant.

[1] *above* King Carol I of Roumania

[2] *above right* Queen Elisabeth, also known as Carmen Sylva, wife of Carol I

[3] *right* Crown Prince Ferdinand with his young bride, Princess Marie, whom he married in 1893

[4] *above* Castle Peles, the
royal residence at the
summer resort of Sinaia in
the Carpathian Mountains;
birthplace of Prince Carol

[5] *left* Prince Carol aged
about three: 'the beautiful
boy with golden curls'

[6] *opposite* Crown Princess
Marie with her two eldest
children, Prince Carol and
Princess Elisabetha

[7] The poet-queen, Carmen Sylva (in white), presiding
over one of her artistic salons

[8] Prince Carol's paternal grandmother, Princess Antonia,
Infanta of Portugal, with her Roumanian and Hohenzollern
grandchildren; Carol (in sailor suit) and his cousin and
lifelong friend, Prince Friedrich, stand at the back

[9] King Carol I and Crown Prince Ferdinand crossing the frontier during the war against Bulgaria in 1913

[10] The Russian and Roumanian royal families at Constantza, 1914. King Carol I and Tsar Nicholas II stand to left and right; Prince Carol and Crown Prince Ferdinand stand behind Grand Duchess Olga, with Princess Ileana on lap, seated between Tsarina Alexandra and Crown Princess Marie

[11] *right* Prince Carol salutes as King Ferdinand receives the colours after the battle of Marasesti in August 1917

[12] *below* Ioana Lambrino, with Princess Ileana

[13] *below right* Prince Carol as a young man

[14] Carol and Ioana Lambrino at the time of their marriage in Odessa, 1918

[15] Paris newspaper front page of 20 August 1919, reproducing Prince Carol's marriage certificate and his letter renouncing the Roumanian throne

LE PRÉSIDENT POINCARÉ DANS LES RUINES DES VOSGES

EXCELSIOR

MERCREDI
20
AOUT
1919

En aucun cas, il ne peut être juste de nuire à quelqu'un.

UN ROMAN D'AMOUR A LA COUR DE BUCAREST

LE PRINCE HÉRITIER CAROL ADRESSE AU ROI UNE LETTRE D'ABDICATION
LES RAISONS DE LA RENONCIATION DU PRINCE A LA COURONNE ROYALE

Trois pièces officielles : 1° L'acte de mariage du prince et de Mlle Lambrino, enregistré à Odessa, en langue russe, le 31 août 1918; 2° La lettre de renonciation; 3° Le prince, photographié avec sa femme.

(VOIR, EN PAGE 2, LE RÉCIT CIRCONSTANCIÉ DE CET ÉVÉNEMENT SENSATIONNEL ET DE SES CAUSES)

TRADUCTION DE L'ACTE DE MARIAGE

EXTRAIT DU REGISTRE DES MARIAGES POUR L'ANNÉE 1918

DEUXIÈME PARTIE

N° du registre des mariages : 444.

Mois et jour : Août, 31.

Profession, prénoms du père, nom de famille et religion du marié et le nombre des mariages précédents : le colonel du 8° régiment de chasseurs de l'armée royale de Roumanie, Charles-Ferdinand (Ferdinandovitch), fils de roi, en premières noces, Orthodoxe.

Age du marié : 23.

Profession, prénoms du père, nom de famille et religion de la mariée et le nombre des mariages précédents : jeune fille noble, Jeanne-Constantin (Constantinovna) Lambrino, en premières noces, Orthodoxe.

Age de la mariée : 22.

Qui a célébré ce mariage : l'archiprêtre Meleti Chabetsky, assisté du diacre Alexandre Brodovitchon.

Noms des témoins : du marié, l'ex-sous-lieutenant Eugène Meleievitch Charofsky et le gentilhomme Henri Vassilievitch Serdich ; de la mariée, le capitaine d'état-major Serge Meletievitch Charofsky, du 8° régiment de grenadiers de la Tauride du général-feldmaréchal grand-duc Michel Nicolaievitch, et le sous-lieutenant de réserve Constantin Mihailovitch Sentroff.

Signature des témoins (facultatif).

Signatures :

Le supérieur archiprêtre : MELETI CHAROFFSKY.

Le diacre : M. FILIPPOVITCH.

Sur les deux timbres, de 10 copecks chacun, on lit la date : Août 31/1918.

EXTRAIT DU REGISTRE DES MARIAGES MENTIONNANT L'UNION DU PRINCE CAROL DE ROUMANIE ET DE Mlle JEANNE LAMBRINO

TRADUCTION DE LA LETTRE D'ABDICATION

PHOTOGRAPHIE DE LA LETTRE D'ABDICATION DU PRINCE CAROL. — ENTRE LES DEUX FEUILLETS : LE PRINCE ET SA FEMME

[16] Prince
Nicolas in British
Royal Navy
uniform

[17] *below* King
Ferdinand at
Castle Peles

5

Were It Not
for the Child

In retrospect, it is easy to see how the matter of Carol's marriage was mishandled on both sides. Carol himself blew hot, then cold, caught in the conflict between his duty to his country as heir to the throne and his duty to his wife and now to his forthcoming child. Politicians and eminent people in Roumania were more or less content to regard the problem as a family matter, although there was concern that it could in certain unfavourable circumstances affect the monarchy itself. However, the King and Queen, like their son, were indecisive, firm only in their determination that Ioana Lambrino would never be Queen of Roumania. They stalled for time, hoping that something would turn up to help them, that their son would lose interest in his wife when he realized what a sacrifice he must make to keep her.

Much of their attention was anyway focused on world events that were of far wider importance to Roumania than the fate of two young people. These events required the absence at crucial times of some of the leading figures in the domestic drama, as for example when the Queen so ably joined her country's representatives at the Peace Conference in Paris which was reshaping the map of Europe. As a result of this reshaping, Roumania more than doubled its size and population, acquiring the whole of Transylvania and most of Bukovina from Hungary (now detached from Austria), Bessarabia from Russia and the southern part of Dobruja that had been lost so recently to Bulgaria. Such was the reward of having chosen the winning side.

Czechoslovakia, Poland and Yugoslavia became countries, newly created or reconstituted, on Roumania's border. Their stability was an unknown factor. The other borderng countries were defeated Bulgaria and Communist Russia, now the Union of Soviet Socialist Republics. In such circumstances, the isolated Roumanian monarchy looked far from secure, despite the enormous prestige of Queen

Marie. Carol's problems thus came at the very time when the Roumanian monarchy – and more important, the Roumanian people – needed stability. Any questioning of the line of succession to the throne might upset the balance and perhaps bring an end to the monarchy itself.

The young heir apparent meanwhile received the news of his wife's pregnancy with great joy. She had thought about aborting the child but he wrote to her, forbidding such an action. 'We have wanted this so much,' he protested. 'Why at a whim seek to destroy the fruit of our passion?' Ioana's pregnancy helped to clarify Carol's mind. He knew now at last where his first loyalty lay and was determined that his future should be with his wife and child. Early in May he had given Ioana the jewellery that Queen Elisabeth had bequeathed to him with the intention that it should be handed on at his betrothal to the future Queen. It was symbolic of his new purpose to stick by Ioana.

He proposed that he give up the succession and depart the country with her. This was not at all what his parents had in mind. They did not dare put the dynasty at risk at such a crucial time; in any case, as far as they were concerned, the marriage was officially over. For them, the matter was settled by the Tribunal of Ilfov, which had been set up to examine and annul the marriage, a tribunal at which neither Carol nor Ioana participated.

The prospect of soon becoming a father galvanized Carol into activity, if not into sensible action, for in his distressed state of mind he behaved with increasing wildness. Ioana described an occasion when he 'threw himself beneath his horse in the hope, if not of killing himself, of at least wounding himself seriously'. She spoke of this as 'one of those dramatic gestures' that were more in keeping with the actions of a spoilt child than with true courage, although Carol may have been simulating an accident or making it appear worse than it was. This striking of dangerous attitudes, doubtless brought on by stress and to attract attention to his cause, was, however, hardly likely to help his wife and baby.

Even more grave, when in May the King suggested that his son should join a trade mission to Japan, with the obvious intention of getting him out of the way temporarily, Carol took a revolver and shot himself in the leg, not seriously but badly enough to immobilize himself and make it impossible to travel. Ioana noted that neither King nor Queen visited their son following his self-inflicted accident, but there can be no doubt of their concern, for Marie sent her loyal friend Stirbey to ask Carol to wait three months – not six, as stated by Ioana – before abdicating his rights and going abroad, allowing time to effect the necessary legalities and to prepare public opinion. Carol regarded any delay as excessive but he accepted his mother's suggestion to take a holiday with Ioana in Monasteria, on the Danube, where he could recuperate while his demands were being considered in Bucharest. On 15 June, the couple arrived at their holiday home, where they enjoyed themselves thoroughly. The Queen's proposal was a typical stalling tactic: if Carol would not accept a delay, she could at least keep him happy and out of the way until some opportunity arose to deal with him or until he again brought the issue to the boil. It was not long before a pretext was found once more to separate him from Ioana.

Extraordinary events had been occurring in Hungary. Three months earlier, while the Peace Conference was still in session in Paris, Lenin's disciple Bela Kun seized power in Budapest and set up a revolutionary government on Bolshevik lines. Although he had no truck with the old political leaders, he was careful not to antagonize the army officers and actually managed to enlist their reluctant support to some extent for a reorganization of the military.

The dangers of this development were felt more keenly in neighbouring Roumania than among the world's statesmen in Paris, who sent South Africa's General Smuts to negotiate with Kun. When it became clear that Smuts's intervention was unlikely to restrain Kun's excesses, the Roumanians decided to take a stand themselves against the ruthless Communist regimes that were threatening both the country's eastern and western borders.

Roumanian forces entered Hungary, quickly pushing Kun's troops away from the Roumanian border and occupying the Hungarian borderland. This protective action brought international criticism and speedy word from Paris that under no circumstances must Roumanian units proceed to Budapest. That Roumania was justified in her alarm at Hungary's motives became evident, however, at the end of May when Kun attacked Slovakia, part of the newly created Czechoslovakia. As Dr Seton-Watson wrote, 'In this he followed the double aim of saving Slovakia for Hungary and establishing direct contact with Russia across Galicia.'

At last the major Powers in Paris took notice of the danger and issued an ultimatum to Kun, who realized that he had gone too far. He dutifully withdrew his troops from Slovakia, but it was not long before he threw them against Roumania, in what Seton-Watson described as 'a gambler's throw', reckoning doubtless that inter-national opinion would be less inclined to support Roumania while it was actually occupying a particularly fertile area of Hungary.

Roumania was not unprepared for the attack. In any case the morale of the Hungarian army had been shattered by their withdrawal from Slovakia, and they were no match for the Roumanians. It took the Roumanian troops precisely five days to smash the 85,000-strong Hungarian forces and bring the revolutionary government to an end. The Roumanians proceeded to occupy Budapest and Kun fled to Vienna, hardly to be heard from again. Had Kun succeeded, the Communist system would probably have been established throughout the area immediately after the First World War instead of after the Second.

It was these problems with Hungary that provided the royal family in Roumania with the excuse they needed to interrupt the idyll of Carol and Ioana in Monasteria. The Prince was recalled to his army duties, with the Minister of War, Vaitoyanu, and Joe Boyle being sent by the Queen to ask him to rejoin his regiment.

Carol was at first intransigent. He banged the table angrily, declaring that the mobilization order was entirely political, that the army was involved more in a police action than a war, that he had a pregnant wife to protect, and that he was unwilling to acquiesce until his future situation had been clarified. Nevertheless, as soon as his visitors had departed, he decided to return to Bucharest, determined first to do his duty and then renounce the throne.

He may well have been influenced by his mother, who wrote to him: 'For the last time, in the name of all you hold sacred, I ask you is it possible that you can let your regiment go to the front without you ... have you lost all sense of honour and duty ...? Is it not better to die, a bullet in the head, to be buried in good Roumanian soil, than to betray your country? Carol, where is the little boy with golden curls who was the most beautiful gift I gave my country at the age of seventeen? ... At this time when I go among the wounded at the front, is it possible that instead of being at my side you will flee the country you are betraying, like a thief, like a man who has never known honour? One day, Carol, you will understand all the dreadful things you are doing. How can you achieve happiness at the price of your humiliation? Make another effort, become a man again, leave with your regiment, fight like a soldier, redeem your honour and show the world that you are the man I believed you were at least a year ago.

'Carol, Carol, do not break my heart.'

This highly emotional appeal brought forth the following reply: 'No one knows better than I the seriousness of the situation. I see it better than you all, for I know that my duties are heavy. The idea that my regiment should leave without me at its head in the middle of the fight is very hard to take. I have never refused to leave for the front and I am ready to rejoin the regiment as soon as my situation with Zizi is clear and precise.

'The whole question could not be simpler and clearer were it not for the child. I do not want to leave her in this painful and ridiculous position. I must spare the woman I have chosen for life as much humiliation as possible. In my case I can never admit that this child is other than legitimate, and whatever happens I shall always recognise him. . . .

'I want to settle this matter, and the very next day I shall join my regiment. So you will see that it does not depend only on me. . . .'

Carol's departure for Bucharest may also have been influenced by his assumption that any military action must be over in a few days, perhaps a month at most. He may, too, have considered that he would be in a stronger bargaining position if he had been seen to do his duty to his country. His desire to save Ioana 'as much humiliation as possible' was put at risk, however, as soon as he was no longer at her side. She reported that the chauffeur he had left behind was taken away from her, that her house was watched by police, that attempts were made to suborn her servants and that her mail to and from Carol was intercepted.

One letter that did reach her may have given her pause for thought. 'I am completely faithful to you,' it read. 'Have no fear on this point and above all do not believe what anyone says to you on this subject. They are only lies and the last weapon they have invented to make you renounce me.'

It was at this time that Carol took independent steps to force the issue of his future. He had finally come to the conclusion that he must if necessary give up everything for his wife and child. He probably reckoned that by formally announcing an intention to abdicate his right to the throne, he would bring the matter to a head. It was one thing to dither when he was first married, but he could not now afford to wait when his wife was four months' pregnant.

While in the capital, he consulted two senior politicians, Take Ionescu and Alexandru Marghiloman, about the correct form of an act of renunciation. He was not concerned to discuss the issue but only sought advice as to procedure. Marghiloman reported the matter in his diary entry on 31 July: 'I was woken at midnight by Ciocardia. He was summoned by Prince Carol to Cotroceni. Boyle had delivered a condemnatory letter to the Prince from the Queen: exile in Switzerland, all legations forbidden to marry, etc., if he did not go to the front. The Prince replied that he would do so immediately but that he wants first to settle his matrimonial status . . . he wants to renounce the throne. I have been asked for a formula. . . . The Prince is absolutely firm. He also wants to settle by will the situation of his family. . . .'

Marghiloman drafted a statement that Carol chose to accept in preference to that drafted by Ionescu. On the Prince's instructions, copies were made and distributed to the King and to Prime Minister Bratianu, among others. Significantly, a copy went also to the Socialist leader Dragou, in the certain knowledge that its contents would thereby be disseminated. In fact it was reproduced in a Paris newspaper, *Excelsior*, and copied by a Bucharest newspaper, whose edition was immediately seized by the police. The statement, dated 1 August 1919, addressed to the King and signed 'Carol, Prince of Roumania', was short and to the point:

'By virtue of a natural right implicity recognized in article 83 paragraph 2 of the Constitution, I hereby renounce my title of hereditary prince to the throne of Roumania, both for myself and my heirs, as well as all rights recognized by the Constitution as pertaining to the heir apparent.

'I remain the servant of my country and, in putting my sword at its service, I beg Your Majesty to give me a place among the soldiers who are now at the front.'

To complement this dramatic gesture, Carol also executed a will in favour of his wife and wrote to her: 'Leaving for the front to resume command of my regiment, we do not know what may happen. I want all the world to know that the child you are carrying is mine and that despite the annulment of our marriage, I still consider myself your husband.'

Having made his announcement, Carol left for the front. Coincidentally, the train in which he travelled to Hungary crossed with that in which the King was returning to Roumania from visiting the troops, but by then the enemy was already in disarray.

Five days later, Marghiloman was summoned to Cotroceni by the King. The audience lasted two and a half hours and the first subject discussed was the Crown Prince's purported renunciation of his rights. Matters had now reached a point where a draft document had actually been prepared for the King in the event that his son's abdication was to be allowed to proceed.

Marghiloman reported that the King was very unhappy, accusing his son of having put a wall between them. Ferdinand was bitter about Ioana, whom he said would deceive Carol 'whenever and as often as she wishes'. He believed that his son was also seeing another woman, but that Ioana completely dominated him: 'The sound of her voice is enough to make him forget everything.' One might take the remark about another woman more seriously if the King had not also said that he did not believe that Ioana was pregnant and that when Carol realized this, he might come to his senses. Ferdinand was clearly not facing reality and was therefore incapable of dealing dispassionately with the problem.

What he apparently had in mind was that Carol should be allowed to renounce the succession – although he agreed that his son should continue to be known as Prince – and leave the country for at least three months. If he wished to marry Ioana or anybody else, he would have to do so abroad. Apart from begging the question of whether Carol was already married, the King's attitude again revealed the hope that, given enough time, his son would see sense. Perhaps, he seemed to be thinking, the boy will return in due course without a wife, but at worst with a wife whose marriage abroad might be regarded as morganatic if ever Carol resumed his old status or some alternative royal dignity. Ferdinand in effect was clutching at straws. His confused attitude was further revealed when he attacked the allegedly evil influence of Carol's old tutor, 'the anarchist Mohrlen', whom Carol still trusted.

If the King was resigned to giving way to his son, such was not the case with the Queen, who still felt that she could change the course of events. She did all she could to suppress the news of Carol's intentions, although the Socialists had already leaked his announcement to the press. Popular opinion had not yet had time to form and whereas government ministers and informed observers were largely on the side of the King, prominent people felt inhibited in offering advice unless it was sought. The question of the succession was still at the time considered a matter for the family.

Carol had been determined to resolve his situation, but it was allowed to simmer dangerously. With the brief war over, he was confined to an army camp at Bistritza in Transylvania, with the clear indication that unauthorized departure would be regarded as desertion. Ioana was forbidden to visit him, although she made an unsuccessful attempt to do so. In the meantime his mother kept up the pressure. She wrote him a long letter on 19 September, in response to letters from him asking to be allowed to rejoin his wife, which very clearly explained her position:

'Returning from Bicaz last night, I was given your two letters. They reached me so late, I cannot understand, and you mention having written three times, yet I received only two letters.

'What astonishes me about them is their extraordinary tone. You seem to want to play the accuser, quite forgetting that you are the one who is misbehaving, not me. You had given us a formal and signed statement, saying that you would do your duty in a dignified way as long as your father considered the country needed you, that is to say till it was out of its difficulties, and that at the end of that time you would honestly declare if you had changed your mind or not, and then by your good behaviour you would have won your right to what you call your happiness and *we* consider your misfortune.

'Instead of that you behaved on every occasion beneath yourself, your position, your education, sinking lower and lower, till you put yourself entirely into the hands of an association of people who have no code of honour and who have dragged you down from your level to theirs. One day you will realise this, now you apparently cannot. You broke loose from all ties that had been dear and holy. You denied your country, your sisters and brother, your traditions and your duty at an hour when more than at any time in its history, Roumania was in need of its rulers. You talked of morality, of regeneration, of leading a benighted people towards light, you judged your father, criticised all those who after all were trying to do something (even if badly) for their country, then just you, who were to have been their example, their hope, you desert your post at a moment when your country was the most humiliated and your parents were fighting a deadly battle against overwhelming odds, to run away, after a woman! And then to make an absolutely unjustifiable action appear less monstrous, you coat it over with some heroic talk of how you were going to try and deliver your country from the other side!

'Seeing the mess you have got into by your own want of character, you consult some vicious little lawyer recommended to you by the pack of thieves amongst whom you have fallen and throw a document into the world which is to rid you of every obligation towards your country and family. At the moment most convenient to you, you chuck over everything, regardless of the harm you are doing, and instigated by others, you intrigue with the Socialists, thereby hoping to weaken your father's position. Then when you feel desperate, you turn round and want to play the accuser, the one who has the right to kick up any scandal to gain your own ends.

'They have been rotting you to the core, all those fine friends you now so proudly associate with – you who I had hoped were going to be the leader of the country towards light. Oh! I wish you would see yourself as others see you – just a love-sick weakling who has lost all sense of honour and duty.

'Now after ignoring all my prayers and entreaties, when you are at the end of your tether, you turn to me for help that God knows I would like to give you and I am still just and ready as ever to give you if you come back to your senses, but under the present conditions I cannot see how any change can be made by your father in your military situation. You are now in the hands of the army which has explicit instructions that for any act of desertion or wrongdoing you are to be treated and punished just the same as any other officer, and I your mother as Queen cannot change this.

'I am called abroad and although the inner political situation and the position with the Allies is very difficult, I have to do my duty as I had at one time hoped you would do yours. I have missed you bitterly at every turn and cannot realise that I must learn to work without what had been my right hand for so many years. I shall probably be gone for a month and because of the desperate and offensive tone of your letters, I feel it necessary to let you know the exact position of Papa and myself so that you should not commit some rash and foolish act which would destroy you, trading on the false belief that at the last minute we would relent.'

This letter made no attempt to see anything from Carol's viewpoint, and the bitterness felt by Marie shows in her reference to 'some vicious little lawyer'; in fact her son had consulted two of the most respected figures in the land. The Queen had made the speech for the prosecution, unaware (or unwilling to admit) that there was a case for the defence. Perhaps she saw everything from her point of view in essentially black and white terms; perhaps she merely chose to ignore facts that did not suit her argument. Whatever the truth, her attitude was painfully clear. She would not agree to Carol rejoining Ioana and if he tried to do so, he would be treated as a military deserter.

Not content with letters, the Queen sought the help of a close friend of Carol, an army officer named Mugur, whom she sent to

Bistritza to plead with him. She also again used Joe Boyle, who on one occasion spent three days trying to convince Carol to change his mind about abdicating. Marie was quite determined, and she was a very powerful personality and widely respected. She admitted later that 'I must seem a tremendously ambitious woman who got her way, destroying my son's happiness because of my formidable pride'. There seems no doubt that Carol's behaviour towards his mother in later years was coloured by his harsh experiences at her hands at this time. Yet to Marie, she was only acting in her son's best interests, which in her mind coincided with the best interests of the State.

Carol, torn between conflicting duties, could do little but protest, but his efforts to put his case seemed in vain; no one appeared willing to listen. He wrote a series of letters, seeking the support of leading political figures, but only one even replied. As Ioana wrote, what was the point of fighting on?

Christmas came and Carol was still a virtual prisoner at Bistritza, although his parents came to visit him. He informed Ioana that he had written to his mother, asking her to let him go to Bucharest for the birth of their child. He received no reply.

Ioana gave birth on 8 January 1920 to a boy. They called him Carol Mircea, after his father and his baby uncle who had died so young.

6

The Great Sacrifice

What may seem, and often was, the peculiar behaviour of the principal characters in the marriage drama can to some extent be explained by the verdict of the Tribunal of Ilfov, which met in 1918 to consider the subject of Carol's marriage to Ioana. Before and since, there has been a common misunderstanding that the Roumanian Constitution prohibited the marriage of the heir apparent to a Roumanian national. Even Carol's youngest sister, Princess Ileana (now Mother Alexandra), told me: 'The stipulation that no member of the royal family, male or female, was permitted to marry a Roumanian was a law in 1866, laid down by the country when inviting a foreign ruler.' But there was no such law. The 1866 Constitution, to which she was presumably referring, and which was unanimously adopted by the National Assembly, required Carol I's descendants to be brought up in the eastern Orthodox faith, but there was no mention in this Constitution of conditions of marriage.

Princess Anne-Marie Callimachi reported in her book that when Ferdinand wished to marry Helena Vacarescu, the Prime Minister told him that the heir presumptive 'must marry a foreign Princess, equal in rank and birth, who can be his future Queen. The Constitution is quite definite on this matter.' But in fact the Constitution ignored it. Hannah Pakula was similarly mistaken when she said, 'The writers of the Roumanian Constitution, fearing that one Roumanian clan or faction might gain control of the throne, specifically prohibited marriage between members of the royal house and their subjects.' She was right about the thinking behind the preference for a foreign marriage but wrong about any specific prohibition. It was only subsequent to Carol's marriage to Ioana Lambrino and the birth of their son in 1920 that this and similar matters were dealt with formally by an Act of Parliament, dated 4

January 1926 and promulgated in the *Official Monitor* the following day.

Guy des Cars made a possibly more significant point when he wrote that the heir to the throne 'can only be married with the authorisation of the government, ratified by Parliament'. This idea may have arisen from the fact that the Roumanian Constitution was based on the Belgian, which provided that the Crown Prince needed the consent of the King to marry; but nowhere was this promulgated in Roumania. The possibility of the heir to the throne wishing to marry without the monarch's approval probably never occurred to anybody.

Ioana herself reported a conversation between King Ferdinand and Carol in which he told his son that she was not sufficiently noble to become Crown Princess. It is odd that the King should have advanced this argument instead of the one about her being a Roumanian subject, although perhaps he made that point also. Carol protested that the Lambrinos were more noble, knowing their aristocratic background, but Ferdinand clearly equated nobility with being foreign.

There was never any doubt that the Tribunal set up to look at the whole issue of the marriage would act as a rubber stamp to the King's wishes. As Ioana had been shrewdly told, 'The King will obtain whatever verdict pleases him.' The Tribunal was there in effect to annul the marriage, and annul the marriage it would do. It did, however, accept the fact that, contrary to popular belief, neither in the 1866 Constitution nor in any law enacted in Roumania prior to Carol's marriage to a fellow Roumanian was there a legal restriction on his freedon to marry. What was claimed, undoubtedly correctly, was that Carol's marriage to a fellow Roumanian was against the spirit of the Constitution – but that in no way invalidated the marriage in law.

If the marriage was not constitutionally unlawful, another reason had to be found to annul it, and a number of arguments were advanced before the Tribunal. One was that Carol, being a soldier at the time, had not obtained the consent of his commanding officer. However, it was highly doubtful if a marriage contracted without military consent could actually be invalidated on that ground, even though it might incur some disciplinary action, and the argument did not seem to have swayed the Tribunal. Indeed, it agreed that the marriage had been correctly conducted in accordance with prescribed local laws in the presence of witnesses. What it finally pronounced was that the marriage was void by reason of secrecy.

This verdict relied on article 174 of the Roumanian Civil Code, which required that an announcement of marriage be made in the newspapers. It was a very narrow legal point. The article could hardly have been intended to apply to a marriage contracted abroad; and in any case the Civil Code did not provide that lack of publication was in itself cause for annulment. Had Carol participated in the legal proceedings, he might well have pointed out that in any case the Roumanian consul in Odessa had been made aware of the marriage before the event. Carol had taken immediate steps to inform his father after the event, and although the elopement had of course been meant to be secret, this was not contrary to law. Paradoxically, too, the royal family had at first preferred to suppress news of the marriage and would have been horrified had an announcement appeared in a Bucharest newspaper. According to Ioana, when the new edition of the *Almanach de Gotha* appeared, which listed the marriage, Queen Marie was furious: 'It's another dirty Boche trick!' she yelled.

The proceedings of the Tribunal had been political rather than juridical. They took only a quasi-legal form, for the two people principally involved took no part in them, nor was there any right of appeal from the resulting judgement. Indeed the verdict was never officially communicated to Carol, although a copy was sent by messenger to Ioana. Had Carol been legally represented, there were issues that might have well been raised on his behalf. He might even have argued that the Tribunal was incompetent to deal with a marriage validly contracted in a foreign country and in the eyes of the Church. He would certainly have been able to respond to the charge of clandestinity which the Tribunal finally selected as its reason to annul the marriage.

The verdict of Ilfov was actually given in December 1918 but it was not officially registered in Bucharest until 13 April 1919, and it was only on 7 May that it was reported in the *Official Monitor*. The delay in seeming to give effect to its judgement may have been partly due to the fact that the King and Queen hoped that Carol would walk away from the marriage of his own accord; partly to give them time to try to buy off Ioana; or perhaps even because so few people knew about the marriage that to announce its annulment might have caused more problems than it solved. Ironically, the marriage in

Odessa was not officially registered in Roumania until the day of the registration of its annulment.

At all events, from 7 May 1919 onwards, the King took the view that the marriage was legally over, whereas Carol and Ioana were uncertain about their legal status. This may explain why on occasions, under pressure, they seemed to acknowledge the annulment when in fact all they were doing was to recognize the legal position in Roumania if Ilfov was accepted. At no time did they regard themselves as other than man and wife, and at no time did Carol deny his unborn son.

The official annulment was legally highly suspect, but even so did it have legal authority in Roumania? Was the judgement so perverse that the annulment could not be regarded as effective, in which case Carol Mircea, my father, could have become King of Roumania, or is the fact that it was recognized by the Roumanian establishment sufficient to defeat its inherent weaknesses, in which case the line quite properly descended from Carol's second marriage?

The fact that Carol remarried did not necessarily affect the legal position of his heirs. Even if he eventually consented to the annulment, this does not imply that he ever regarded his first marriage as having been invalidly contracted. Carol always recognized Carol Mircea as his legitimate son.

These legal matters were tested many years later, after Carol's death. In the first case, my father sued Carol's third wife, Magda Lupescu, and his own half-brother, by then the former King Michael, in Lisbon. In April 1955 the court decided that my father was the legitimate son of King Carol II and that he was entitled to have succeeded him. In considering the validity of the Tribunal of Ilfov, the Portuguese court made the points that neither Carol nor Ioana had participated in the proceedings, that the outcome was contrary to their wishes, that the Tribunal had failed to take into account their honest belief in the correctness of their actions, that the marriage was contracted in good faith, that there had been no violation of Roumanian law and that the verdict had been given for political, rather than legal, reasons.

In a second action, brought in 1957 in Paris, the French court supported the Portuguese judgement. Many of the same points were argued. It was stated that there was no known precedent for a marriage to be annulled on the ground of clandestinity where the parties had acted in good faith, and that in this case it was enough that the wedding had been celebrated publicly in the presence of witnesses. Once again the court spoke of political considerations and said explicitly that the Ilfov judges had obeyed reasons of State.

These matters are now academic but the later legal cases point to the considerable significance of the original debate about Carol's marriage and its annulment. It is interesting to note that the courts in Lisbon and Paris were not invited to consider the issue of whether at any time Carol had renounced the succession for himself and his heirs, presumably because if the heirs of the first marriage were thereby excluded, so too must have been the heirs of the second marriage. In any case, any attempts at renunciation were not officially recognized or accepted; and even had they been, the fact that Carol subsequently became King would have negated them.

A major reason why such ardent endeavours were made to suppress the news of Carol's attempt to renounce the succession is revealed in Marghiloman's diary entry for 8 January 1920: 'A son has been born to Madame Zizi Lambrino. . . . It is still hoped to detach the Prince from his beloved and to persuade her to give him his freedom. . . . No one wants the continuity of the dynasty to rest on a single head.' With Carol no longer in line, the future of the monarchy would rest on sixteen-year-old Prince Nicolas; and if anything should happen to him, a foreign prince would again have to be imported on the death of King Ferdinand, since the succession was through the male line only. What had been welcomed in 1866 might not prove acceptable to Roumanian public opinion more than fifty years later. This was the strength of Carol's position, if he but knew it; and perhaps it explains why, despite his difficulties, he had boasted to his fellow army officers that nothing would stop him becoming King of Roumania.

The weakness of his position was that his parents were able to keep him in the army, separated from Ioana, and to apply constant pressure to get him to put his duty to his country above that to his wife. One can almost hear the arguments put to him: 'Are you prepared to give up the unique opportunity to become King of what is now one of the most important countries in Europe? Are you willing to sacrifice the privileges and the pleasures of such a position and to turn your back on a country that needs you? And for what – for a woman? You are a man whom God has placed in a position of wealth, power and influence. It would be criminal to reject all this for the sake of a woman, no matter how much you love her. Do you not also love your country and your parents and your fellow officers and your good friends, who all look to you for support? Throughout history men have loved women, and sometimes fallen out of love with them. Even if she has been faithful to you, have you been completely faithful to her?'

No doubt these and similar arguments were advanced with a mixture of threat and cajolement, depending on the speaker. No doubt too it was urged on Carol that it was in Ioana's best interests as well as his own that he should leave her. There is no question also that suitable financial arrangements were proposed for Ioana and the baby.

The question of Carol's faithfulness to Ioana is interesting; there is too much evidence of other temporary liaisons for his fidelity not to be doubted. Indeed it is almost certain that he had a son by another woman in 1918, the year of his marriage, but although the child was conceived before he was legally committed to Ioana, he appears not to have told her about his secret love affair of such recent date.

Public knowledge of this matter did not surface for four years, and even then the facts were obscure. Marghiloman referred in his diary to a scandal involving a woman named Leonescu and her husband, a stationmaster in Bucharest. There were accusations of bouncing cheques and a large-scale swindle, and the judge in charge of the investigation discovered a batch of letters from Prince Carol to the woman which referred to 'our children'. Marghiloman went on to say that Carol had met the young woman 'at the time of the Lambrino intrigues'; he reported that she 'was thrown into the arms of Carol, from which followed a pregnancy and an arranged marriage' with the stationmaster.

Returning to the matter eight days later, he wrote: 'I learn . . . that in the letters that were seized, the Prince recognises the paternity of – why in the plural when only one is of the age to be his responsibility? – the children of Madame Leonescu. The Prince writes that he would like to have called the last one – aged four – Caesar, but that he agreed to Silviu at the behest of the mother. Madame Leonescu had relations with the Prince before his marriage – at the time one wanted to separate him from Zizi Lambrino – and continued after his marriage. The young lady, dressed as a soldier, was introduced to the Prince while he was commanding in the north. . . . I recall that it was rumoured at the time in Bucharest that the Prince had a child by a Transylvanian girl: this must be little Silviu. The woman was married to a stationmaster.'

Marghiloman than gave details of the money presumably paid to the woman and her new husband to buy her off. 'This was the time,' he concluded, 'when the Prince was writing me the letter in which he put himself and his wife Zizi under my protection!'

There are·a number of inconsistencies in this story that cast doubt on it. In his first entry, Marghiloman said that Carol had met Madame Leonescu at the time of the Lambrino intrigues; in his second, he admitted that the couple had had relations before the Lambrino marriage, which must have been the case if Silviu was aged four at the time of the diary entries, assuming of course he was Carol's child. It is difficult to know what reliance can be put on Marghiloman's other statements that Carol continued to see Madame Leonescu after his marriage to Ioana. It is easier perhaps to accept his comment that the relationship with Leonescu was still continuing at the time of the scandal, because it might well have been revived.

What is puzzling, however, is that Carol should have written so very many letters to Leonescu. Of that there is no doubt. Unfortunately, a judge was prevailed on to hand over the correspondence to a representative of the Palace, and the letters were suppressed, perhaps even destroyed, so that they cannot be inspected; it is clear, however, that many of them must have been written after Carol's marriage to Ioana, even if one cannot say for certain that some of them were written at much the same time as the Prince was writing to his wife. He was a passionate and inveterate letter writer, if nothing else.

We can only imagine Carol's state of mind when he was put under such great pressure to abandon his wife. His actions are open to differing interpretations. In any case his situation was outside normal experience. He was heir to the throne and millions of people might be affected by his decision; and the pressure on him was from the most powerful people in the land. It would have been more surprising had he not succumbed. Whatever his feelings for Ioana, even in his bemused state he must have weighed the apparent security of his position as Crown Prince against the uncertainties of life in exile with a woman he could probably never leave in such circumstances, even if they tired of each other.

At all events, the day before the birth of his son to Ioana, his parents visited him at the army camp in Bistritza and he finally told them that he was ready to make 'the great sacrifice'. He had taken the decision to put country before love, and he declared his intention to resume his royal duties, thereby effectively abandoning his earlier attempt at renunciation.

Even at the last minute, however, he was assuring Ioana that he would never desert her. 'The other day Boyle was here,' he wrote. 'He tried every way he knew to force me ... to renounce you. ... Courage, my darling wife. All will be well, I am sure, and we shall soon be the happiest and most united family possible.' The letter ended with the words 'Yours for life.'

Life turned out to be less than a fortnight. Ioana then received what she called 'the letter of rupture and abandonment'. It announced that Carol was yielding to pressure and obeying his duties towards the country. He said that he was convinced that in the long term his decision to sacrifice himself was in her best interest, and he was renouncing 'a union to which his heart nevertheless remains faithful'. He offered her his undying friendship.

He was telling her clearly that he had put his head before his heart, and it can only have been the more painful to her that his decision came almost simultaneously with the birth of their son. In her published memoirs, she wrote that she was told later that Carol's letter was dictated to him, that he kept stopping and trying to insert a softer word here and there; and that he was in tears at the time and consuming large amounts of alcohol. She admitted, however, that this story might be apocryphal.

Undying friendship was not at all what Ioana wanted. Although she claimed that she was distressed by the publicity, it is almost certain that it was she, at the instigation of certain opposition politicians, who provided the newspaper *Epoca* with a copy of the letter that Carol had written to her when he left for the Hungarian front, in which he admitted that he was the father of her child and that he had never ceased to regard himself as her husband. The newspaper published a facsimile copy only eight days after the birth of the baby.

The letter caused a sensation because it was the first public indication that the Crown Prince had a son. The name of the father on the child's birth certificate was unprecedentedly left blank – 'another danger overcome', according to Queen Marie! In fact not many people in Roumania even knew that Carol had married. As in Britain in 1936 when references to King Edward's interest in Mrs Simpson were kept out of the newspapers although it was widely reported abroad, so in Roumania news of the marriage in Odessa had gone largely unreported.

By publishing Carol's letter, Ioana had in fact provided him with an opportunity, should he wish to seize it, to rally support in the country, particularly among anti-government factions; but Carol either regarded this as too dangerous a game or perhaps he had already made up his mind, despite his ardent protestations to the contrary, that his future must be without Ioana. His declaration to his parents may have been more genuinely based than his much trumpeted love for the mother of his child. At any rate, publication of his private letter served only to incense him. Somewhat peevishly he wrote another letter, to Professor Murnu, for publication in the newspaper *Universul*, complaining that his personal letter to Ioana had not been intended for publication. Ioana, however, was not concerned with the law of copyright. She had made her point and told the world that Carol had an heir.

It was to no avail. The authorities, and possibly Carol himself, were now more than ever determined to keep her out of the way. Carol was to be sent on a long journey across the world, in the hope that he would be able finally to put his marriage behind him. This would also provide further time for the authorities to see what best could be done with Ioana, especially now that she had a baby. This time there was no bullet in the leg. Carol agreed almost willingly to join a trade mission that would keep him out of the country for seven or eight months, although he exacted a promise from his mother that she would do what she could to help his wife and child.

He set sail from Constantza in the early morning of 21 February 1920. He had not seen Ioana for well over six months, since the day he left Monasteria for the front, and they would not meet again until 1925 in Paris. She never forgave him for not at least visiting their child once before his departure, a fact that even surprised Queen Marie.

7

The Spell
Is Broken

Carol was accompanied on his foreign tour by an entourage of eight people, including a political minder named Filodor, who doubtless reported his actions to Bucharest. The ship first called at Piraeus, enabling the party to explore the Ancient Greek monuments in and around Athens, before visiting Egypt. In Alexandria, the Prince reviewed a guard of honour, and in Cairo, the Sultan entertained his visitor privately in his palace, serving Turkish coffee. Egypt at the time was still a British protectorate, and Field Marshal Allenby gave the Prince a spectacular military welcome. Carol also visited the Pyramids and other historical sites, before proceeding to Aswan, Luxor and Ismailia. He then embarked for Port Said by steamer and met the daughter of Ferdinand de Lesseps, whose vision had created the Suez Canal.

While in Cairo, he wrote to Ioana. 'My life is nothing but a torment,' he told her, 'and an eternal remorse. My thought is only for you, my darling, and for the cradle I adore and for which I suffer so much. I have such mad bouts of despair that I do not know what to do and think. . . . The awareness of duty is but a consolation for the heart.'

At Port Said, the party joined a larger vessel that stopped briefly at Massawa in Eritrea, *en route* for Ceylon. At Massawa, he wrote again to Ioana. Two letters in such quick succession hardly indicate a desire to break with her, suggesting that he had made a conscious decision to play the game by his parents' rules and to their orders, while not deserting her in his heart. He continued to write in loving terms, possibly out of a guilty conscience, or, as Ioana suggested, from a feeling of homesickness.

'My life away from you is despair,' he now declared. 'I am, you must know, the unhappiest of beings. . . . I think only of you and our little one and I have only one misgiving, how you put up with this frightful separation. Eight terrible months worse than all the tortures of hell . . . but I still keep my head high and my heart young and so crazy about you. . . . I have your adorable photograph, which smiles at me above my bunk . . . my stubborn thought flies always to you two darling creatures. . . . Always and always your Boysky.'

After a brief visit to Aden, the party reached Ceylon on 10 April 1920 and spent a week on the island, mostly in Colombo and Kandy. Next they embarked on a British cruiser for Bombay, where the authorities put out the red carpet: a squadron of native cavalry paraded in their colourful turbans, followed by a selection of British army units in India. Carol was taken to visit many of the famous sites of the country, including the Taj Mahal and the Red Fort in Delhi. His party were the guests of the Maharajah of Patiala in his enormous palace, where they were greeted by a guard of honour from their host's private army and were escorted on elephants to a magnificent tiger hunt. Simla, Kashmir, Srinagar and Calcutta all followed, and then the royal tourist and his entourage set sail for Rangoon.

In Burma they visited the famous pagodas and proceeded to Penang, where Carol was received by the Sultan of Johore. They then sailed to Hong Kong and Shanghai, before leaving for Japan. The Prince was certainly seeing the world and after his initial declarations to Ioana he did not seem during all this activity to have found the time or inclination to write to her.

She reported an important visit at about this time from General Averescu, who was again Prime Minister, to discuss her future. One suggestion was made to the effect that her marriage should be declared morganatic, which would automatically have excluded her children from the succession. Although she expressed interest in this idea, she heard nothing more on the subject. A number of writers have referred to the morganatic nature of the marriage, but in fact this was never more than a point of discussion. The marriage and the subsequent annulment were either valid or not, but there was never a morganatic contract.

The royal family and the authorities were clearly waiting to see what Carol would do on his return, hoping that time was on their side and that the longer the young people were separated, the more chance there was that the Prince's ardour would cool, that he would meet someone else, or that Ioana would leave him. She reported a proposal of marriage from an unexpected and unwelcome source which she rejected angrily, suspecting that the suitor had been put up to it.

There was of course always the possibility that absence would make the heart grow fonder, especially as there was a baby whom Carol had never seen. Meanwhile, schemes were afoot to bring other young women into the Prince's orbit. Marghiloman quoted Stirbey as saying that this was 'one of the projects of the Queen'. In his diary entry for 17 July, he wrote: 'Stirbey does not regard the Prince Carol affair as being ended; he suspects him of wanting to keep the woman and the crown. It will not be settled unless the Prince returns married.'

Carol wrote again to Ioana from Japan, apologizing for 'so long a silence'. In the near-four-month interval between 30 March when he wrote from Massawa and 23 July when he wrote from Kyoto, he had lost none of his remarkable facility to declare himself in emotional terms, but Ioana now sensed a more detached tone: 'I again write to you, my love, a few words. They are poor words to express the heaviness of my heart and mind. What are you doing, you and the boy? I am completely destroyed by the lack of news. . . .' (Could she not have said the same to him?) 'My love,' he continued, 'love of my life, I am sometimes overcome with dreadful presentiments; you have not a friend around you, I fear for you and the child. Not that they would dare touch you, but the suffering. I am so tired and can write no more. . . . For ever and ever my heart is yours. Your Boyky who kisses you so many times.'

Following the visit to Japan, Carol went to Hawaii and on to New York, where a dinner was given in his honour on 20 August by William Nelson Cromwell, who had founded the Society of the Friends of Roumania. ('Isn't old Nelson Cromwell a delightful old chap?' his mother wrote to him from Sinaia on 11 September in a letter that mentioned almost everything that she thought could possibly interest him – except Ioana, who might not have existed!)

Carol went on to London, where he stayed at the Ritz Hotel, from which address he wrote to Ioana on 9 September – a letter surprisingly not quoted in her memoirs: 'Courage and patience,' it advised. 'That is the constant message which I keep repeating and which must seem pretty useless to you, but it is true. I adore you and I do not forget you. . . . We must act with extreme prudence. Know that my heart is entirely yours and that in everything I do, even if it appears to the contrary, it is all for you! I only ask that you break with those who have done us the greatest harm' – he included Serdici in this category – 'and to whom you have fallen innocent victim. . . . You would have confidence in me if you knew what I think of you. . . . My darling, you are all my life and all my love. Thank you so much for your dear letter. Love me and obey me. . . . A thousand mad kisses to you and the boy. Yours forever, Boykie.'

One cannot be entirely sure about the background to this particular letter, but it seems that Carol was concerned about the company Ioana was keeping and the friends with whom she was surrounding herself, even if they were old friends of his. Perhaps knowing that he would soon be home, he did not want to find Ioana at the centre of a little court that was intriguing against what he thought might be his best interests. There is no trace of the letter from Ioana to which he referred; she did not mention in her book ever writing to him, and there is no means of knowing when it was sent or received, or if indeed it was the only letter she despatched during his world voyage.

What would have attracted her attention was the phrase 'even if it appears to the contrary', with its implication that he might do something that would seem to be against her. Exactly what he had in mind is hidden behind his sugary sentiments. 'I adore you,' 'Know that my heart is entirely yours,' 'Everything I do . . . it is for you!', 'You are my life and all my love,' 'Yours forever.' How is it possible to reconcile these expressions with a letter from the same writer sent from Zurich barely two months later?

This letter read: 'It is not a conqueror who writes to you but a loser. I have fought to the end for what I believed to be our happiness. Returning to the country, I saw that I had no chance of getting my way; I therefore surrendered. Life will tell me one day if I was right. You must not believe from this that my affection for you has lessened. All my life my heart will tell me what you have been in my life; I shall always recall the bright days of our passing happiness. The spell is broken; I have turned a new page.'

He ended with the words: 'You need have no fear for yourself. You must think of the boy's future. That way you will find a happiness that will help to alleviate the sorrow of our inevitable separation.'

What Carol was telling Ioana, with an honesty that had earlier been lacking, was that he had decided to leave her for another woman, effectively acquiescing in the possibly illegal annulment of their marriage. Yet how could he have changed course so rapidly? Was he sincere in saying that he had been defeated, that the decision was forced on him unwillingly? Or had he all along never intended to return to her, in which case his protestations of love were not worth the paper on which they were written?

Was Carol a mad romantic or a ruthless hypocrite? Could he have been both at the same time? Perhaps the political adviser Filodor had the answer when he described him as having 'the naivety of a boy of eighteen'. Marghiloman made the following entry in his political diary on 29 September, just before Carol returned to Roumania; 'Filodor tells me that the Prince returns cured and totally determined to forget his loves in order again to become Crown Prince. But as he is extremely susceptible where women are concerned . . . he must be married and above all removed from the influence of his old friends.'

Extremely susceptible and naive he may have been, but Carol was widely regarded as an intelligent man and it seems almost incredible that he can have been deceiving Ioana up to the very last minute, unless perhaps he was deceiving himself as well. If he had intended finally to abandon her, surely he could have prepared her for what was to come? One is drawn to the conclusion, despite some indications to the contrary, that he did indeed have a genuine change of heart, that he really did fall in love suddenly, and most fortuitously as far as his mother was concerned. The timing could hardly have been better, for he met the woman who was to become his second wife within three weeks of writing to Ioana from London and only days before his return home.

The rumours reached Ioana that Carol's new girlfriend was Princess Helen of Greece, known as Sitta. Ioana waited anxiously for news but Carol made no attempt to see her. In fact he deliberately kept her at arm's length, refusing to intervene when she was asked to return Carmen Sylva's jewels, saying that the matter was out of his hands. She angrily refused the request, pointing out that apart from her son, the jewels were the only souvenir she had of Carol. Eventually she was given a pension but the value of the jewellery was deducted from the capital sum on which interest was paid to her.

Carol wrote one last letter to Ioana at the end of November, two months after his return, confirming that the stories about Helen were true. He was still in a sense protesting his innocence, seeming even now to say 'I was pushed' rather than 'This was my choice':

'Do not think that I gave up without a fight . . . it was only when I saw that I was alone that I surrendered. Yes, my poor little one, it is true that I am engaged, and to a Princess. It is so much against my principles that I am myself most astonished. . . . I have found someone who understands me and who shares my views on life. She has agreed to console a badly bruised heart.

'I should like to have waited, to leave a little time to soften things, but circumstances beyond our control have made us act more quickly. . . . Yes, such is life. . . .'

On 2 July 1921, by which time Carol had remarried, a settlement was drawn up by which Ioana was granted 500,000 French francs as expenses and a capital sum of 2,200,000 francs was set aside for her. Twice a year a French bank was to pay her five per cent interest on the capital, which she was not allowed to touch for twenty years. The logic behind this was presumably that she should have a guaranteed supplementary income from the Roumanian government while her son was growing up, during which time the capital sum was withheld as a guarantee of her good behaviour. It was also necessary for her to live in France, or at least outside Roumania, to receive the money. As an incentive for her further to break the connection with Carol, she was, however, allowed to withdraw 800,000 francs from the capital if she remarried.

There were other conditions, the main one of which was that she should not either herself or through another party divulge the circumstances of her marriage or the settlement. In the event, she did not remarry and she only published her memoirs of the relationship after nearly thirty years, although she was sorely tempted to tell her story much earlier. Following Queen Marie's highly successful visit to the United States towards the end of 1926, it was suggested to Ioana that her autobiography was what today we might call a hot property. Even the great film-maker, D. W. Griffith, expressed interest in movie rights, and a contract was prepared by American journalist John McHugh Stuart to act as agent to exploit all rights in the book. This contract remained unsigned, and doubtless Ioana and her advisers balanced carefully the potential value of the rights against the sacrifice of the income from the Roumanian government which must inevitably have followed such exploitation.

Whether or not Carol himself was instrumental in securing the agreement for Ioana, he cannot have been unaware of what was being done to persuade her to leave the country. He must have shared in the royal family's relief when she finally decided to make her home in France, and no doubt the financial compensation helped to ease his conscience where she and their son were concerned.

8

A Kind of
Deliverance

'At first I saw little of him and he showed not a vestige of interest in me.' Such were the words of Princess Helen of Greece, referring to Prince Carol of Roumania when their paths crossed on the last leg of his world trip. The Greek royal family were in exile at the time. King Constantine had been forced to give up his throne in 1917 in favour of his second son Alexander, who was virtually a puppet king, and he was now living with his wife and other children in Switzerland.

Although he was closely related to Queen Alexandra, who had married the British King Edward VII, Constantine had not espoused the Entente cause in the First World War as vigorously as his Prime Minister, Venizelos. This may have had more to do with the fact that he preferred Greece to remain neutral than that his wife, Queen Sophie, was a sister of the Kaiser. However, Constantine's popular following inside Greece was less powerful than the support that Venizelos received from the Entente nations, notably France, and in exile he and his family had to live down a possibly unfair reputation of having supported the German side in the war. It was a humiliating and unhappy time for them.

Prince George, Constantine's eldest son, had long been attracted to Carol's sister, Princess Elisabetha. They had first met in Bucharest in 1911 when Elisabetha was sixteen, and three years later she had turned down his proposal of marriage. Now in 1920, coming up to twenty-six, she was still unwed. It was a source of anxiety to Queen Marie, to add to her worries about her eldest son, and her delight was great when George, by now thirty-one, again proposed to Elisabetha and this time was accepted. Although the fortunes, and especially the finances, of the Greek royal family were at a low ebb, their family pedigree was impeccable.

Thus it came about that Queen Marie was in Switzerland when her son arrived in Zurich on his way back home and was introduced to King Constantine and Queen Sophie, Princes George and Paul and Princesses Helen and Irene. Marie invited George and the two girls to visit Roumania, and Carol travelled with them and his mother on the royal train to Sinaia. Helen, who was then aged twenty-four, went reluctantly, only because her father encouraged the visit, 'so that it will be obvious to the world that my children are not treated as pariahs, even though I am'.

The Greek party was installed at Queen Marie's summer residence, which gave Carol and Helen the opportunity to get to know each other. Helen described him as 'retiring and not very affable', but that he was beginning to find her attractive is suggested by his insistence on accompanying his mother and her Greek guests when they were forced suddenly to return to Switzerland, in exceptional circumstances. All the while, he made no attempt to see Ioana.

The exceptional circumstances were that within days of Carol's return to Roumania, both King Alexander in Athens and Queen Marie's mother in Zurich died. Alexander, trying to pull his dog away from a gardener's pet monkey, was badly bitten by the monkey and succumbed to blood poisoning. Within twenty-four hours of the first news came the report of the second death.

As soon as Helen heard about her adored brother's sudden and bizarre death, she determined to rejoin her parents. When it became necessary for Queen Marie also to leave for Switzerland, arrangements were made for her to travel with the two Greek Princesses, accompanied incidentally by the faithful Stirbey. Prince George was to remain behind in Roumania with his fiancé and King Ferdinand. It was at this point that Carol insisted on accompanying the travellers.

It was while he was in Switzerland on this second occasion that he asked Helen to marry him, and she accepted him. Whatever her early impression of Carol as not being very affable, both his sister Ileana and his mother noticed his interest in the Greek Princess. Helen was a beautiful young woman, dark-haired, tall and stylish, and it is not difficult to imagine any man falling for her; moreover, here was a woman of whom his mother was bound to approve. There is no doubt also that Carol was a man who required the companionship of a woman, and although it is not to be assumed that he had been deprived of all sexual contact since he had left Ioana, he had had no opportunity to form a continuing relationship. His last letter to Ioana reads almost as if he was taken by surprise by finding himself in love and after all the emotional confusion and the pressures put on him over the past few years he had decided to take advantage of this happy circumstance to regularize his position, even at the cost of sacrificing the mother of his child.

Queen Marie was overjoyed. She may well have had some part in bringing the two young people together, but she can hardly have plotted such a perfect result. Queen Sophie, on the other hand, was less enthusiastic, and even warned her daughter against the marriage, perhaps because she had just lost a son and did not want virtually to lose a daughter so quickly. She may also have been concerned about Carol's past and her daughter's motives in accepting him. King Constantine, however, agreed to the match, with the proviso that Carol was 'quite finished' with Ioana.

Given the way the marriage eventually developed, it is important to consider the attitude of Helen at this stage. If Carol was in love with her, was she in love with him? Or was she too being pragmatic, perhaps looking on marriage as a means of escaping her exile? In his authorized biography of Princess (later Queen) Helen, Arthur Gould Lee quoted her as admitting that 'I was attracted to him, and felt that later I could come to love him. But what made me really decide to say "yes" was the thought of Alexander. All through the exile my one hope had been to go back to the country we both loved, but now he was no longer there I felt I could not face Athens. . . . To marry Carol and go to Roumania . . . seemed in these days of sorrow a kind of deliverance.'

Carol, at this stage anyway, certainly seems to have loved Helen more than she loved him. On 26 November Marghiloman wrote: 'The newspapers announce the engagement of the Prince with the pretty Princess Helen of Greece. . . . The Prince has remained in Lucerne. Young Berindey states that he is madly in love with his fiancée.' Carol wrote his final letter to Ioana from Lucerne at the end of the month.

The sudden death of Alexander had caused much more than personal sorrow; it produced a political crisis in Greece. At the end of October Marghiloman had reported the current view that Venizelos was willing for eighteen-year-old Prince Paul to assume the throne, on condition that King Constantine and his eldest son Prince George, now engaged to Princess Elisabetha, remained in exile. He merely wanted to substitute one figurehead king for another. Young Paul, however, insisted that his father was the rightful King of Greece. This provoked Venizelos into overplaying his hand. He put the issue to the vote, seriously overestimating his own popularity – and perhaps also underestimating the hold that the royal family had on the Greek people. In the result, announced less than three weeks after Carol's engagement, Venizelos was badly defeated and left the country. In December 1920 King Constantine regained his throne.

What had only recently seemed like two minor alliances now assumed an altogether different complexion, for the restored Crown Prince of Greece was to marry a Roumanian Princess and the rehabilitated Crown Prince of Roumania was to marry a Greek Princess. It was almost as if the pieces of an enormous jigsaw puzzle had suddenly fitted into place, binding the Greek and Roumanian dynasties.

The first wedding took place in Roumania on 27 February 1921 and the second on 10 March in Greece. The Orthodox Church required that when brother and sister married sister and brother, the ceremonies must take place almost simultaneously, but special dispensation was obtained for a short delay. Carol and Helen were married in the Metropolitan Cathedral in Athens. King Ferdinand was unable to be present but as his mother recorded in her diary, it was she who had saved her son, so the important thing was that she was on hand!

Helen no longer needed marriage to escape her exile from Greece or to restore her royal dignity. Indeed her marriage would effectively provide an alternative exile, since she would still be living abroad, only in Roumania rather than in Switzerland. She had, however, given her word. Arthur Gould Lee reported her as saying, 'I was now beginning to feel that I did love Carol', which suggests that her heart was not wholly behind the wedding, and he also recorded her last-minute doubts. One does not know to what extent one can rely on what Helen told him, which may have been coloured by her interpretation of subsequent events, but it is certain that she entered matrimony in good faith and presumably with high hopes.

By the time the Greek honeymoon was over and the couple returned to Roumania early in May, Helen was pregnant. She gave birth prematurely to a son on 25 October, not much more than seven months after the marriage.

9

Lamentations

The marriage of Carol and Helen soon turned out to have problems. The premature birth of their son, named Michael after the great Roumanian hero Michael the Brave, had been very difficult for Helen, and left her very weak. For a brief time the couple lived in a small chalet in the grounds of Castle Peles in Sinaia, until in December 1921 they moved into a house of their own in a fashionable part of Bucharest, which was 'fitted out' by Harrods, the famous London store.

As when he had been living with Ioana, Carol devoted most of his mornings to his army duties, but he seemed to have been less happy at home with his second wife than with his first. He had far more in common with Ioana than with Helen, who was quoted by her authorized biographer as saying that 'Carol's background and interests were fundamentally different from mine' and that 'our temperaments were not quite so attuned as I had at first imagined'. Carol particularly enjoyed reading and listening to music, and he had his superb stamp collection, but Helen's tastes were more artistic – she liked decorating, for example – and she shared his mother's passion for riding. Carol, like his brother Nicolas, was far more interested in riding in cars, especially fast sports models.

In fact Helen's heart never seems really to have left Greece. Perhaps she was homesick in Roumania or perhaps she concluded quite early on that she had made a mistake in marrying Carol. There is no record of her ever having said so – but all the indications are that he was at first more in love with her than she with him, and that she gradually withdrew from him. In later years she was to blame Carol for the collapse of their marriage, attacking him in particular for his womanizing, but the faults do not seem to have been so one-sided. For such a virile man as Carol, who enjoyed – and needed – a woman's company, it was probably expecting too much that he accept her absences from his side – indeed from Roumania – for lengthy periods.

She first sought the King's permission to visit Athens with her son when the baby was not yet three months old. She wanted to see her father, who was unwell, and permission was a formality, but she remained in Greece for four months at the beginning of 1922, far longer than had been expected. It was rumoured that during her absence Carol had formed a liaison with the wife of an army officer, but if this were true, it is not so surprising when it seemed as if she had taken the first opportunity to distance herself from him, for whatever reason.

Any impression that Carol was nothing but a playboy is, however, quite false. Whatever his private life – and promiscuity was far from unknown, was even an accepted tradition, in Roumania, especially in the circles in which he moved – Carol was always at the heart of public life. Perhaps his greatest error was a lack of discretion. His parents too led their separate private lives to some extent, but without attracting the scandal that attached to Carol and that has helped obscure his many public activities.

As early as 1913 Carol had been instrumental in founding the Roumanian version of the Boy Scout movement and in 1918 he helped create the Sports Federation for young men between the ages of eighteen and thirty, as well as a charitable organization to help students. He also took a continuing and active interest in the Roumanian air force, having realized its potential importance during the very early years of aviation, and played a leading part in introducing the first air corps into the military in the early twenties.

In 1921, the year in which he married Helen, he set up the Royal Cultural Foundation, in whose activities he took the greatest interest, being particularly concerned to foster Roumanian culture both at home and abroad. One of its aims was to safeguard the traditions of village life in the countryside; another was to translate foreign literary works into Roumanian. Carol also set up a publishing house to provide educational books for the peasantry. In October 1922, he founded the Philharmonica Orchestra, with eighty-four members, under the direction of Georges Georgescu.

It was the way he did things, perhaps more than what he did, that invited opprobrium. There was undoubtedly a reckless streak in his nature which made him careless of consequence. For example, he came very near to espousing the cause of the National Peasant Party, under the leadership of Juliu Maniu, and actually spoke out against Bratianu and the Liberals. King Ferdinand to some extent shared his son's political convictions, which were in sharp contrast to those of Queen Marie, but the King was careful not to adopt a public position.

Although Roumania did not have the British type of constitutional monarchy, where the royal family was precluded from adopting political stances, close involvement with one faction was extremely unwise and dangerous, particularly for the Crown Prince. The position of the King and Queen was slightly different. Whereas Carol's heart may have been in the right place politically, in that his political actions were motivated by genuine concern for the country, his head most certainly was not. His judgement at this time is questionable and it cannot have helped his personal cause and reputation that Bratianu's Liberals returned to power in January 1922.

His mother had long shown her preference for the Liberal Party and she maintained a very close personal relationship with Prince Stirbey, the Prime Minister's brother-in-law, but she was far more adroit than her son in walking the political tightrope. When she was seeking to play an active political role, there was far more at stake. Carol's strong dislike of Bratianu was to some extent because of his mother's involvement with Stirbey and because he regarded him as something of a dictator who supported his mother and effectively restricted his father's authority; but it was also because Carol genuinely espoused the cause of the little man, the peasant, against the powerful urban interests represented by the Liberals.

While Helen was in Greece, Carol's middle sister Mignon became engaged to King Alexander of Yugoslavia; they were married in Belgrade in June 1922. This union was favourably viewed by the public in both countries since it consolidated the Little Entente that had been completed during the previous year. The first stage had been a mutual defence pact signed in March 1920 between the two new nations, Czechoslovakia and Yugoslavia; a similar agreement was made the following month between Czechoslovakia and Roumania; and the third treaty, signed in June 1921, was between Roumania and Yugoslavia. This three-nation alliance was effectively crowned by the linking through marriage of the two monarchies.

The Greek relationship through the marriage of Carol and Helen further extended Roumanian influence and, with Carol back in the fold, the enlarged and potentially prosperous post-war Roumania, with its strong Balkan connection, was becoming a power to reckon with in Europe. This was symbolized by the coronation of King Ferdinand and Queen Marie on 15 October 1922 – after Ferdinand had been on the throne for eight years. The ceremony, the first of its kind in Roumania, took place at Alba Julia in Transylvania, a town historically associated with the defeat of the Turks in 1599, and among the foreign guests were the Duke of York from England and Field Marshal Foch from France. The Duke, who later became King George VI, found the occasion 'very picturesque'.

Not everyone in the country, however, supported the expensive, indeed extravagant, affair; and even before it had taken place, new events in Greece had shown that there were serious cracks in the foundations of Roumania's new alliances. Less than three weeks before the coronation in Roumania, King Constantine was deprived of his throne for the second time, after Greece had been defeated by Turkey in a war begun by Venizelos. It was hardly consolation that he was forced to abdicate in favour of his son George, which meant that Carol's sister Elisabetha was now Queen of Greece, for the future of the Greek monarchy was now very uncertain, and George was King in name only. In the ensuing crisis the former King's supporters were ruthlessly pursued; Prince Andrew (father of Prince Philip, Duke of Edinburgh) was among a number of prominent people in Greece who were arrested and tried by court-martial. The outcome of the trial was predetermined. Six convicted politicians and generals were shot and the fate of Prince Andrew was in the balance.

This time Constantine chose Sicily for his place of exile. Helen's immediate instinct was to join her parents in Palermo, but she could not decently do so until after the coronation in Alba Julia, which she attended with Carol. She made it absolutely clear where her main loyalty resided, however, by leaving Roumania at the first opportunity. She felt unable to desert her father at the time of his second defeat.

Helen's extreme concern for her family was understandable, but it meant that again she was temporarily leaving Carol. Something of her state of mind is obvious from a twelve-page letter, running to over 2,000 words, that she wrote to Carol on 3 and 4 December 1922 from Palermo. (This 'endless' letter, as she herself described it, has been slightly edited here for sense.) There is no doubt that she was under very great tension because of uncertainty about Prince Andrew, her uncle and godfather; had he not been related to King George V of Britain and King Alfonso of Spain, he would probably already have suffered the fate of others who had fallen foul of the new regime in Athens.

'My own darling,' Helen wrote, 'I can hardly collect my thoughts to write to you coherently. The emotions of these last days have been almost too hard to bear. . . . Our one terror now is for Andrew. Those inhuman fiends . . . will always find means to condemn him. The worst of it is they are completely indifferent to the impressions their dastardly acts are causing in Europe.' She was, she said, 'absolutely desperate'.

She continued at length, through four pages, with a story, which she was at great pains to refute, that she was unsafe in Italy; she feared that if this suggestion were transmitted to Bucharest, she would be called back home. 'I nearly got a fit,' she declared, 'as you can imagine. . . . My sweetness, this story has upset me to such a degree and made me worry so frightfully, I don't know what to do with myself . . . perhaps I am worrying for nothing. . . . Darling, please forgive me boring you with all this but I was in such despair, I had to pour it all out on you and want you to know all the details. Besides, my darling, Mama's state simply breaks my heart. I could not possibly leave her just now, I really honestly do not find her well enough, her nerves are in a pitiable state and a mere nothing would cause an absolute breakdown.'

Helen was obviously determined to remain with her parents, especially with the doubts about her uncle's fate, and she returned more than once to the same themes. 'This suspense,' she wrote, 'is so ghastly, we have meals in Mama's salon, not feeling at all inclined to sit in a room crowded with strangers who stare so.' (The family were in a hotel.) 'One trembles every time the door opens, expecting from one moment to the other to hear the worst about poor Andrew who is in such danger. I pray that something should be found to save him. Oh! it would be too ghastly if anything should be done to him. Can one imagine such infamy? One would think, after slaughtering six men . . . they would be satisfied. I suppose you know the details about their last moments, poor miserable men, and their families; it makes one's heart break to think of them. Poor, poor Andrew, after doing his duty and showing splendid conduct . . . this is what he has to suffer. It's too too cruel. . . . You can imagine the state we are in and I simply could not leave Mama just now, I am so terrified of her getting ill. Uncle Georgie of England telegraphed he would do all in his power to help Andrew but what can he do?' (In fact Britain broke off diplomatic relations with Greece and was instrumental in saving Prince Andrew.) 'The revolutionaries declare any foreign intervention will be fatal. Oh! what terrible things one has to hear. My heart feels turned inside out.'

There was a sudden, almost startling, change of tone in the letter. 'I must', she said, 'tell you some other things besides these lamentations,' but she completed the letter the next day with further references to the same topics. Fortunately, she had been woken with the news that 'Andrew has been degraded and banished', which, since it meant that his life was spared, was a matter for rejoicing. 'To be degraded by those people can be no humiliation,' she believed, and then she again pleaded with Carol not to heed any suggestions for her to return home. Her main preoccupation, apart from concern about her uncle, was her almost obsessive desire to remain in Italy, which she constantly attributed to the need to protect her mother. She had got so nervous, worried and jumpy, she said, on this account that she could hardly sit still. 'I get my attacks all the time from worry. Mama says it's nothing, she used to have it continually and it comes from anaemia.'

The only reference to her son was at the end: 'Kiss my little sweetums,' she requested, 'I hope he is well, I miss him and you so much, my two darlings.' The letter closed with the words: 'All my love and thousands of kisses, your own Puss.'

From these extracts, it is clear that the pull of Italy was far stronger for Helen at the time than the pull of Roumania; it was more important for her to be with her parents than with her husband and child. No doubt she reckoned that little Michael was well looked after by his nanny and other members of her household and needed her less than her more vulnerable parents. Her father was a dying man, which was excuse enough to want to remain at his side, but it was the need to support her mother that she used to justify remaining in Sicily. Even allowing for the stressful circumstances under which this letter was written, it almost betrayed terror at the possibility of being summoned back. Indeed, who is to say when she would have returned had her father not died at the beginning of 1923? He had already suffered an attack of apoplexy, which went unreported, and he suddenly collapsed and died on 11 January, not six weeks after Helen's mammoth letter. The events of the last four months had finally destroyed him.

Helen's desire to be with her parents was without doubt genuine and cannot be attributed in any serious way to a wish to be away from Carol. Her letter to him was clearly couched in affectionate terms and did not suggest any coldness towards him. It is more than possible that she knew about his infidelities, which were an almost open secret, but they do not seem to have been a reason for her remaining abroad. In fact in the section of the letter not concerned with her 'lamentations', she went so far as to ask: 'Why aren't you here, my darling? I need you so badly to protect me from worrying. I keep wondering if you are lonely and want me. I do miss you so dreadfully but I do wish I had not married you just now (it's not true!) but what I do wish is that you were Mr X and we could go where we liked.' That hardly sounded like anything but a declaration of continuing love.

Carol may, however, have wondered about a reference in the letter to a young man. 'The Duke of Aosta's son is one of the most charming boys I have ever met,' she wrote, 'very good-looking, one metre ninety-nine without shoes on and a wonderful figure. He ... does all he can to cheer Mama up and is as kind as possible. He is on the go all day, has service in the early morning, university in the afternoon and rides and bathes and comes to see us in his spare time. He has a motorbicycle which he tears about on. . . . We only saw him three days, then he left for a week . . . and has not yet returned. You would love him.'

It seems rather strange for a married woman thus to describe a young man to her husband. Was his inclusion in the letter because he helped to divert her mother or was there possibly some other reason for mentioning him and even giving his measurements? Perhaps Helen was desperate to introduce some light relief, some contrast to the darker thoughts that were preoccupying her. She also referred to 'a most charming lady' called Princess Trabbia who had lost two sons in the war. 'Her husband is the great person here. They have fifty-seven titles . . .' Apparently this lady also visited 'Mama and is so kind about all our affairs', which may be the reason for her inclusion; or perhaps the Duke of Aosta's son and Princess Trabbia were the only people Helen met, since she admitted that she did not particularly like Palermo and said that the family had not been outside the grounds of their hotel.

Helen's letter is in general rather a puzzling document. The constant references to her mother rather than to her father, who was an obviously very sick man, may simply indicate a particularly intimate mother-daughter relationship. But it may also be that Helen thought Carol would more easily recognize the need to look after one's mother as a valid excuse to remain abroad and that, concern for Prince Andrew apart, the real purpose of the letter was to anticipate and frustrate a recall to Roumania on the grounds that she was at risk in Italy.

There is also Helen's curiously detailed description of the Duke of Aosta's son. It seems highly improbable that there was any sort of liaison between them at the time; if there had been, she would have been unlikely to mention him, unless she were troubled about any rumour reaching Carol's ears. Yet, however innocent and casual their relationship, she seems to have been very smitten with this young man, perhaps more than she was aware of. A letter written nearly four years later from King Ferdinand to Queen Marie hints perhaps that this had been the case. The King was staying at the time at the Ritz Hotel in Paris, from where he wrote on 26 August 1926 to 'My own Maddy', the affectionate pet name he used for Marie in the family. He reported dining with their son, who was in France at the time, in the private room of a restaurant, where they discussed, among other matters, the state of Carol's marriage. Ferdinand wrote that Carol had confided 'something very painful, making allusion at an affection which he believes Sitta has for the Aosta boy. He did not accuse her of having gone too far but he said there had been a change in her since she came back from Palermo. He told me still other things which I cannot write but which I will tell you when I come back. You can imagine how painful this conversation was.'

Prince Nicolas in his diaries wrote that 'Duke Amadeo delle Puglie, son of the Duke of Aosta, was a charming man, tall, handsome and very likeable. . . . As things between Carol and Helen were already deteriorating quite seriously, it was very possible that these young people were attracted to each other, that they should even have fallen in love and planned a separation from Carol at Helen's initiative.' Nicolas claimed to have heard this story both from his mother and from the Queen of Spain.

Perhaps too much has been made of this matter. In any event, Helen returned to Roumania after her father's death, bringing her mother and younger sisters to stay for a while in Bucharest with her. They spent much of their time together and Helen seemed to be more in the company of her mother than of her husband, whether from choice or necessity. Absence in the case of their marriage had not made the heart grow fonder. Carol noticed a definite change in Helen's attitude towards him.

It is indisputable that he had been seeing other women, almost openly, while his wife was in Italy. This could hardly have surprised her, but she may have begun to be worried by the rumours that were now reaching her. The name of one woman in particular was soon on many lips. She was Elena Tampeanu, the divorced wife of an army officer, who became known to history as Magda Lupescu.

10

The Black Hour

We can only know a fraction of the truth about the extraordinary relationship that developed between Carol and Magda Lupescu. There are different versions of nearly every story about them, many of which have little or no basis in fact, so that it is often a question of deciding what is most probable. As was the case with King Edward VIII and Mrs Simpson, people took up a position according to their personal view of the association, and were inclined to believe either the best or the worst about them. In Roumania, a far less politically stable country than Britain, there was, however, less consensus among the population and opinion was much more violent. The Carol-Lupescu affair became a political football and the confrontation between the Crown Prince and the government grew so bitter that Bratianu and Stirbey may well have been responsible for spreading what today would be called disinformation.

It did not help the cause of truth that the story attracted the attention of newspapers throughout Europe and North America. Journalists are not renowned for their accuracy, and dubiously romantic versions of the facts were later repeated, even by supposedly serious writers. It was an Italian journalist, mistaking Lupescu for somebody else, who is said to have given her the first name of Magda, after which she was rarely known by her real name of Elena. Because her false name is how she became known, it is how she is referred to here. Nor can one always rely on the evidence of the people themselves concerned. For example, in Magda Lupescu's driving licence, she described herself as a 'housewife' and took nine years off her age!

Exactly the same questions can be asked about Magda Lupescu as Wallis Simpson. Did she set her cap at the Prince? Was she an adventuress who was determined to trap him, or did she simply respond to his interest in her? Did she love him? And the questions are just as difficult to answer – in fact even more so because she was the victim of a sinister campaign designed to destroy her, and through her Prince Carol.

Magda Lupescu was born in September 1899, making her almost six years younger than Carol. Her Jewish father, named Wolff, adopted the Orthodox faith in order to be allowed to own his own shop in Jassy, where he set up as a pharmacist and changed his name to Lupescu, a Latinized version of his original surname. Her Viennese mother, also of Jewish origin, had become a Roman Catholic. Both parents had thus distanced themselves from the disadvantages of being Jewish in what was often an anti-Semitic society but this did not protect Magda from being vilified by Carol's enemies as a Jewish whore.

Although not everybody agreed that she was beautiful, she was a woman whom many men found exceptionally appealing. Her glory was her red hair, with green eyes to go with it, and she is said to have walked with a provocative swing to her hips. At the age of eighteen, she married an army lieutenant named Tampeanu, but the marriage was unsuccessful and her husband divorced her, alleging infidelity. Thereafter she resumed her maiden name.

Conflicting stories circulated of when and where she met Carol. She herself claimed that they met as children when her father had taken her to tea with Carmen Sylva, but it is most unlikely that the Queen would have entertained a country pharmacist, and the story seems to have been either a fantasy or a deliberate attempt on Magda's part to pretend that her origins were grander than supposed. The evidence from several entries in Carol's diaries is that they first met each other in March 1923 and that they began a serious relationship on 14 February 1925. There is no reference in the diaries to the circumstances of the first encounter but both Lupescu's biographer and Carol's brother Nicolas referred to a photographer named Postmantir, a friend of Magda's who worked for one of Carol's charitable organizations. Although he did not formally introduce the couple, it is believed that he was responsible indirectly for their coming together.

In any event by the middle of 1925 their friendship could no longer be ignored, and although Carol's marriage had the outward appearance of normality, particularly in the obvious love of both parents for their young son Michael, in reality it was already on the rocks. As Helen herself declared, 'It was plain that Carol's indiscretion was being discussed quite openly. Rumour was rife, and many wild and extravagant tales were being circulated round the city.' It was not long before articles, critical of the liaison, began to appear in the newspapers.

The seeds of much of this adverse comment were planted by Carol's opponents. As Helen readily admitted, her husband had the interests of his country at heart; she referred, for example, to his 'active support of welfare work, and his practical interest in social, racial and economic problems'. However, Magda Lupescu gave Carol's enemies an excuse to attack him for having shown that the interests of the Roumanian people did not coincide in his eyes with those of Bratianu and the Liberals.

Carol was never a man to play safe. It may not even have occurred to him that his flaunting of Lupescu made him a vulnerable target. He probably thought that his position was so secure, inviolate even, that he could get away with doing exactly as he wished. Had he been more discreet or played his cards more diplomatically, he would have escaped much of the opprobrium heaped on him by the people he had made his enemies. He may well have thought that what a man did with a woman was his private affair, and this might have been true had he not been Crown Prince or had he not adopted political positions.

Ever since the Liberals had returned to power at the beginning of 1922, Carol and Prime Minister Bratianu had been on a collision course. The Bratianus had been powerful figures in the land since before the monarchy was established. It was said at one time that they ran Roumania like a business, which opinion was responsible for the famous comment that 'Roumania is not a country; it is a profession.' Carol saw their hereditary pretensions as offensive, in much the same way that certain Americans referred slightingly to the Roosevelts or the Kennedys, and he regarded Bratianu as a man who, if not actually a dictator, would readily have assumed the role in favourable circumstances. He went so far as to assert that his rights as heir to the throne took precedence over those of the Prime Minister and, more dangerously, he threatened that he would break the power of the Liberals when he succeeded his father.

He went even further on one occasion, vowing that he would send Bratianu and Stirbey into exile when he became King. This was when he had, however, been mightily provoked. In April 1924, his parents undertook a goodwill tour of western Europe, a situation when the heir to the throne would normally have been expected to be the leading figure in the Regency Council automatically set up to act in the King's absence. But Carol was pointedly excluded. He rightly regarded this as a deliberate insult, which could only be interpreted as an attempt by the Prime Minister to diminish the Crown Prince's role and power. Almost worse was the confirmation of Carol's belief that Bratianu so controlled the King as to gain his consent to the public humiliation of his own son. The fact that the Queen may have pressed this initiative on her husband did nothing to assuage Carol's indignation at what he regarded as a pitifully weak royal response to political pressure.

To an extent Carol brought Bratianu's wrath on himself, and he should not perhaps have been surprised that the Prime Minister and his supporters fought back and even fostered anti-Semitic feeling against Magda Lupescu as a means of getting at him. Although it may not have been entirely his choice and to some extent he was manipulated by opponents of the Liberals, Carol inevitably found himself at the head of a group hostile to the government, a sort of 'Prince's Party'. This opposition group attracted many Socialists and a number of extremists, enabling Carol's enemies to dub him 'Bolshie Carol' on the basis of the company he kept, although his ultra-conservative, some might say reactionary, upbringing hardly qualified him for the role of revolutionary, and it is arguable if his alliances were more right-wing than left-wing.

In a modern constitutional monarchy, it is of course quite unacceptable for the heir apparent, indeed for any royal person, to indulge in active political activity, let alone actually to take sides. Even though one cannot consider Roumania in 1925 in terms of, say, Great Britain or Sweden, nevertheless Carol's behaviour, however well meant, was politically naive and often verged on the reckless. His parents seem to have made surprisingly little effort to guide him and when there was an attempt to restrain him, it was usually in respect of his relationships with women rather than for political reasons.

The King was all for a quiet life. Insofar as he was aware of what his son was up to, he appeared to believe that matters should be left to run their own course. The Queen was probably better informed about Carol's activities because of her close friendship with Stirbey, but she was becoming increasingly estranged from her son, who blamed her for supporting the politicians he despised and whose policies he felt were ruinous for Roumania.

At one time a rumour was rife that Carol had quarrelled with Stirbey and had actually struck him in the face. This story, though probably untrue, caused Marie great distress, and was indicative of the war of words that was served like a tennis ball by enemies of Bratianu and returned by his friends. Carol was himself partly to blame for the extent to which his opponents were prepared to go to discredit him; if he had used the influence of his position more subtly, rather than so challengingly, he might even have persuaded them to alter course.

A revealing episode of the lengths to which Bratianu was willing to go concerned the purchase of aeroplanes for the Roumanian air force. Carol, who had become its Inspector General, was a natural choice to head the first commission charged with obtaining new aircraft for the service. Although the French were the main suppliers of military equipment to Roumania at the time, the commission spread its net widely, eventually opting mainly for Dutch Fokker machines. All would probably have been well had not one of the new foreign planes crashed during a display flight, whereupon Bratianu, incited perhaps by French interests, charged Minister of War Madarescu not only with purchasing faulty machines but of accepting bribes from foreign manufacturers. The Prime Minister knew perfectly well that, in making these serious accusations, he was implicating the Crown Prince, and he was willing even to sacrifice one of his own ministers to achieve that object. Carol responded by demanding an official inquiry, which in due course absolved the members of the commission of any misconduct.

The result of Carol's behaviour, both in political and matrimonial matters, was to divide the country into two nations, one for which the Crown Prince could do no wrong and the other and more powerful group for which he could do very little right. Basically, he had the people behind him but not the establishment. Meanwhile, the strain in his marriage, as he and Helen gradually drifted apart, cannot have been helped by her distress over the declaration of a republic in Greece in March 1925, after George had reigned for little over a year. It was not long before he and Elisabetha returned in failure to Roumania.

The latter part of 1925 turned out to be crucial for Carol in more ways than one. In August his mother described him as 'a changed man, an ill man, a haunted man', but she did not elaborate on the reasons for her observation. It clearly upset her that her son was on bad terms with her own political friends, but this may not have worried her unduly in the context of Roumanian political life; she seems to have underestimated, or even ignored, the dangerous schism that beckoned. She was far more inclined, and probably rightly, to attribute her son's condition to his matrimonial problems, but it was not until October, after her daughter-in-law had confided in her for the first time certain facts about the marriage, that she explained to Stirbey that Carol's problem 'is one of those intimate troubles which might become a public one'.

Until then Marie had not been over-concerned about her son's extra-marital activities; they were only a serious issue if they put his marriage at risk. She had now, however, to face the reality that Carol had withdrawn completely from conjugal relations with his wife in favour, it now appeared, of one woman. There might have been safety in numbers but it seemed that Carol had found a woman to whom he was prepared to be faithful.

Maybe Lupescu had captured his heart as no woman had done since Ioana Lambrino. He had been deprived of his first wife's companionship for long periods; his second wife had absented herself for weeks at a time. When he fell in love with Lupescu, nobody this time succeeded in separating them, and she filled his urgent need for female company. He proved with her how faithful he could be to a woman he loved and whom he was allowed to love. In this sense she was very good for him, even if not for Roumania. Carol was determined, now that he was in his early thirties, that he would no longer allow anyone to wreck the great love of his life. Magda Lupescu became to him a symbol of his adulthood and independence, indeed of his power in the country. If he could not enjoy the woman he loved, to what did all his status as Crown Prince amount? It followed from that that if he could not live with her, he might as well give up his rank and privileges.

Of course he had first to regularize his position with Helen, as they both knew; and it was at this time that they began seriously to think about divorce. But once again Carol's position, if only as father of a child who was in line for the throne, made it difficult for him to act without looking over his shoulder at his other responsibilities. What he resented most of all, and what he was not prepared to accept, was that he required governmental consent for his private conduct. His personal behaviour was, as far as he was concerned, his own business and he was not willing to put the matter of his relationship with his mistress to the judgement of his enemies. They in turn sought to use the relationship to embarrass him. It became a weapon in their hands, which is why one cannot separate the personal issue from the political one. Each was part of a larger issue, and in assessing Carol's strange conduct at the end of 1925, this must be borne in mind. His actions can be interpreted as being motivated solely by his determination to be with Lupescu; or they can be interpreted as only the excuse for a showdown. I personally believe that what he did, he did for love.

October was a critical month. It marked Queen Marie's fiftieth birthday, which was the occasion for an enormous celebration that Carol could hardly have missed, only a fortnight after his own thirty-second birthday. A week before the great party for the Queen, Carol spoke separately to both his parents about his mistress. Having recently been alerted similarly by Helen, the news came as no great surprise, but the gravity of the position was all too apparent. The King's first reaction was to threaten to send Lupescu as far as possible away from Bucharest. There were stories that she was ordered to leave Roumania, that she refused and that threats were made to kill her, although if such threats were made, it is very doubtful that they were intended literally. It was Ioana all over again as far as Ferdinand was concerned, only now his son was of an age to know better and Carol now had his own strong following in the country.

On 7 November Carol and Helen made their last joint public appearance, at a flower show in the capital. No innocent spectator would have realized that anything was wrong, but matters were fast coming to a head. Within a fortnight an event occurred that helped Carol to a momentous decision. He was handed an excuse to leave the country without causing a single eyebrow to be raised. In England, Edward VII's widow, Queen Alexandra, died and the obvious candidate to represent the Roumanian royal family at the funeral was the Crown Prince.

The idea that he should have been accompanied by the Crown Princess barely seems to have arisen. The necessity of fulfilling a royal duty offered a distraction from Carol's affair with Lupescu and the occasion was looked upon as an opportunity to separate the couple for a brief time while the problem was being considered. This was precisely the tactic that had been employed at the time of Carol's marriage to Ioana Lambrino. A further excuse for Carol staying away presented itself. His young sister, Princess Ileana, was at school in England and he could conveniently remain there for a few days after the funeral on 27 November before returning with his sister, at the end of her school term, for the Christmas holidays.

Although Carol was highly nervous that Bratianu might seize the opportunity of his absence abroad further to discredit him, he saw how to turn the situation to advantage; he may even have felt that circumstances were playing into his hands. He immediately made arrangements to meet his mistress in Paris and though the exact details of her departure are unclear, it appears that even if Bratianu's spies knew that she had left Roumania, they were uncertain about her destination. They do not seem to have been the most efficient operatives, perhaps because they spent more time in watching Carol. Bratianu was convinced that his survival as Prime Minister and that of his party depended on distancing the Crown Prince from the throne, so he sought to obtain whatever ammunition he could to hurt Carol, whose every move was monitored.

When Carol arrived in England, he was surprised to find that his affair with Lupescu was discussed openly in the newspapers, with a freedom altogether impossible at home. It was almost as if Magda Lupescu had become a British national issue. The popular papers saw the 'royal scandal' as a matter of great human interest for their readers and Carol suspected that some of the more malicious gossip had been fed to the British newspapers by his enemies in Roumania.

The day of Alexandra's funeral was bitterly cold. Carol walked through a snowstorm directly behind King George V, the Kings of Belgium, Norway and Sweden, and the Prince of Wales, the future Edward VIII. During the following week he was a guest of the British royal family.

Helen wrote to him on 3 December, using careful language because she suspected that her courier was a spy. Her letters to Carol at this difficult time testify that she was a generous-minded and lovable woman. She revealed in the letter that Carol had telegraphed instructions for his car to be sent to him, presumably in France, by train. 'I do wish you would write me a line when you have time,' she said, 'and tell me if you have decided anything and how things are proceeding.' She was presumably referring to their marriage. 'The snow has arrived with a vengeance,' she wrote, 'it's too disgusting and dark, dreary and altogether insupportable, and frightfully cold. I see by the papers you had the same weather for the funeral. You and Ileana must have felt in your element.'

Carol was certainly not in England when this letter was delivered to him because on 4 December, when he should have collected his sister, he telephoned her at her school to say that he had to leave for France, doubtless having made alternative arrangements for her return home. He met Lupescu in Paris, collected his car and drove with her to Milan, where they stayed in separate rooms at the Hotel de Ville. It seems highly unlikely that he acted on impulse, all the indications being that he had planned this journey, a sort of honeymoon trip, before leaving Roumania for the funeral.

The news that Carol was in Italy, in the company of a woman, did not take long to reach Bucharest, where it seems, astonishingly, to have taken nearly everyone by surprise. Even more astonishing is that at first the woman in question was not thought to be Lupescu. There were even reports that Carol was back with his first wife, Ioana.

As soon as the identity of Lupescu was established, the Italian newspapers had a field day. It was now that she was wrongly reported as being called Magda, the name by which she would thereafter be widely known. Another journalist related that she had signed the hotel register as Princess Lupescu – an implausible story given that Carol wanted to keep their tryst secret, although in this respect he must have been unusually trusting since his car was not exactly insignificant or unidentifiable.

On 12 December Carol wrote a fateful letter to his mother from Venice, which she described as 'a dreadful letter that tore our lives to pieces'. From the shakiness of his English (as well as the spelling and other mistakes that have been corrected here for clarity) it was clearly written in turmoil.

'Mama dear,' he began, 'By this letter I'm frightened that I'll cause you all great sorrow, but since I've been abroad and I've had time to think things over, my decisions have become firm.' He went on to say that no one else had influenced him: 'it is a clear-headed and sure decision taken only by my own will, this I'm ready to swear on the Bible before God.

'I have thought a lot about what you told me and what you wrote to me before leaving; I must also say that I have often found life very difficult to stand. Deception is not the word for what I've felt, and all the same I've put all my energy to go on with my work. But even in the flying, which has been my great passion, I've had deception after deception; it's a thing Sitta can tell you, and she could also tell you how often I have told her that I couldn't stand it any longer.

'Now the last events of the last months have come on the top of everything and have disgusted me still more of everything. I've learnt to know people, and to see that one cannot trust even the most honest.' He then pointed out to his mother that she herself had told him that people were turning against him, notably in the army.

'You can work yourself to death,' he complained, '. . . then everything crashes. Well, better crash than disconsideration; I like better to leave everything and that is my decision. I'm sorry for all the sorrow that I'll give you, but I'll not come back upon my decision. I'm young enough, I've never been frightened of work, and I'll manage to make a life for myself.'

He then made the astonishing suggestion, which further indicated his state of mind: 'The best solution I've been able to imagine is that one should find a way of declaring that I've been killed in a motor accident, let's say drowned in the Lago Maggiore, so as to make things pass without any scandal.

'I want you in your trouble to have as little enemies as possible. As I'll be dead for many, let me be dead for everybody. I'll know how to disappear without leaving any trace.

'Again pardon me,' he concluded, 'but don't ask me to come back on my decision. I've got many reasons for it.'

There can have been no ulterior motive for writing this quite extraordinary letter, in which he naively offered to disappear from the face of the earth. It was not part of some ambitious plan to defeat his enemies back home. He was declaring straightforwardly that he was weary of fighting them and was ready to surrender in return for a life of peace – and presumably of love, although not once did he mention Lupescu.

The letter – yet another example of Carol's dramatic tendencies under pressure – marked the culmination of all the turmoil under which he had been living, albeit partly of his own making. He would probably have behaved very differently if in the past he had been allowed to be with the woman he loved, but the attempts to distance him from Ioana and Magda, as well as Helen's absences, had turned him into a rebel, which was contrary to his nature and upbringing, and which set up terrible conflicts for him, driving him from one indiscretion to another.

There is no doubt that Carol was infatuated with Lupescu and could not tolerate a further separation; and there was no way he could return home with her until he had regularized his position with Helen. In any event Magda Lupescu might never be accepted in Roumania, even as his wife following a divorce from Helen. By putting his mistress before all, he was of course playing right into the hands of his enemies. Perhaps he considered that he had lost the battle. In any case, if he had to choose, his choice was clear. He decided that he would renounce the succession.

There is no way of knowing when this idea first occurred to him, although it was not unfamiliar to him from the time he had sought to give up his rights when he was married to Ioana. No doubt the possibility of a second renunciation had been in his mind for a long time, but whether he left Roumania for Queen Alexandra's funeral with the intention of remaining abroad or whether he acted on the spur of the moment is a moot point. It is very unlikely that his decision was part of some deep scheme to rally support back home, although to an extent that was its effect. More probably it arose from a gradual realization that he preferred to spend his life with the woman he really loved and that the only way to achieve this was to exile himself.

At all events he prepared a document for his father, officially renouncing the throne. On this occasion it was not easy to brush it aside or suppress his intention, particularly with Bratianu ready to pounce on such a heaven-sent opportunity to pull the troublesome thorn out of his flesh. Carol in fact sent the renunciation to Helen, to pass on, along with a letter to his mother. The news was received in Roumania on 21 December. Helen was devastated because, although she knew that her marriage was over, she wanted to save Carol from himself and his opponents; she was very much on his side and understood him better than did his parents. She was told, somewhat cynically, that for her this was a first experience; for others, it was second time round!

Three days later both Helen and Marie wrote to Carol. Both letters are very moving in their different ways. Helen made the excellent point that Carol still enjoyed great support in the country. 'You will say perhaps that I have no right to talk to you this way after all there has been between us,' she wrote, implying perhaps that she had some part in the breakdown of the marriage, but her letter was obviously concerned and loving, and written on her own initiative. It was the letter of a dear friend:

'I really don't know what to think or to say,' she declared. 'Are you quite sure you have thought everything over quietly and calmly before taking such a terribly serious step? Carol dear, one day you will regret it bitterly. Have you thought of all the consequences that may result from such an act to the country, especially in these moments when things are in a rather critical state?' She told him that his decision had brought great grief to his parents and that his father was hurt that he had sent no word apart from the official document of renunciation. 'I want you to have your eyes open,' she said, 'and I have the feeling towards you that one has for a person who wants to drown himself because life is too hard for him and who one would do everything in one's power to save.'

She went on to ridicule his suggestion of pretending to be dead. 'Fancy,' she pointed out, 'if afterwards the truth came out in all the foreign newspapers, as it absolutely surely would, what light would we family show up in? No, Carol dear, that is a crime against religion and all one's inner feelings, as I am sure you will admit yourself if you think it over well. I beg you and implore you to think everything over again, because, don't forget, whatever people say, you are popular here, and fancy what a grief for all those who love you and expect great things of you when they hear of this, especially the army. I must tell you quite honestly I did not think you would ever really do this thing. I thought at the last your love for the country would triumph over all the misunderstandings and deceptions you have had.' There was an implication here that Carol may already have discussed renunciation with Helen.

'If you do feel you would like to change your mind,' she continued in practical fashion, almost as if Carol were her son rather than her husband, 'why don't you say you need a six-month holiday? The papers you sent can always be destroyed.' Was she perhaps inviting him to have a six-month fling with his mistress before returning to the fold? 'Again, I repeat, you may be angry with me, Carol dear, for writing like this, after all there has been between us, but I wonder if you have asked yourself: Has a man the right to do this vis-à-vis his God and his country? There may be terrible reproaches you will make yourself later; look reality in the face now and ask yourself if you are happy in this decision you have taken. If not, don't hesitate one moment. If you are, that is another question. I only want to point out all the things you might not have thought of. How will you live, my dear, where and on what? What sort of life will you make for yourself when you have been used to having everything you want? I want you to know that nobody has seen this letter or asked me to write it, only my conscience tells me what to say and the feeling that one day you will regret this step. Keep it to yourself and believe that all these words come from a heart that wants your good, whatever happens.'

There was not a mention in the letter of the woman who must have been very much in Helen's mind while she was writing it, and only the briefest reference to their son: 'Baby went into your room yesterday and kept asking "Where's Papa?"' 'Well, Carol dear,'

Helen concluded, 'I must leave you to think things over quietly. God bless you and help you, with love from Sitta.'

Queen Marie's letter, in which she pointed out that her husband had been 'so near to death this spring', was almost twice as long, more sentimental and reminiscent of earlier communications, but nevertheless powerful. Like Helen, Marie did not mention Lupescu by name, although she could not resist one brief comment that 'the face of sin is crowned by hair of flame!'

'What can I say to you, Carol my boy?' was how she began. 'What can a mother say to a son who is stabbing her in the heart for a second time. . . ? You have everything: a country that needs you, a grand future to make yours, a lovely home, a beautiful and good wife, an adorable child, parents who loved you, whose right hand you ought to have been, parents who are going towards old age, who have given their lives to a mission you were to have completed.

'All this you give up, tear to pieces, throw away as though it were so much rubbish, and for what?

'You try to delude your own self and others with words: you speak of mistrust of others towards you, unfairness, no acknowledgement of your efforts, no comprehension of your human needs! Words, words, you know yourself that they are but words, you know that you had more than your share of the good things of this world, more of your share of love, indulgence, help, money, prestige, credit, and if you were not given more still, it was because you would not take it because you preferred mean flatterers and blood-suckers rather than those who, having in view your good, stood up when danger was at hand to call out "Beware!" because they loved you, Carol, because they believed in your future, because they wanted to make of you a man! Who of us has not occasionally had to listen to reason, to follow a hard advice, to give up something, to sacrifice part of their dearest desire?'

Where Carol was concerned, his mother would have made a marvellous prosecuting counsel. Like many successful people, she had the ability to see all things from her viewpoint, in black and white. Her friends were perfect; her opponents were flatterers and blood-suckers. 'Love, Carol,' she told him – and here she was speaking with some authority – 'does not mean the blind giving-in to all a man wants. . . . As I told you during that sad last interview in Sinaia, what I cannot understand is what is your conception of life? What is your conception of duty? What is your idea of love? Is love for you simply indulgence, simply a letting yourself go to your animal appetites till you are sick of the one who satisfies you, and then you pass on? Is there no fidelity in your code, no restraint, no accepting of duty, no keeping of promises given, no moral limit, no straight road you want to keep to? Nothing, nothing at all? No ideal, no vision, no dream of the future, only lust, only giving way to each passion which flits across your path?

'Then, my boy, you are right to go, then we cannot understand each other, for we speak a different language, then indeed you are not worthy of standing above others, of being chosen as a leader for a people who need a shepherd, who need one capable of sacrifice, one who will love them enough to overcome himself for their sakes. If you recognize no duty, no fidelity, no obligation, then you are indeed unworthy of carrying on the torch.'

Marie of course was quite right to address these questions to her son, but she may for once have underestimated the quality of his love for Magda Lupescu, whom she saw as just another in a long chain of women but who in fact held a special place, almost a unique place, in Carol's affection. Mother and son did indeed speak a different language, perhaps because Carol did not have his mother's great strength of character at that time. It is interesting to note that his relationship with his father was never anything like as close as that with his mother; it is impossible to imagine Ferdinand upbraiding Carol in similar terms to those used by Marie. It seems indeed to have been Carol's fate only ever to have become emotionally involved with women. He was able to cope successfully with men, even his opponents, on an entirely different and unemotional level.

As her letter continued, Marie became more and more emotional, often repeating the same points. 'Everything needed you here, everybody needed you here, you were born to a glorious inheritance, but you are casting it back in their faces, and for what, for whom?' She pointed out that he had a son, 'and in your letters to your wife and your mother you say no word of him, you do not even send him a kiss. You abandon him, you throw him out of your life, and with him the sweet woman you swore to love, honour and protect. Not a word to ask us to look after them, not a word to recommend them to the country's heart, to the country you have betrayed. Not a word of love or thanks either to your father . . . only a cold turning upon him in accusation of having been undervalued, misunderstood by him and others.'

There was a great deal of truth in these accusations. Carol had completely cut himself off from his first wife and son, and now he was about to repeat the process. No doubt he had weighed this problem in the balance and decided that his children would be well cared for, but these were occasions, rare in his life, when he could not both have his cake and eat it. In the first case it had not been his wish to abandon Ioana; in the second case he probably did not feel that his actions would entirely cut him off from Michael, but it is true that he did not mention the boy when he wrote to his mother from Venice.

Marie had not finished with him. She was determined to deliver the knock-out blow. 'This is your mother's parting wish,' she stated: 'may you never live to realize the hideousness of the act you are committing and the utterly monstrous inhumanness of the way you are doing what you do. The world is wide, there are many wanderers on the face of the earth, many outcasts, many prodigal sons, you are going amongst them, turning your face towards what, with whom? I do not know – I, your mother, I do not know! Can there be any real happiness in it, Carol, can there?'

There was more of the same. She told him that she had fought for him in the past, 'stood up like a tiger defending her cub, stood up and faced a world of hate, for your sake, Carol, for your sake, because I believed in you. . . . If you consider that life owes you everything and that you owe it nothing in return, then, Carol my boy, you had certainly better go, you are not worthy of the trust God laid in your hands, not worthy of being a man amongst men, not worthy of being a Prince, a husband, a father, a son.

'And as goodbye, only just this, Carol: although the world is wide, a mother's heart is wider still, and even broken to pieces, trodden upon until it is but a bleeding rag, it can still be found beating at the hour of need. . . . I kiss you for a last time on your forehead, Carol, a last mother's kiss.'

Marie was in danger of losing her case by overemphasis. One has the impression that Helen was genuinely distressed for Carol: Marie may have been more distressed for herself. She concluded her letter with these words: 'Even if as Queen I must cast you from me . . . there may come one day, that hour of need, the black hour when you will weep alone, abandoned as you abandoned others today. Your Mama.'

These letters did not cause Carol to alter his decision. Bratianu meantime had persuaded Ferdinand to order his son to return home alone. General Angelescu, Marshal of the Court, had been sent to Milan to try to persuade Carol to return to Bucharest, but the Crown

Prince had had experience of even tougher negotiators. Mugur was also employed for this purpose but Carol would not even open the door to him. The young lieutenant wrote a series of short letters on the hotel notepaper, imploring Carol to see his 'most devoted friend', but all he got for his pains was a note to say 'You will have to bring me home in my coffin.'

It seemed that there was no possibility of remedying the situation and, urged on by Bratianu, a Crown Council was summoned to Sinaia on the last day of the year to accept Carol's 'irrevocable renunciation to the succession to the throne and of all the preroga-tives appertaining to that rank, including membership in the royal family'. Carol had got his way, but so had Bratianu. The timing of the renunciation caused Marie to remark bitterly: 'Here is my son's New Year present.' At about the same time, Magda Lupescu was telling a reporter: 'I have no responsibility in what has occurred.'

One of the reasons why it was easier to accede to Carol's request on this occasion was that the dynasty was no longer dependent only on Prince Nicolas, since Carol had his four-year-old son Michael (as well of course as a son by his first marriage who was not recognized for the purpose of the succession). Young Michael was now declared heir apparent and a Regency Council was set up, with Nicolas at its head, to act in the event of Ferdinand's death during the child's minority.

All these steps were ratified quickly by Parliament, on 4 January 1926, indicating Bratianu's anxiety to get rid of Carol as soon as possible. It seemed that there was no going back.

11

The Maddest Gamble

An irrevocable renunciation it may have been on paper, but it is abundantly clear that there were many people, both inside and outside Roumania, who were unwilling to accept the reality. Many Roumanians now heard for the first time that Carol had renounced the succession before, and they perhaps considered that this new renunciation had as much chance of sticking as any earlier attempt.

What the renunciation did in effect was to polarize opinion in the country. There were those, in all walks of life, who could not visualize Roumania without Carol. The sick and ageing King was a representative of the past; Carol was a symbol of the country's future. Even those who did not approve of his personal conduct saw their future as more secure in his hands than in those of a child under the Regency of the lesser known and the less popular Prince Nicolas. Paradoxically it was Carol's notoriety, his very visibility, that gave him his strength.

Even those close to the throne, including the Queen's private secretary, maintained contact with Carol in exile, making it clear where their allegiance or their interests lay. Important figures in the country remained constantly in touch with him; even a man of such high moral principle as the statesman, Juliu Maniu, while not condoning Carol's extra-marital relationship with his mistress, came eventually to see that the future of the nation would be better safeguarded by Carol's presence in the country.

Roumania was split into two almost equal camps, pro-Carol and anti-Carol, holding irreconcilable opinions about his behaviour. The views were reflected in the foreign press but whereas inside Roumania Carol was the victim of an almost scurrilous propaganda campaign, outside the country his cause was widely heralded. For example, the Vienna correspondent of the London *Daily Express*, referring to Carol as a prisoner of dictator Bratianu, ran the story

that in 1924 the Prime Minister had forbidden the Crown Prince to
leave the country, causing Carol to reply that he did not take orders
from Bratianu. He also referred to the incident in which Carol was
alleged to have hit Stirbey, supposedly after his mother's friend had
reproached him for his behaviour with Lupescu. The same source
stated that Carol had written to his mother to ask who ruled in
Roumania, the Hohenzollerns or the Bratianus?

Carol and his friends were almost as adept at propaganda as their
enemies. Many stories of this sort, only partially true or sometimes
downright false, were circulating widely. Carol himself gave an
interview to a well-known journalist named Bogholm in which he
said that his decision to renounce the throne had been taken not, as
claimed by the Roumanian government, for sentimental reasons, but
for political reasons. He spoke of a long-standing struggle between
himself and the Bratianu brothers, 'the true masters of Roumania for
many years who were supported,' wrote Mr Bogholm, 'by Queen
Marie.'

The London *Times* also saw a political motive behind Carol's
actions, referring specifically to the way he had been treated in the
matter of the purchase of Dutch aircraft. The French newspapers
were the friendliest towards Carol and also the most sensational in
the way they reported the renunciation. *Le Matin*, which carried a
long report of the Bogholm interview, described Carol's decision as
unpopular inside Roumania. 'The Prince was loved by all and enjoyed
great popularity,' according to the newspaper's special correspondent
in Bucharest.

Exactly how Carol saw his future when he decided to renounce
the succession, whether he did so for sentimental or political reasons
or for a mixture of both, is a matter of speculation. I incline to the
opinion that he acted to some extent impulsively and without too
clear a view of the likely repercussions. There is no doubt, however,
that he was ready and willing to take advantage of favourable
circumstances as they arose, and almost before the ink was dry on
the papers he had sent to Roumania announcing his decision, he
must have been having second thoughts. He was not the only one; as
early as 25 February 1926 the *Chicago Tribune*, which described the
renunciation as 'the maddest gamble ever undertaken by the heir
apparent to a throne', was forecasting that 'Carol may soon be Prince
again'.

Far from consolidating Bratianu's position in the country, Carol's
exile and loss of status badly rocked the boat. Queen Marie was

particularly worried at the stories of personal conflict between her son and Stirbey, who was violently attacked by a French journalist as 'a Roumanian Rasputin'. Writing in *Le Quotidien*, Pierre Gascouin referred to Carol as a weak and pleasure-loving man, not without faults but basically honest, who lacked the wisdom and character to deal effectively with 'Bratianu and his camarilla'. Because of this, he could only employ 'childish indignation against a dishonourable regime'. While canvassing the political reasons for what he regarded as Carol's brainstorm in renouncing the throne under pressure, this same journalist insisted that Stirbey's evil influence had been at work behind the scenes.

Gascouin's shrewd portrait of Carol contrasted sharply with his sensational and exaggerated picture of Stirbey, based probably on an article that had appeared in a new Bucharest newspaper which referred to Stirbey's 'occult influence'. Marie was determined if possible to quash such stories at source, and she called on her son for help in suppressing some of the bad publicity that was affecting even the King. In one of her typical letters, dated 24 January, she told him that 'there is one thing you could do for your father's sake. . . . You must know that what makes his cup particularly bitter is that many rise up to accuse him of having punished you beyond your due; they will not and cannot understand that his act was only accepting with bleeding heart your own demand to be set free, and around this a thousand wicked intrigues build themselves up to make his life a torture.'

Of course she ignored the point that it was not necessary to deprive Carol of membership of the royal family. She went on to ask her son to write either to the Prime Minister or to the Patriarch to 'express your sorrow or even indignation at the way your name is being used to make your father's work or duty more difficult,' and to request everybody to 'rally around the King and the son you have left to the heart of the people'. She virtually dictated the sort of letter she expected. 'I ask you to write this letter,' she said, 'you can even in it ask it to be published so that your voice may once more reach every heart.'

No better indication could be provided of Carol's hold on the Roumanian people and the disastrous effect his renunciation was having on the monarchy and the government, who found themselves blamed for Carol's behaviour.

'Most noble', his mother continued, 'would be to write the letter to Bratianu, so as to prove that it was not because of vulgar discussions between your father's government and yourself that you threw everything over, but if you cannot rise to that height, write it to the Metropolitan who is one of your son's guardians in case of your father's death.'

Carol did in fact respond to this appeal, addressing the head of the Church rather than the Prime Minister. His letter, which was published in the newspapers, said that he had renounced the throne for his own reasons and that those who sought to blame his father were committing 'a great sin before God'. It is highly revealing that it should have been found necessary to beg a young man who might be said to have deserted the country, and who had been brutally dismissed from family membership, to come to the aid of the regime.

His mother had written to Carol previously, on 2 January. Although she declared that 'this is not to be a letter of reproach', she could not resist upbraiding him at some length for his misconduct, and she made what may have been one of her rare references to Magda Lupescu: 'Do not let whoever you may cast in your lot with destroy your very soul.' She made it clear, however, that she did not want to break with her son. 'In what way,' she asked, 'can I still be your mother? . . . If the hour of despair comes, do not be afraid of crying out to me. My heart has not abandoned you. . . . If I can help in any way to make the new life easier, in any way, I am always there for you. . . . Keep in communication with me directly or through others if you will, but never let me quite lose sight of you.'

His wife Helen was no less determined to keep in touch. In fact she wanted to visit Carol, although she did not appear to have had any particular plan in mind, but he was not keen to see her at that time and the government did not want her to go. As Marie said in her second letter, Helen 'has behaved with a quiet dignity, worthy of her golden heart, forgiving disposition and admirable education. Of course,' she added, 'we cannot know what took place intimately between you, that remains a mystery as everything in your behaviour is a mystery.' Helen wrote to Carol on 3 January. 'I curse the day I received your letters,' she told him, 'and did not have the sense to throw them in the fire without showing them to anybody. Looking back now, I see how wrong my attitude was towards you. Don't you see that all my life will be one big remorse that everything is my fault, that I have brought this dreadful calamity on to the country and ruined your life? Carol dear, if at the end we had decided that our lives could not be lived together, could we not have found some other solution? . . . I am writing to you quite openly, my dear, and would like you to keep this letter quite to yourself and destroy it afterwards.'

Fortunately for us, the letter was not destroyed. It is open to more than one interpretation and must speak for itself. Helen continued: 'When that day we had the exploration together, I see now I ought not to have said no categorically as I did to your proposals to me. I was wrong in everything, even the last day when you threatened to leave for good. I thought that once abroad, the different atmosphere and life would put new strength in you and that by yourself you would see that such a step was out of the question. . . . I see now I ought to have been more explicit; then I thought that after all there had been between us that I had no right to say straight out you must come back. Oh! if only one could put back the wheels of time.'

She went on to say that when she learnt about the Crown Council, she started fighting. 'I fought for you like a wild tiger,' she said. She had begged the King to delay proceedings but 'other forces were at work', although she believed that Ferdinand longed to give his son another chance. Even now, the day before Parliament was set to ratify the decisions of the Council, she had not abandoned hope.

'Another thing you must know,' she continued, 'is, extraordinary though it may seem, that this thing has gained you a popularity of eighty per cent! Everybody is convinced that there is some political, deep plan behind this and that you are being sacrificed. Of course they say you ought never to have done such a dreadful thing but they are beginning to murmur against Uncle Pa' – her term for the King – 'for taking this decision without giving you another chance, that even a criminal is given a few weeks. There are many political things too which I dare not write. Of course some say it is on account of the girl, others because we did not get on and I had deserted you and treated you badly.'

Helen further told him that both his parents 'want to do everything they can to make your life supportable', but the King could not himself go back on the decision. 'That must come,' she said significantly, 'from outside, from the people.' If Carol did return, matters could be arranged, but she dared not write too openly.

An extraordinary passage in this long letter is the following: 'Carol dear, if by doing this thing you had me at the back of your mind, you don't realize that by so doing you have sacrificed me as well, because had I wanted to leave before, I would have left the boy in your hands. Now, how can I leave the poor little boy without a mother as well? . . . Oh Carol, if you have done this for me, it was a sacrifice that would put you personally among the martyrs, but dear, sacrificed on the wrong altar. I feel at the bottom of my heart I may have been the cause of this decision ... why did we not face the difficulties together? How blind one is, and one sees clear too late.'

Was Helen blaming herself for Carol's behaviour, and if so why? Unfortunately there is no further evidence to help elucidate the true meaning behind the words.

What is evident is that, although in exile, Carol was never out of the thoughts of his countrymen, and certainly not out of the thoughts of his parents and wife. Although officially he was now simply Mr Carol Caraiman, almost everyone continued to address him by his royal title and whenever possible to maintain contact with him. 'Royal Highness,' Mugur wrote to him on 3 January, 'what a noble title. I use it for the last time,' but this did not stop him from using it the following day or from addressing Carol as Prince in his later communications, usually on Prince Carol Cultural Foundation notepaper.

It is interesting to note that while Bratianu sought to remove all photographs of Carol from public places, Carol's name continued to be associated with the charitable institutions with which he had been connected. The Cultural Foundation, of which Mugur was one of the leading lights, is the most notable case in point. The fact that Carol was now a private citizen did not deter Mugur and others from keeping him well informed about activities in Roumania and from seeking his advice, help and even instructions. For example, during the first half of 1926, in the first six months following the renunciation, Mugur wrote on average a letter a month on Cultural Foundation business.

On 1 February he wrote to say that the Foundation was desperately in need of funds. On 22 March he promised help to fight 'the adventuress Lambrino' after Carol's first wife had instituted a claim for damages against him in the French courts, taking advantage of the fact that he was now resident, at least temporarily, in France; the arrival of Carol and Lupescu in Paris from Milan on 25 February had been very widely publicized, and the resultant legal action was a thorn in Carol's flesh, although the claim eventually failed. On 17 April Mugur declared that he was 'staying here to look after this Foundation that you created; for us you remain its soul and through it we serve you with passion'. He also gave information about publication of the Bible in Roumanian and of 'books for the masses', which would require a special company to market them, and also news of the Philharmonic Orchestra. 'I will send you in the future and regularly information on all our activities and projects,' he said, again expressing the hope that he could soon meet Carol, perhaps with General Condescu, Inspector General and administrator of the Foundation. On 5 June he reported in even greater detail, and said that whenever and wherever the name Prince Carol was mentioned in connection with the Foundation, it brought applause, showing the public's love for their lost Prince.

This last letter contained the excellent news that the paper *Universul* planned to print a 'cultural page' every Sunday in collaboration with the Foundation. This meant that each week, under a heading bearing the name of Prince Carol, would appear material intended mainly for minority opinion but which would constantly remind readers of their former Crown Prince in exile. Carol's enemies were either not powerful enough to stop this or did not consider it politic; in either case it represented a victory for him and his interests.

Mugur may have had an ulterior motive for keeping in touch with Carol, wanting to know what was happening in France so that he could report back to his friends in Bucharest, whoever they may have been. It was not just he, however, who kept in contact with France. Dinu Cesianu, head of the Sports Federation, wrote on 20 January and again on the 25th to the 'man who has honoured me for many years with his friendship and his total confidence'. Two months later he was telling Carol that 'Madame Lambrino was very badly advised to attack your Highness . . . by enemies of the dynasty'. On 22 April he sent a letter via General Condescu, who was visiting France, in which he reported the proceedings of the Sports Federation, held the previous Sunday and attended by Prince Nicolas; and he wrote of his high hopes that the new sports stadium would be ready by the autumn of 1928. On 26 June he sent a telegram to inform Carol that the Federation was about to lay the foundation stone of the building, and offered the Federation's gratitude and thoughts for him with affection. Three similarly informative letters followed in July and another in September.

Someone else who maintained a close relationship by correspondence was Paul Theodorescu, one of the most senior officers in the air force. In a letter dated 2 April, he thanked Carol for a message he had received. 'Your good wishes', he wrote, 'have been received with high satisfaction by our comrades, who were in doubt about your Highness's feelings and thought they had been forgotten.' He also said that he had presented the official report on the Roumanian air force to the King as being the work of Carol. On 5 June, in more personal vein, he referred to young Prince Michael. Apparently the boy had entered the room, spotted Theodorescu and said in English: 'This is the officer who used to work with Daddy, but when will Daddy come?' 'Like him,' Theodorescu wrote, 'the whole of Roumania is asking the same question.' He also reported a remark of Admiral Scodrea: 'If Prince Carol were here, I would have a navy to direct.' 'Our airmen say the same things,' he commented.

Carol's hold on the armed forces was strong, although they were loyal to his father. It is said that Carol knew the names and personal details of every officer in the army, with many of whom he had a close rapport.

Enclosed with a letter dated 9 July from Theodorescu was a copy of the first issue of an aeronautical magazine, supposedly Carol's brainchild. Twice in this letter reference was made to his return from exile. Eleven days later Theodorescu reported the annual celebrations of the air force, whose 'officers spoke about you with much affection which the whole army has for you also'. There was no secret where Theodorescu's sympathies lay. He was almost sycophantic in his support, but he had good reason since he knew from personal experience that, without Carol, there would have been no effective air force. He knew better than anyone how much Carol had done for the service. He gave an example in a letter dated 30 September, in which he reported an accident involving 'probably the best pilot in the Roumanian air force', both of whose legs had been amputated. 'Thanks to your recommendations,' he commented, '. . . the new laws dealing with pensions include provision for people killed or maimed in action. Now they or their families will receive a pension according to rank.'

Even Queen Marie's private secretary, Eugeniu Buhman, kept in frequent touch with Carol. While some of his letters were replies to Carol's who was particularly concerned to protect his stamp collection, he was surprisingly friendly. 'I believe that your Royal Highness does not even suspect the popularity and the love that all classes of our country have towards your Royal Highness,' he declared on 7 June. 'We are all waiting impatiently for your Royal Highness to retake his place among us.'

Marie can hardly have been unaware of her secretary's contacts with her son, although she might have been surprised at his effusive sentiments. The point is that few people inside Roumania, except his opponents, took serious notice of Carol's renunciation. It had taken his defection to bring to the surface his popularity in the country, which had the effect of galvanizing his enemies into even more vicious attacks on him. His irrevocable renunciation was never a reality.

It was only on official documents that he was referred to as a private citizen and his influence was that of a privileged person – a VIP. In his absence abroad he was, for example, able to obtain letters from the various legations in Bucharest to assist him in his travels. Typical was a document from the British Minister in Bucharest, stating that Carol planned to visit England in the company of the Inspector General of the Roumanian police, in itself an extraordinary association in the circumstances; His Majesty's Minister presented 'his compliments to the Chief Officers of His Majesty's Customs at Dover (or Folkestone) and would be glad if such facilities could be granted to Monsieur Carol Caraiman, who is proceeding to England'. Monsieur Caraiman was even able to use the diplomatic bag for an acquaintance of his to send his shooting guns from London to Paris!

Even to the authorities, Carol was Prince in all but name. His parents never broke off contact with him and, especially when they realized the effect in the country of his renunciation, they hoped for reconciliation. This was extremely difficult, however, while he remained married to Helen but enamoured of Magda. 'Carol, my boy,' his mother asked in a brief note sent in May, 'what are these underlying forces separating us? Remember that divided we fall.' It was almost as if she were saying 'Come back, Carol,' but unfortunately he could not return on his own terms.

Marie wrote him an unusually chatty letter, without the regular haranguing, on 17 July. 'You know I was always a good fighter,' she told him, '. . . but I am no more as young as I was; it is uphill work.' She revealed that he had recently met his sister Elisabetha, and speaking of his brother Nicolas, said, 'Nicky has a rather difficult time of it as he has to learn many things that he thought he would never have to know. It is like beginning all over again at a disadvantage. He is willing but he is hot-tempered and often does himself harm in public.' If Carol had faults, so too did his younger brother, who had returned to Roumania in 1922 after completing his education at Eton in England; but he had not remained permanently in the country since then because he had joined the British Royal Navy, where his duties were very much more to his liking than participation in official Roumanian activities. At this particular time he held the rank of captain in the British Navy and had command of a gunboat.

Marie seems to have kept strictly to herself the contents of the letter that Ferdinand wrote to his wife from Paris in August, after a secret meeting with his son. Carol's first action on meeting his father again, so the King told his wife, 'was to take both my hands and kiss them, and his eyes were full of tears . . . he is very much *au courant* about things in Roumania and he judges them with passion. Of course he felt sore about the aviation.'

According to the King, Carol had gone on to discuss his marriage, saying that he was unhappy because it lacked the tenderness that he needed. He admitted that he had not confided fully in his parents, but Helen knew the situation. 'I told him,' Ferdinand said, 'that he probably also from his side did not try to get near his wife and found consolation in another way which must have offended her. . . . He told me the last time he tried was when Sitta came back from England but that then she refused. . . . His one idea is to get separated from his wife, and there must have been conversations between them before of which we did not know everything. He says she knew his intention of not coming back and that it has been to a certain degree arranged between them.' Carol had then made the surprising assertion that he had separated himself from his wife 'to make things easier' for her.

This letter is the only record of what Carol actually thought about his marriage, or claimed to have thought, and it must of course be read in conjunction with the reference, previously quoted, to the son of the Duke of Aosta. As Ferdinand said to Marie, 'What shall we believe?'

The King added that Carol 'feels himself not quite out of our hearts. . . . He asked me to find ways that he might be more in communication with me, and I think I ought to do it to influence him . . . we must talk it all over when I come and we must keep very close together to try to help him . . .'

Before he left Paris, Ferdinand sent his son a recent photograph to remind him of 'your old Papa'. Not much more than a month later, Marie passed through Paris on her way to the United States, accompanied by her children, Nicolas and Ileana, and met Carol. He elaborated to her on what he had told his father about his marriage; he said that Helen knew about his plans, which provided an excuse for her to divorce him. Marie tackled her son about his interference in Roumanian politics and he assured her of his loyalty to his father.

Prince Carol in Egypt on his world travels in 1920:
[18] *above* The royal party visiting the Pyramids
[19] *below* Field Marshal Allenby's march-past of British
troops to welcome Carol to Egypt

[20] In India: Prince Carol's party setting out on a tiger hunt as the guests of the Maharajah of Patiala

[21] In Japan: Prince Carol with the future Emperor Hirohito

Ileana

[22] *above left* Princess Elisabetha and Crown Prince
George of Greece on their wedding day, 1921

[23] *above right* Princess Ileana, Carol's youngest sister,
in 1928

[24] *below* Princess Helen of Greece with her and
Carol's son, Michael, who became King at five years old

[25] Elena (Magda) Lupescu, Carol's mistress

[26] *below* Carol and Lupescu in Nice during his first exile from Roumania

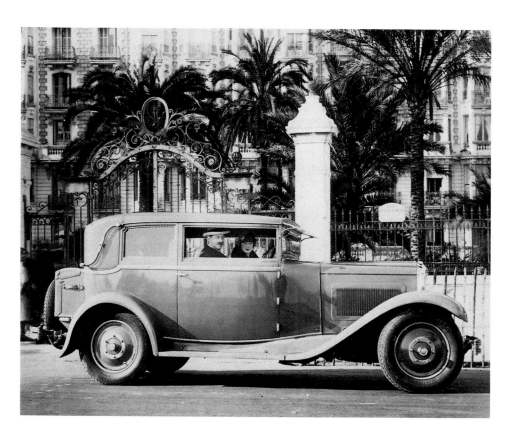

She agreed to a show of public support for him by allowing him to see her off at the station the following day, much to the annoyance and embarrassment of others in her retinue. This was more than the government back home could tolerate and she was formally forbidden to visit Carol on her return. Instead, she wrote a letter, enclosing a Christmas present, saying that the King had instructed her not to see him. 'I must obey,' she said, 'considering how ill he is.'

Clearly, although there were two camps, for him and against him, Carol simply did not disappear from public view even if he was out of the country. Indeed he had never been more conspicuous in some ways. There were those who wished to humiliate him but many more who preferred to maintain respectful contact with him.

His influence inside Roumania was doubtless greater than he had realized. While he was going the rounds of the fashionable French resorts, accompanied by Lupescu, his defection brought a political backlash in its wake, much to Bratianu's surprise. The Prime Minister had assumed that, in ridding himself of his most powerful focus of opposition, his path ahead would be smoother. Quite the opposite was the case. The Liberals were blamed, not altogether justly, for Carol's behaviour, and even the legality of the renunciation was debated openly.

Bratianu and the Liberals had been in power since January 1922 and had seemed to many people to have become immovable. They represented business interests and the big cities. Their main opposition came no longer from the Conservatives, the party of Marghiloman, or from Averescu's Populist Party, and certainly not from the very small Socialist Party led by Dragou, but from the National Peasant Party, with Juliu Maniu at its head. This grouping, which became the effective party of the working classes, had grown from the alliance in 1925 of the National Party under Maniu and Vaida-Voevod, the Peasant Party under Mihalache and the National Democratic Party under Jorga.

Carol's renunciation and exile had a remarkable and almost immediate effect on the fortunes of the Roumanian political parties. It undoubtedly played a big part in the backlash against the Liberals which brought about their defeat in the March elections. This was in effect an immense victory for Carol, whose interests thereafter were even more closely linked with those of politicians like Maniu and Jorga in particular.

Bratianu was forced to resign and in normal circumstances Maniu would have taken his place, but in March 1926 the King was still free to choose whichever Prime Minister he wished, or whom he could safely impose on the people, whatever the election results. Ferdinand, perhaps under advice from Bratianu, was not yet prepared to entrust the government to Maniu, and in this he was supported by the Queen. He did not believe that the National Peasant alliance could deal with the crisis in the country and he opted for a strong man, the country's wartime hero, General Averescu. Although he had the support of but a handful of deputies in Parliament, Averescu became Prime Minister.

Had Maniu come to power, indeed had the wishes of the people been recognized, Carol would very probably have been recalled home within four months of his renunciation, even though Maniu did not approve of Carol's morals. The problem of Lupescu was a real one but in those circumstances some accommodation would probably have been reached. It can be argued therefore that his father's decision to select Averescu was the cause of Carol remaining in exile, and the hand of Marie was seen in this by many critics. Both the King and Queen would doubtless have been delighted to have had their son back on their terms, but they regarded it as too risky in a volatile situation to allow him back on his own terms.

Throughout the last half of 1926 and the first half of 1927, the political situation in Roumania was fraught with problems. At a time when the country needed a strong figurehead, the King, never a powerful personality in his own right, was an ill man. The Queen, a more dominant character, was concerned about her husband's health, the eclipse of her political friends and her son's conduct; she spent about two months out of Roumania on her visit to the United States, for which she was criticized by some people, although she proved as always to be an excellent ambassadress for her country.

On her return at the beginning of December 1926, she learnt what she had long feared, that her husband had developed cancer. It was cancer of the bowel. Carol's German cousin, Frederick of Hohenzollern, writing to him from Freiburg on 27 January 1927, said that what made the King 'sink so low was not only his illness but above all the pain caused by your having left'. Although Carol's conduct may have contributed to Ferdinand's deterioration, such a heavy accusation must have been hard to take.

Early in April 1927, the King received the last rites of the Church but although he survived, the writing was now on the wall for all to read. The country faced the prospect of a child monarch and a Regency under the leadership of the young and inexperienced Prince

Nicolas. It seemed that only the return of Carol could guard against this eventuality. Neither option commended itself to everyone in the country, and in May Averescu offered an alternative solution when he obtained the backing of certain sections of the army to stage a coup that would have installed him as the head of a military dictatorship. The exact circumstances of this manoeuvre are very uncertain because of the secrecy of the preparations, and precisely what would have happened to the monarchy had the coup succeeded is yet another matter of speculation. It does not appear, however, to have been organized to bring Carol back to Roumania but rather to secure strong government at a time of critical weakness. It is certain in any case that Carol would not have been party to any act of disloyalty against his father. While Ferdinand was alive, Carol was unable to consider certain actions that might be open to him after his father's death.

It should be emphasized that when Carol renounced the succession, he had no reason to suspect that his father would not remain on the throne for many years to come. Had he known that the King's health would deteriorate so suddenly, it is most unlikely that he would have left the country.

Whether Averescu was the instigator of the attempted coup or whether he was persuaded to lead it by elements in the army is also unclear. He was known to admire Mussolini, who had seized power in Italy in 1922, but he was always a great patriot and indeed he accepted the position when the King, literally rising to the occasion, summarily dismissed him as Prime Minister on learning what was planned. He may have relied on Ferdinand's illness to have prevented the King either from discovering the plot or from taking any action, but once Ferdinand made a stand, Averescu probably concluded that he could not rely on the army in the face of active royal opposition. It is not inconceivable that had Averescu won the day, Carol might have been obliged to return home and call on the armed forces to restore his father to the throne.

Apart from the failure of the coup, Averescu does not appear to have suffered personally, and he later threw in his lot with the National Peasant Party to oppose the Liberals. Even now the King could not bring himself to appoint Maniu or one of his supporters as Prime Minister. Instead he invited Stirbey, who was not a professional politician despite his relationship and close connection with Bratianu, to act as chief minister pending elections. The Queen, who for once had no hand in the appointment, realized that nobody would believe this.

The elections on 24 June 1927 resulted in victory for the Liberals, quite reversing the voting of the previous year and clearly demonstrating the volatility of an electorate that only fifteen months before had rejected Bratianu in the wake of Carol's renunciation. Perhaps it was a case in a crisis of supporting the devil one knew. The outcome meant that there was now no prospect that Carol would be asked to return. Had Maniu won, the situation might have been different.

Carol meantime was living openly with Magda Lupescu in France. Motor cars, music, cards and his stamp collection were his main interests, but above all he loved her and she knew exactly how to get her way with him. She seemed able to cast a spell over him. They were very much a married couple in appearance and behaviour but he was strongly under her influence. Nevertheless, he desperately wanted to return home and even managed to enlist his mother's support, but there were too many conflicting interests. If it had really come to a decision to let him resume his responsibilities without Lupescu at his side, it is doubtful if he would have agreed, although in December 1926 she had offered to sacrifice herself if Carol was restored to his former status. Not everybody took this declaration seriously.

Very early in the morning of 20 July 1927, King Ferdinand died. In normal circumstances his son Carol would automatically have succeeded him. Now his decision to leave the country and renounce his rights must have seemed to him a stupendous act of folly, for instead of being King of Roumania he was a private citizen living with his mistress in a foreign land.

12

The Right to
Intervene

The man who, had he behaved himself, would now have been King was not permitted to attend his father's funeral or to comfort his mother in person. He had to content himself with attending a memorial ceremony at the Roumanian Church in Paris, along with representatives of the French government and members of the diplomatic corps. There were some shouts outside the church when Carol appeared of 'Long live the King!' Among the mourners ironically was the dead King's former mistress, Helena Vacarescu.

The long obituary notice in the London *Times* contained these words: 'The political worries of his later years were enhanced by domestic trouble. The Crown Prince not only differed from his father's ministers on several matters connected with military training, but also in 1925 once more indulged his taste for amorous escapades.' The same notice observed that Prince Nicolas 'was educated at Eton and in the British navy and has many friends in this country'.

The King's will was dated 2 July 1925 but there was an important codicil dated 11 January 1926. Properties were left to the Queen and the other children, and there were bequests to cultural and educational institutions, as well as to all the churches in the country. Carol's legacy originally was the estate at Sinaia and Castle Peles, together with all the King's personal property, but the codicil changed the situation.

'It has seemed good to Heaven,' it read, 'to afflict the country, the Queen, and myself with a great sorrow in the renunciation of the throne by Prince Carol. I can never forget my grief at having to take such a decision, which nevertheless was demanded by the interests of the State and of the Crown. The new situation thus created makes necessary the following change in my will: I annul the bequest of castles and real estate to my son Carol because these are absolutely necessary to the future King of Roumania. Prince Carol will be given his share in money and in State securities. I pray God to help my son in the new life which he has chosen, despite our wishes, and to grant that his choice may prove happy for himself and for Roumania.'

The fact that this codicil was added within days of Carol's renunciation indicates perhaps that the King knew that he did not have long to live; or it may have been no more than palace efficiency. Ferdinand also left a letter for the Prime Minister, in which he referred to Carol in the following terms:

'My love for Roumania does not permit me to consider my duty ended with my life and I must think of what the future may bring forth. God has willed that the Crown shall pass to my grandson, who is yet a child, and the burden of government will fall first upon Prince Nicolas and the Regency Council. I call upon all good citizens to do what lies in them for the peace and progress of our country.

'I cannot look into the future without thinking with fatherly love of my dear son Carol, to whom I wish a worthy and happy life in the new destiny he has chosen. I do not doubt that he and every good Roumanian who loves his country will strive to help the progress of the kingdom during the reign of his son and his successors. For the peace of the country, I have sacrificed my fatherly desire to see him again and I charge him to keep his promise not to return without the permission of the government. Let my son Carol respect scrupulously the legal conditions made by his renunciation of the throne and the sacred duty of a Roumanian son and a father to respect the undertaking that he has given of his own free will.'

Carol wrote to his mother on 27 July to say that he was broken by his father's death and exactly a month later, with questionable taste in the circumstances, he wrote to say that Magda Lupescu was ill with despair and that she had nearly gone blind at the news! This may have struck Marie as somewhat exaggerated at least, but she may have been even more astonished to have received a long letter written nine days earlier from the stricken lady herself. No doubt Carol and Magda were trying to ingratiate themselves jointly with Marie now that she was not constrained by her duty as consort of the monarch.

'Madame,' Lupescu addressed her, 'I am writing to your Majesty and I beg her to forgive me and not to consider this letter as lacking in respect and commonsense.... If during all this time I have remained close to Prince Carol and suffered side by side with him, it is because I loved him and respected his sadness. It is precisely because of this deep love that I would never have believed that I would be so severely judged and that I would be considered as the cause of all the unhappiness that has befallen the country and your Majesties.

'I have been a friend, a companion and on occasion a true and faithful counsellor. I have always believed that a mother's love is the strongest feeling there is in nature and I have therefore tried to reconcile Prince Carol with his parents. . . . If he has heeded the advice I have given him, it is because he has always maintained a feeling of profound respect for his parents. . . . I should like to dedicate my life to helping others who suffer, and to give me the strength I humbly beg your Majesty to send me her blessing. . . .'

Within a few hours of his grandfather's death, little Michael, not yet six years old, was proclaimed King in Bucharest and the Regency came into being. In a different era and in different circumstances, Queen Marie or even Princess Mother Helen, as she was now officially called, might have been appointed Regents, but although, contrary to what has been written elsewhere, there was nothing in the Constitution to prevent the appointment of a female Regent, such a role was not widely considered suitable for a woman at the time. The strongest royal figure obviously available was therefore the young, inexperienced and virtually unprepared Prince Nicolas. He was assisted by the Patriarch Miron Christea and by George Buzdugan, the country's senior judicial figure and the most politically able of the three. They were widely regarded as a weak team who lacked the authority of Carol himself and who might have difficulty in safeguarding the interests of the nation. Inevitably this put greater power into the hands of the politicians.

There was considerable anxiety outside the country about the stability of Roumania under a child King and there were fears that the Hungarians and the Soviets might take advantage of the situation to press old claims to Transylvania and Bessarabia. In these circumstances Carol made an important statement to a French journalist which was first published in *Le Matin* on 31 July 1927. He complained bitterly that he had not been allowed to attend his father's funeral. 'Did those responsible for this inhuman gesture,' he asked, 'fear that my presence would provoke trouble in Roumania? It is still very far from my mind to foment any agitation in my country.' He went on to say that he had renounced his rights for 'a reason of dignity' and that, in serious circumstances, he had been forced into his decision by people and means about whom and which he did not wish to go into detail. He now deplored the consequences of the action he had been obliged to take.

The situation in Roumania, he declared, had altered radically since his renunciation. At the time there had been no fear for the health of the King and the country appeared to be secure. Now matters were different and there was grave concern about its future. He then announced his position:

'I consider that as a Roumanian and as a father, I have the right and the duty to see that the greatness of the nation ... shall not suffer any damage so that my son may collect a secure heritage when his time comes.

'This situation gives me the right to intervene personally. I am, and have always been, a loyal and ardent patriot. In my heart is a fervent desire to be of use to my country and not to provoke unrest, but I shall never be able to refuse to obey the wish of my people and to respond if they appeal to me.'

Carol had effectively thrown down the gauntlet. He obviously now bitterly regretted the renunciation, or at least its consequences, and he sought every means to present it as involuntary. He continued to claim that the decision had been imposed on him and even went so far as to state that he had never renounced his right to the succession. This attitude fanned international speculation about his return to Roumania, forcing Bratianu to issue a statement that Carol would not be restored to power. 'The succession to the throne,' he said, 'is a constitutional problem. Once settled, it cannot be reopened.'

Bratianu reacted angrily when an emissary from Carol, a former government minister named Mihail Manoilescu, was arrested at the Roumanian frontier and found to be carrying letters, addressed to prominent citizens, informing them that Carol's renunciation had been forced on him. Although the letters were in Manoilescu's handwriting, Bratianu recognized the work of Carol. The affair attracted international notice when Carol publicized the arrest. 'I consider that the Roumanian people have a right,' he said, 'to an accurate account of the situation and to the declaration that I have made in France. That was the mission that I confided to Manoilescu.' Manoilescu was tried and acquitted in November on charges arising out of this matter.

Bratianu, whose prestige received a severe blow, believed that Carol, through his agent, was engaged in a plot against the government. For his part, Carol regarded Bratianu's reaction as evidence that he was rattled because of the support for their former Crown

Prince among the Roumanian people. In any case the Prime Minister was sufficiently worried by the situation to make a statement to the *Daily News* in London and to broadcast a communiqué throughout Europe.

There is no doubt that Carol was in touch indirectly with many of the leading politicians in Roumania, at least among the opposition parties. His contacts in Roumania were sending him back disturbing news. For example, Emil Otetelisanu, a civil servant who later became a junior government minister, wrote on 12 October that conditions had deteriorated in the three months since Ferdinand's death. He said that the government could only maintain itself 'by terror and abuse' but that unfortunately the opposition parties could not agree on policy, leaving Bratianu very much in the driving seat. It appeared, however, that Averescu might support Carol's return on certain conditions, one being that 'Your Majesty' (as so many supporters now addressed him) 'renounce a certain liaison'.

Although practised in the art of renunciation, this was one renunciation that Carol did not welcome. It must have been increasingly clear to him, however, that, despite the Liberals, he had a very good chance of returning home as King if he were prepared to leave his mistress, and it is certain that he considered this course and probably even discussed it with her, notwithstanding his infatuation for her. He doubtless reckoned that a temporary abandonment might suffice and that once he was King, he could do as he pleased. If to Henry IV of France Paris was well worth a mass, to a private citizen named Caraiman the throne of Roumania must surely have been worth at least the pretence of separation from Magda Lupescu.

Otetelisanu also referred to conditions in the army as 'frightening' and told Carol that 'the mass of officers are allied to our cause'. He expressed the view that Bratianu was only waiting for a propitious moment to install a republic, with himself at its head. 'It is up to us,' he wrote, 'to hasten the end of this odious regime.'

Letters like this, containing information that has to be read with some reserve, confirm that there was a plot against the government which Carol either instigated or of which he took advantage. He would have been less than human if he had turned a deaf ear to all the representations made to him since the death of his father, especially now that he wanted to return as King. 'Now more than ever,' Otetelisanu finally said, 'the hope of our nation is directed towards your Majesty. The country is on the edge of a precipice. News arrives from Bessarabia, from Bukovina and above all from

Transylvania that our very national unity is endangered. The economic situation in the country is disastrous. We are a poor people in a rich land ... threatened by enemies without and also by discontent within which grows every day. We must not lose time. Your Majesty may be able to change this state of affairs in one minute. It is your historic mission. We others are ready to fulfil our duty.'

An only slightly less partisan letter was sent the following day from Virgil Magearu, a friend of Manoilescu who had met Carol in Paris and relayed their discussions to two opposition politicians, Maniu and Mihalache. It made the startling accusation that Bratianu had told French journalists that Carol was in liaison with the Russians, through the intermediation of Madame Lupescu 'who is a Soviet agent'. It also assured Carol that 'we all continue to believe and hope that we shall very soon have your Highness's accord in order to hasten the coming of the hour of joy when we shall receive King Carol II in the country'.

The uncertainty in the country adversely affected Roumania's ability to borrow money abroad. As Stirbey wrote to Marie on 10 December, 'What is holding back credit is the fear of political upheaval.' It was, he said, over 'the question of Carol'.

Before this, however, an unexpected event of crucial importance occurred. On 24 November, just four months after the death of King Ferdinand, his almost exact contemporary, Prime Minister Bratianu, also died. He succumbed to blood poisoning following a severe throat infection, originally diagnosed as tonsillitis.

More than one foreign newspaper referred to him as a dictator or to his government as a dictatorship, but this was very unfair to a man who had played a prominent and valuable political role in the country for over thirty years. Every newspaper made the point that his death had removed Carol's main rival in Roumania – his 'sworn enemy' according to the New York *Herald*, his 'most formidable opponent' according to the London *Daily Mail*.

Unable to speak, Bratianu on his deathbed had in writing nominated his younger brother, Vintila, the country's Minister of Finance, as his successor. This perhaps says something about nepotism and his assumption of the royal prerogative, and gives some credence to those who complained about his dictatorial or proprietorial tendencies. Fearful of disruption in the country, the Regency Council immediately endorsed the dead Prime Minister's wishes. Prince Nicolas was unlikely to have been able to influence the other Regents in support of a candidate more favourable to his brother, and there is no evidence that he tried or even wanted to do so, although at this time he was still to some extent under his elder brother's thumb, even if he had swallowed some of the unpleasant propaganda that had been circulating about Magda Lupescu.

Vintila Bratianu at once declared that there would be no change in the dynastic policy of the government, but his word did not carry the weight of that of his brother and the authority of the administration was further reduced by the fact that a key member, Foreign Minister Titulescu, was critically ill with double pneumonia.

There was great confusion in the country. The armed forces, whose officers had not been pleased at the arrest and trial of Manoilescu, could be relied on to defend the nation if an attack came across the Soviet frontier but their loyalty to a weakened government opposed to Carol, whom many regarded as one of their own, was an uncertain factor. The opposition parties, now joined by Averescu, could be relied on at most to try to keep matters on an even keel until such time as new elections, as they hoped, returned them to power. They might be willing to put the question of Carol on ice for the moment, but it could not be shelved for ever, especially when their interests were to some extent inevitably involved with his. One solution much canvassed at the time was to allow Carol to return not as King but as a member of the Regency Council.

There was also the problem that Carol had an unknown number of impatient supporters in the country, with many potential followers waiting on events. There was a very real danger of serious trouble.

Carol probably regarded Bratianu's death as facilitating his return home. Paradoxically, however, it had the effect of delaying the resolution of the problem, because it forced the government and their political opponents to close ranks to protect the nation at a vulnerable moment in its history.

13

'My Time Will Come'

'Your personal enemy is no more,' wrote Prince Dimitri Soutzo, '. . . the whole country is for your Royal Highness . . . there is not a stream but a river of seventeen million Roumanians flowing to bring back Prince Carol. . . . But at present, since the death of Bratianu, all hearts and minds are turned towards Paris; all who are young, clean and idealistic await their King; and if you do not respond to their many appeals at this very propitious time, you will bring discouragement and disappointment into all their hearts.

'Give a sign to all of us who are waiting for you to act, and as quickly as possible, so that we can organize your triumphal return.'

Now that his father was dead, Carol had no qualms about pursuing his own interests inside Roumania. His strategy was clear: he wanted to return as King. The tactical question was how to achieve this objective. Letters from the likes of Soutzo encouraged him to precipitate action and it is anybody's guess what would have happened had he responded immediately to such appeals. The last thing he wanted, however, was to embroil his country in a civil war against opponents who would resist him in the name of his own son, a civil war moreover that might invite unfriendly foreign intervention. It was worth waiting in the hope that the opposition parties would come to power and invite him back.

Of all Roumanian politicians, Mihalache was the one who seemed most supportive; at Manoilescu's trial, he had told the court that the country was in favour of Carol's return. Jorga and Maniu, although both disapproving of Carol's personal life, foresaw the possibility that his return might be in the country's best interests. Averescu, probably the most pragmatic and opportunistic of the opposition leaders, was always a man to keep open his options.

Carol had reasonable hopes therefore that he would get his way by sitting tight, although he was not helped by the fact that newspapers in Roumania, which were not supposed even to criticize the government, were strictly forbidden to discuss the possibility of his return. The government actually used the army to confiscate offending journals. What he may not have reckoned with is that almost all the serious politicians were patriots who, in a crisis, would put Roumania's interest above all else. He had to convince the waverers that his interests and those of the country were identical, otherwise they would, at least in the short term, shelve or postpone a resolution of the Carol question, or give it a lower priority than he wanted.

His waiting policy created considerable frustration among his followers in Roumania, and by the spring of 1928 he himself was becoming exceedingly impatient. He had shown in the past an inclination for dramatic behaviour in face of opposition and there was always a danger that he would do something silly, or be pushed into reckless action by others.

In fact he badly damaged his cause by a serious misjudgement during a visit to England, which began on 28 April. Carol may have thought that Britain, with its tradition of tolerance and dislike of dictatorship, would warm to his cause. His family had many connections with England, and was not his mother a granddaughter of Queen Victoria? He may have been impressed with the supportive letters he had received from London, for example that of Newton Rowe, a young man writing from the Royal Colonial Institute, who had recently returned from Samoa where he had launched a publicity campaign 'against a dictatorship which had become established there', resulting in the setting up of a Royal Commission of Inquiry. 'I should like particularly to serve in your cause,' he told Carol, 'because I have the greatest detestation of anything in the nature of a dictatorship such as appears to prevail in Roumania at the present time.' Or there was the letter, written five days later from the United Service Club, from Colin Ballard, a former military attaché in Bucharest. Fearing that it was unsafe to use the post, Ballard had entrusted the letter for delivery in person by a journalist on the staff of the Chicago *Daily News*. He assured Carol that 'if I can do anything for you or your royal house, it would be a privilege and pleasure to serve you'.

Whether Carol involved either of these men in his English adventure is unknown, but certainly he arrived in Dover from Ostend on the SS *Jan Breydel* on 28 April 1928. Travelling as Mr Carol Caraiman – and not in the name of Jones, as reported in the less reliable newspapers – he was admitted for two months for the purpose of visiting friends. In his party were his hosts, Mr and Mrs Barbu Ionescu – not Count and Countess, as again romanticized in the popular press – and Magda Lupescu, together with her father and younger brother and six servants. A report from the immigration officer who admitted them noted that one of the party had been heard to forecast momentous events in Roumania on 6 May, eight days later.

They drove at once to the home of the Ionescus at South Godstone in Surrey. Ionescu was a man of somewhat dubious credentials. There were stories that he was related to, or even the son of, a former Roumanian Prime Minister, but the name by which he was known may not have been that with which he was born. In an article published in January 1974 in the French magazine *Histoire pour Tous*, Jacques Delaunay claimed that Ionescu had previously been known as Maurice Leiba and Leibovici. A British Foreign Office minute, dated 24 May, referred obliquely to his 'activities as a keeper of disorderly houses in Putney', but for all that he was a Roumanian citizen who had been allowed to live in Britain for a number of years. Another Foreign Office speculation was that Ionescu, who was 'not considered straight by the Roumanians in this country', might endeavour to interest Carol in questionable business transactions. Whatever the truth, Ionescu was financing, either wholly or in part, the visit of Carol and his entourage to England, and despite his pretensions, he was undoubtedly a wealthy self-made businessman who was known to have extensive interests in the catering industry both in England and on the Continent.

In Carol's position, he had to gather support wherever it could be found, and there were many opportunists willing to offer him a hand in the expectation that their reward would be great if his cause prevailed. For others, keeping contact with Carol was a form of insurance. There were people in very powerful positions who took a serious interest, or who even had a stake, in the future of Roumania, such as Henry Deterding, the head of Royal Dutch Shell; and the position of the first Lord Rothermere, the newspaper magnate, must be examined in this context.

If Rothermere had been involved in Carol's plans prior to 28 April, it is surprising that his *Daily Mail* did not immediately report the arrival in Dover and scoop the rival press. In fact the British newspapers did not seem to be aware at first of Carol's visit to England and it was not until the late editions on 1 May that they reported his presence in the country. The visit was extensively featured the following day, not always very accurately. The *Daily Sketch*, for example, said that Carol had visited Croydon Airport, which may possibly have been true in view of subsequent events, but it also claimed that he had been accompanied by a member of the Roumanian Legation, which is inconceivable. In fact it is clear from Foreign Office records that, on learning of Carol's arrival, the Roumanian Chargé d'Affaires at once asked the authorities to be kept informed of his movements, a course that was agreed to after some internal debate.

Not only were the newspaper accounts inaccurate, they were also contradictory. We know for certain, however, that on the Monday after his arrival, Carol had tea and danced with friends at the Savoy Hotel in London and that two evenings later he took a box at the theatre to see *The Monster*, starring Ruby Miller. This provided the *Sketch* with the headline: 'Madame Lupescu in Royal Box'. The report makes amusing reading:

'A crowd of people, mostly girls, gathered outside the Strand Theatre last night set up a cheer when Prince Carol and Madame Lupescu got out of their car there. They had motored from Godstone with their hosts, Monsieur and Madame Ionescu, and arrived shortly after the play commenced. The party entered by the entrance to the royal box, outside which there was an awning and a crimson carpet. When the curtain rang down for the first interval of "The Monster", it was noticed that Madame Lupescu was dressed in an ermine coat with fox collar and cuffs, and that she was smoking a cigarette. . . . During the interval Ruby Miller was received by the Prince, who congratulated her on her good French. Monsieur Ionescu presented her with a giant bouquet of roses and carnations, and another member of the party presented her with a silver cigarette case containing Roumanian cigarettes.'

Even in those days, the people surrounding Carol were clearly not unpractised in the modern art of public relations. The hands can be detected here of Ionescu himself and of Sir Oswald Stoll, who owned theatres and who had an interest in publicizing the play; he also owned the *Sunday Referee*, which later led to the almost certainly incorrect rumour that he too, like Rothermere, was actively assisting Carol's plans.

'Prince Carol,' the *Daily Sketch* article continued, '. . . had previously met Miss Miller on the Continent.' Referring to Magda Lupescu, it observed that people who had caught a glimpse of her had been 'struck not only by her beauty and her wonderful golden hair but also by her charm and simplicity'. One woman was said to have told a *Sketch* reporter that she could not take her eyes off Lupescu's hair.

Pictures of Carol appeared, many of them showing him in Surrey wearing a grey lounge suit and white spats, usually with a cigarette in his hand or in a holder in his mouth. The reporters who interviewed him said that he wore a black crêpe band on his left arm in memory of his father.

According to the *Daily Mirror*, he had come to England because 'I love your country, because my mother is English and has taught me to love England. There are no political reasons for my visit. I am here as a private citizen enjoying a holiday.' He said something similar to the *Daily News*: 'Please let us understand at once that my visit to this country has no political significance. I have come here in the first place to rest.' To the Manchester *Daily Dispatch* he said: 'My greatest wish is to lead a quiet life free from politics. English people know very well how to respect the wishes of one who does not want to be bothered much.'

These remarks make interesting reading in the light of what Carol must have known he was going to do, for he was indeed planning an overtly political action. It can only be assumed that he was deliberately concealing his intentions and lying to allay suspicion.

Twenty thousand copies of a manifesto, dated 5 May 1928, printed in Hungary and addressed to the Roumanian people, had been brought into England. On the front, under the heading 'Do not forget the son of King Ferdinand', was a photograph of Carol in military uniform, beneath which there appeared his signature and the words 'in exile'. On the verso appeared a twenty-one-point political programme, promising free elections, freedom of the press, the abolition of monopolies, financial help for farmers and other equally worthy and unobjectionable policies. This programme was preceded by the following declaration: 'Today, as a result of falsehood and incompetence, we Roumanians are the laughing-stock of the entire world. The time has come to put a stop to this deplorable state of affairs. The regime of lies, intrigue and tyranny must disappear. Roumania must re-establish a regime of real freedom for all its citizens, without distinction of religion or nationality. This task can only be accomplished by a sovereign brought up in the traditions of the nation, ready for every eventuality and aware of the needs of the country.'

The document also contained a specific reference to Magda

Lupescu. She was not the cause of Carol leaving Roumania and would not prevent him from doing his duty towards the country. His renunciation had been motivated by disagreement as to how Roumania should be governed and by 'unhappy matrimonial strife'. He had also hoped that King Ferdinand would live long enough to have come to the conclusion that his son's political opinions were correct and that he would then have changed the regime, 'as I propose so to do today'. He was certain that his father would have recalled him to Roumania, but now that Ferdinand was dead and the country in danger, 'I want to do my duty to my people and my country. I want to return with your consent. . . . I want to return for my son and to make him a worthy successor of the dynasty.'

It was planned to deliver this manifesto, probably by scattering it from the air, to the congress of the National Peasant Party at Alba Julia on 6 May. It may also have been Carol's intention to land in Roumania and join the peasants in a march to Bucharest; credence is given to this possibility by the statement in the document that he proposed to change the regime 'today'. Indeed more than one commentator has concluded exactly that, although it seems highly unlikely that Carol would have risked such a grave step without the certain support of the armed forces. It was more widely believed that Maniu, who presided at the congress, was involved with Carol, but this too was denied.

The whole business was shrouded in secrecy and it is difficult to establish the truth. What is certain is that two commercial aircraft were chartered on Carol's behalf from Imperial Airways to fly to Roumania on 6 May. Exactly who made the arrangements is unclear; it may have been Ionescu or, as the Foreign Office believed, 'certain British newspapers', the most likely being those owned by Lord Rothermere. It appears also that the arrangements were made at the last minute, which is extraordinary if it had all along been decided to drop the leaflets on a particular date. One aircraft would in any case have presumably been adequate to drop leaflets and it is a reasonable assumption that the second machine was to carry passengers. It may well have been intended for journalists but there must be a distinct possibility that the second plane was for Carol himself: it is known from Foreign Office sources that he had intended to be at Croydon Airport himself at four o'clock in the morning of 6 May.

The expedition was in any event frustrated by the British authorities. Learning that Carol or his representatives had on 5 May endeavoured to charter the aeroplanes, 'to take him and presumably other persons to Bucharest,' according to the relevant Foreign Office minute, 'A stop was put on this at the instance of the Foreign Office by the Air Ministry on the score that the Prince had not received the necessary visa to enable him to enter Roumania.' The manager of Imperial Airways was warned that, in chartering two planes to Carol, the company might be laying themselves open to a charge under Section 11 of the Foreign Enlistment Act which could involve confiscation of the two aircraft.

It is quite clear that the Foreign Office thought that Carol was himself intending to land in Roumania, but in the event he did not even turn up at the airport. There can be no doubt also about the intention to drop leaflets emanating from England. There is considerable doubt, however, about Carol's intention to land in Roumania, or perhaps overfly the country, while the leaflets were dropped. It may have been in his mind when he arrived at Dover, or it could have developed after he came to England, possibly at the suggestion of newspaper interests. The most likely scenario is that Carol did indeed intend to land at Alba Julia and that he must have received certain assurances of support, probably from the military.

Was there any advantage for him in launching such an adventure from British soil instead of from French? Perhaps he concluded his activities would be free from surveillance in England. The Roumanian authorities maintained spies in France and the fact that they told the Foreign Office they were planning to bring over a detective from Paris indicates that they had no such network in England. This may also explain why Carol travelled with three members of the Lupescu family; they could have been a very elaborate smokescreen.

Also, if Lord Rothermere really was supporting Carol, it would have been a powerful reason to launch activities from England. Prince Nicolas, in his diaries, throws some light on the matter. Although written many years later and not notably accurate in detail, the diaries are often reliable in their broad outline. 'On May 6 1928,' he wrote, 'news reached us that Carol was preparing a coup in order to return to Roumania. Everything had been organized by Lord Rothermere, the magnate who had caused such a stir about Transylvania to be returned to the Hungarians, and financially by Barbu Ionescu. The idea was that a proclamation signed by Carol be dropped over Alba Julia on the occasion of a congress to be held there by the Peasant Party, and a second plane to land in the midst of the consequently excited crowd. . . . Implicated in this affair were a number of English journalists and without doubt certain Roumanians.'

Nicolas went on to say that it was widely believed that Maniu had simultaneously presented an ultimatum to the Regency Council but 'there never was a question of such a thing'. He was evidently quite clear in his mind that Carol had intended to land in Roumania on 6 May and had only been prevented from so doing by the action of the British government; he was further certain that whatever support Carol may have had from unnamed Roumanians, these did not include Maniu; and he believed that Rothermere was involved.

Before examining the position of Lord Rothermere, we must look at the consequences of Carol's failure either to return home or even to drop leaflets over Alba Julia, since this caused Rothermere abruptly to distance himself from Carol. The following day, an officer of the Metropolitan Police was despatched to Surrey to tell Carol that he was no longer welcome in England and that it would be best if he would make immediate arrangements to leave; if he did not comply within a day or two, he would be reminded, and if he still did not act, he would be deported, perhaps to Roumania! The officer was unable to contact Carol until next morning, 8 May, on which day the Home Secretary, Sir William Joynson-Hicks, told Parliament that after consultation with the Foreign Secretary, Sir Austin Chamberlain, he had 'caused Prince Carol of Roumania to be informed that his presence in Great Britain is no longer desirable and that he must terminate his visit without delay'. It is interesting to note that he referred to Carol by his royal title, although officially he was a private citizen who had been deprived of the right to call himself Prince.

The story of Carol's appeal to the Roumanian people appeared first not in the Rothermere newspaper but in the Beaverbrook-owned *Daily Express*, another indication that Rothermere may not have backed Carol, unless perhaps he was anxious that his connection be suppressed even at the expense of good journalistic practice. No sooner had the Home Secretary made his statement, however, than the whole affair became front-page news. The story was even reported in the Bucharest newspapers, which had not even been allowed to mention Carol's name for many months. This was clear indication that the Roumanian government regarded Carol's English adventure as a major defeat for him.

It certainly set him back. Whatever his intentions, his cause had not been advanced by the actions of the British authorities. Sir Percival Phillips, who had recently returned from Roumania, writing in the *Daily Mail* on 9 May, described him as 'the most disheartened and crestfallen man – and the most surprised – in all England yesterday'. Carol had told him that he was 'pained and astonished at the suggestion that I have offended against the hospitality of the British government', and he expressed his 'deep regret if anything I have said or done has caused any annoyance to the British authorities'.

Events, Carol said, had forced him to act prematurely. 'If the Roumanian government had resigned, as I thought it would, and permitted free elections, my message would have been delivered at the opening of Parliament. We did not know definitely until a few days ago that the mass meeting at Alba Julia would be held. Not until then was it decided to try to reach the people in that way.' Carol did not mention the idea of himself returning to Roumania.

Phillips asked Carol what he would do next. 'Wait, always wait,' was the reply. 'I have patience. Everything will come out all right.' In fact Carol had told the police officer who visited him that he would appeal directly to the Home Secretary to allow him to remain in Britain, for which purpose he despatched Ionescu with a letter to London, in which Ionescu wrote that the leaflet had been prepared long before as a declaration to be used at the opening of a new Parliament in Bucharest and that any new printing in London had been done without Carol's knowledge. This suggests that the proclamation had been reprinted in England, probably by one of the newspapers, almost certainly the *Daily Mail*. Ionescu visited the House of Commons, hoping to see the Home Secretary, but was interviewed by Lord Erskine. As was to be expected, his representations on behalf of his guest were unsuccessful.

On the same day that the Phillips' interview appeared in the *Mail*, the newspaper came to the defence of its proprietor. It not only denied any involvement on the part of the newspaper magnate but alleged that Rothermere had actually rebuffed overtures from Carol. 'Emissaries of the Prince,' it claimed, 'made desperate efforts to interview Lord Rothermere,' hoping to get the *Daily Mail* to print copies of the manifesto and to charter aeroplanes for its distribution throughout Roumania. Viscount Rothermere, it appeared, had 'refused even to discuss the scheme'.

The newspaper went on to allege that Ionescu, accompanied by an unnamed journalist, had called at Rothermere's home the previous Saturday and told his private secretary that, in return for printing copies of the manifesto and hiring 'a number of aeroplanes' to distribute them, the newspaper would be offered the exclusive right to publish the proclamation. It was also suggested that one of the aircraft should be used to carry a *Daily Mail* correspondent to report on the distribution of the leaflets. No suggestion, incidentally, was made that it was part of the scheme that Carol himself should have returned to Roumania at that time, which would have been a far greater reporting scoop had the *Mail* been granted exclusive rights to cover the event.

The alleged meeting could hardly have taken place the previous Saturday since that was the day on which the planes were due to depart and the leaflets had already been printed, so it is impossible to believe this version of events. In any case, why would a newspaper, the primary purpose of which is the dissemination of news and which was privy to such an amazing plot, suppress such sensational information and even allow the rival *Express* to scoop it, unless of course its proprietor deliberately kept the information to himself or gave specific instructions that it be kept on ice?

Rothermere may well have rejected Carol's overtures but certainly not in the circumstances, or for the reasons, given in the *Daily Mail*. It is abundantly clear that there was contact of some sort between Carol and Rothermere, at least through their representatives. So, if, as the *Daily Mail* admitted, its proprietor was privy to Carol's plans, why did it not report them?

Once the British government took a position against Carol, not wishing him to interfere in Roumanian affairs from British territory, Rothermere was quick to detach himself from the matter. 'It should scarcely be necessary,' declared the newspaper, 'to add that Lord Rothermere had had no communication of any sort with Prince Carol, Count Ionescu, or any of the Prince's assistants, whether by interview, letter, telegram or telephone.'

The *Mail* then informed its readers that Roumania was a country 'where corruption is rampant to a degree which almost passes the imagination of Englishmen and where surprising events may happen at any moment. It might, therefore, be possible for Prince Carol, who has a large number of sympathizers among the military and civilian population, to succeed in recovering the throne which he has several times renounced.'

In an uncharacteristic historical note, the newspaper compared Carol to Louis Napoleon, who in 1840, 'amid shrieks of derision', had landed in France with fifty-six followers and a tame eagle. 'He was promptly captured and his followers dispersed, but nonetheless in 1848 he was French President and in 1852 he was Emperor of the French.' Carol's plans were described as no more crazy than those of Napoleon III, who had also used England as a base of operations.

Before this whole Roumanian incident, Lord Rothermere had shown a keen interest in Hungary. On 21 June 1927, he signed a long article that appeared on the leader page of the *Daily Mail* under the heading 'Hungary's Place in the Sun', in which he argued for the revision of Hungary's post-war borders. This public espousal of a cause that had little or nothing to do with him puzzled his own countrymen and infuriated those nations that had benefited from the Treaty of Trianon which effected the post-war settlement. Roumanians in particular knew that top of Hungary's shopping-list in any revision of frontiers would be Transylvania.

Rothermere's article brought him enormous notoriety and prestige in Hungary, perhaps because he was demanding something for the Hungarians that even their own government was not seeking. His name became famous there. Before the end of the year he had received a delegation from Budapest, bearing a document, supposedly signed by over a million people, thanking him for his efforts; and before the year was out, amazing as it may seem, a proposal was formulated to make him King of Hungary. Just how seriously this was intended and just how seriously he took it, and what chance of success it might have had, is better left to students of Hungarian history. Nothing of course came of it, but it is an extraordinary sign of Hungary's interest in Rothermere and of his interest in Hungary.

It is not inconceivable, therefore, that Rothermere might have agreed to help Carol if he thought it would assist the Hungarian cause. The importance of the Rothermere connection with Carol, if in fact it existed, lies in what deal the two men must have made. Ostensibly there can have been very little meeting of minds between the man who wanted to detach Transylvania from Roumania and return it to Hungary and the man who wanted to return to a united Roumania as King. It has been alleged that Rothermere only agreed to help Carol in return for Transylvania, but if such an arrangement ever was made, Carol could never have intended to honour it because it would have made his position in Roumania untenable. Rothermere must have realized this, but on what other basis would he have involved himself?

Point 16 of Carol's proclamation referred to 'The liquidation of all unsolved problems with our ex-enemies by common agreement so as to keep their friendship and guarantee a long and lasting peace for our own benefit as well as for the benefit of Europe and civilisation in general'. If that was the price that Carol had to pay for Rother-mere's support, it was something very much short of an intention to sacrifice Transylvania, and it was the sort of pious generality that was open to any interpretation.

Doubtless there was kudos for Rothermere in even being seen to try to help the Hungarian cause, but if Carol agreed to vary the terms of the post-war territorial settlement, it can only have been his intention to do so in the most minor particulars. The only other conclusion is that he was ready to use Rothermere and later betray him. The allegation that he was willing to sacrifice Transylvania was surely untrue and may have been given spurious validity by rumours to that effect deliberately spread by the Roumanian government to discredit him.

Although there were suggestions in the British press that Carol was making overtures to the Hungarian government to revise the Treaty of Trianon, the Foreign Office did not believe this. They did, however, at first take the view that Rothermere was 'mixed up in the business'; there was some suggestion that the whole plot may have been concocted by Dudley Heathcote, the journalist whom Rother-mere had employed to promote his Hungarian campaign. Heathcote was referred to as an unreliable source of information who, for his own ends, might have acted in this matter without Rothermere's knowledge.

This seems somewhat unlikely, and it is impossible to accept that Rothermere did not know something of what was going on. In fact the Hungarian Minister in London called at the Foreign Office on 7 May, the day after the congress in Alba Julia, and said, 'in confi-dence', that Rothermere had asked his opinion as to whether he should see Carol, who had requested an interview. Rothermere had told him that Carol 'might prove to be a valuable asset to Hungary'. This appears to be an immediate step by Rothermere, through the agency of the Hungarian Legation, to divorce himself from Carol as soon as Carol's plans had aborted.

Foreign Office wisdom appears to have dictated that Rothermere's involvement should be played down. On 15 May, a letter from the Foreign Office to the British Minister in Bucharest said: 'In writing to you by the last bag about Prince Carol, I indicated that Rothermere had probably had a hand in Prince Carol's activities. It is difficult to inculpate Rothermere but certain other details have come to light. . . .' What those details were was unfortunately not disclosed. On the following day, the British Minister in Prague wrote to the Foreign Secretary to report that general opinion in Czechoslovakia was that Rothermere was behind Carol. A handwritten annotation to the letter, made in the Foreign Office, read: 'Don't let us say anything. This incident is closed, and apart from the fact that we have no evidence to justify saying that Rothermere was personally implicated, in fact there are indications that he definitely was not cognisant of Heathcote's little plot.'

Informed opinion at the time was that Rothermere was involved in some way with Carol. This was certainly the view of the London *Times*. The extent of his involvement has, however, always been a matter of conjecture. He might have been interested in Carol because he saw some journalistic advantage in having a special relationship with him and/or because he saw an advantage for Hungary. Since the *Mail*, however, allowed itself to be scooped by the *Express*, the second consideration is probably what swayed him, and having assisted Carol in some way in the hope of advantage to Hungary and of course to himself as a result, he took urgent steps to disassociate himself when Carol's plans went awry.

A neat postscript is provided by a letter from the Foreign Office to the British Minister in Bucharest, written almost immediately after the aeroplanes were stopped at Croydon. All the indications, the letter said, pointed to the fact that Carol had 'got into the toils of Lord Rothermere'. 'It is amusing to note,' the letter continued, '. . . that whereas the *Sunday Express* rather favoured Carol in a leader on Sunday, the *Evening Standard* and other of Lord Beaverbrook's organs turned right round on Carol by Monday evening: that is, as soon as they knew that Lord Rothermere had a hand in the business.'

At all events, neither Lord Beaverbrook nor Lord Rothermere raised his voice against Carol's expulsion from Britain. Escorted aboard by two detectives, he and Magda Lupescu finally left England by sea on 16 May. He had decided not to return to France for the moment but to take up residence at the Château d'Ardennes, owned by another of his wealthy industrialist supporters, near Namur in Belgium. On arrival he found a letter awaiting him from his mother, who referred to 'the cruel and humiliating happenings in England'. 'It is simply horrible,' she complained, 'that you returned thus to your mother's country!' She did not tell him that she had written a letter to King George V, apologizing for her son's conduct while under his protection.

For once Carol did not take his mother's strictures lying down.

She had said that he was badly influenced by other people, but he replied, on 26 May: 'I am absolutely conscious of my deeds and I am not ashamed of myself, but I am ashamed of the disgraceful behaviour of those who pretend to be honest people at home. I can only consider them as downright fools and dirty pigs. What makes me very sad in all this is that you, who always say that you are a loving mother, let yourself be fooled into every disgusting lie by those whose interests are far from being yours and ours all.'

He went on to accuse her of accepting every version of every story that was unfavourable to him. She had allowed herself to be deceived. Had she understood the real interest of the country, she would have behaved differently. 'It is very sad,' he told her, 'that somebody who has a British education should have such a conception.'

There was reference in both letters to a matter that was obviously of importance to Carol, despite all his other problems. Referring to what he regarded as his personal stamp collection, his mother told him that she had no legal right to hand it over to him because, 'being of enormous value', it was the property jointly of all her children and not just of one. She was not prepared to ask her other children, 'who are living useful lives, honoured lives', to give up their rights for 'one who cast them aside – and for what?' She could hardly have taken a more hostile position in the matter and Carol rightly expressed himself as astonished at her attitude. 'I can only say that it is disgusting,' he wrote.

Almost everything and everyone disgusted him at this time, except of course Magda Lupescu. The matter of the stamps, however, was not the main issue. 'My time will come,' he told his mother, 'and on that day there will be many [who] will be sad that they did not see the reality . . . unhappily you are blinded by a lot of low scoundrels who are leading you astray. From today on I'll defend myself by every means.'

14

'The Country Has No Leader'

Had it not been for Helen's position as mother of the new heir apparent, she might well have instituted divorce proceedings at the earliest opportunity, soon after Carol's renunciation when it became clear that he was living openly in France with his mistress. When her son became King, she was placed in an even more difficult position. She had to consider not only her own interest but that of the boy and indeed of the country. Much as she may have wanted a divorce, she was hardly a free agent.

She was also subject to conflicting advice. Many of Carol's opponents believed that divorce would further loosen his bond with Roumania. Separated legally as well as physically from his wife, and further removed from all connection with his son, he was less of a danger to the existing regime. Carol's friends, on the other hand, realized that while he was still married to Helen, if only in name, there was always the prospect of his returning and resuming his family life, or at least appearing to do so. While he was still married to Helen, he could not marry Lupescu, which might make his return impossible.

Helen's version of events was that Carol had asked her for a divorce soon after renouncing the succession. She had discussed the matter with King Ferdinand, who was opposed on religious grounds and made her promise never to agree. Carol wrote to her again in more urgent terms towards the end of 1927, after his father's death, and this time she consulted the country's leaders, who were all against divorce, taking the view that Carol's subsequent marriage to his mistress would seriously damage the monarchy. One could hardly find better proof of the reality of Carol's connection with the monarchy, despite the fact that he was a private citizen in exile who had been formally deprived of membership of the royal family.

According to Helen's biographer, 'In this unanimous desire to save

Carol from himself, no one gave a thought to the possibility that his wife might want to be free too. But this was of no great consequence, because the idea of initiating divorce had never seriously occurred to her.' Even if that were the case, which seems very unlikely, why did she change her mind barely six months later?

The possibility that Carol had planned to land in Roumania on 6 May 1928 may have opened her mind to the ludicrous situation in which she could find herself, but it is more probable that she positively wanted a divorce and was merely awaiting a suitable opportunity. The thought of Carol returning was horrifying. She took the view that he could not have contemplated coming back even briefly without the assurance of support in the country, so what if he should return and have the power to remain? If he returned without his mistress, would Helen be expected to resume some sort of relationship with him, if only for the sake of their son? If he returned with his mistress, however unlikely that might be, her position as Carol's wife would be intolerable.

Helen may therefore have changed her mind about divorce as the result of Carol's misadventure in England, or at least seized on it as an excuse. On 7 June, barely three weeks after Carol left England, she petitioned for divorce 'with the approval of the high Regency'. Carol was summoned in the name of Caraiman to appear before the court in Bucharest on 21 June, failing which the case would be tried in his absence. It is amusing to speculate what might have happened had he decided to attend the proceedings in person. Would he have been allowed into the country? The fact that his physical presence was never contemplated, however, is implicit in Helen's petition.

She sought a divorce on the grounds that 'My husband has left me and lives abroad where he openly leads a life that is totally irreconcil-able with the dignity of marriage. His behaviour constitutes a grave permanent injury ... that justifies and demands the annulment of our marriage.' There being no defence, the marriage was dissolved on 21 June. It was specifically noted in Helen's petition that she did not wish the court to regulate the method of exercising parental power or other matters concerning 'our child, His Majesty King Michael', although a minute in the British Foreign Office records of the time indicates that she claimed that Carol had signed a document, when he renounced the throne, giving her exclusive control over their son. Presumably, however, the royal family regarded this matter as their concern and not that of any court of law; in any case a quick divorce was what was required and Helen probably did not want to delay the dissolution by discussion of more complicated issues.

Helen never satisfactorily explained her sudden change of heart. She referred to increasing pressure from Carol from the moment he left England and alleged that he had made accusations against her that finally wore her down; but he surely did not suddenly make new allegations that caused her to petition for divorce within three weeks, after having resisted him, if she is to be believed, for over sixteen months. In any case, what were these accusations? Her biographer wrote that the 'nature of the pressure brought upon the Princess Mother, the false position in which she had been placed, and risk of exposing the young King to further mischief' finally persuaded the country's leaders to agree to the divorce.

Prince Nicolas, as a member of the royal family and the Regency Council, should have been privy to events, but in his diary he stated that he did not know where the idea of divorce originated. He speculated that Stirbey had influenced the decision in the belief that divorce would further separate Carol from Roumania; and this is not improbable if the government felt threatened by what had happened in England. The suddenness with which the petition was presented certainly lends support to those who believed that Carol's unfortunate British adventure precipitated the divorce.

Although she was a very honest woman, Helen appears not to have told the whole truth in this matter. She may have had her own good reasons for divorce, or she may have acted under pressure from the government, but it is doubtful if she felt under pressure from Carol. He was in love with Lupescu but he was quite happy to live with her without benefit of matrimony, and indeed he did not marry her soon after the divorce when he had the opportunity to do so. He later said that it was Helen who insisted on divorce proceedings. 'She struck the blow,' he declared, 'when I was publicly belittled,' referring to the fact that the divorce followed very quickly after his expulsion from Britain.

Whatever the facts, young Michael's parents were officially divorced from the middle of 1928. Although, in almost every matrimonial dispute, there are arguments on both sides, Helen had good reason to regard herself as the innocent party, and one can well understand her telegram to her mother when the marriage was annulled: 'Freed at last from this nightmare.'

Following the failure of Carol's initiative in May and the divorce in June, which kept him very much in the public eye, there was great uncertainty inside Roumania, and his supporters were becoming bolder in their opposition to the Liberal government, despite the fact that the authorities at first regarded the British episode as a serious setback to his cause. Carol's friends were to some extent, however, marking time, in the hope and expectation that the government would fall. This was not long in coming. Vintila Bratianu told Prince Nicolas 'that he himself and the Liberal government were tired and wished to resign'. He was asked to delay his resignation while an attempt was made to set up a coalition government, but he resigned on 3 November and a week later, Maniu, leader of the National Peasant Party, was back in power, at the head of a broadly based administration that was intended by the Regency Council to act in the country's best interests on non-partisan lines.

Maniu was the only politician in Roumania, apart possibly from Averescu – who was now appointed Minister of War – with the standing to bring Carol back to Roumania. The question was whether he thought it was in Roumania's interest to do so. His own followers were the most fervent supporters of their former Crown Prince, but Maniu himself was a religious man of high moral calibre who did not approve of Carol's relationship with his mistress. He was also a man of courage, however, who would not allow his personal prejudice to override his judgement of what best served his country. Carol at last had a real hope of returning home without having to take extravagant or reckless action.

The divided country, with its child King and weak Regency Council, was beset with economic problems and badly needed a shot in the arm. With all his faults, Carol was, in the opinion of many intelligent people, even some who were critical of him personally, the only answer. No one else had his stature. Whatever Maniu may have said in opposition, would he, now that he was in power, want to bring Carol back, and if so, how, when and in what capacity?

At the beginning of 1929 it was anybody's guess whether the new year would see the return of the former Crown Prince. Although his divorce from Helen had not been well received in the country, his popularity among the Roumanian masses was undoubted. Only the Liberals were inexorably opposed to him.

Despite the somewhat acrimonious tone of their correspondence, Marie and Carol continued to keep in touch. For example, she sent him a short but chatty telegram on 8 January about her health and the party that had been given for Ileana's twentieth birthday, and informing him that her private secretary would be bringing him some stamps; his stamp collection, apart from being a passion with him, was a permanent point of contact between mother and son. It was also reported that Marie and Carol had lunched together in a Paris hotel in the middle of March while she was travelling in western Europe with Ileana.

Early in July there were reports of a pro-Carol coup inside Roumania, resulting in numerous arrests and the forcible retirement of a number of army officers. These reports were serious enough to force Carol publicly to deny his involvement. Maniu was determined to arrange matters in his own way and in his own time, and he was not willing to be pressured into premature or precipitate action. The demonstration in favour of Carol – coup is too strong a word – was designed to force Maniu's hand, and he was obliged at least to appear to react strongly.

In fact, however, although he seemed to be well in control of the situation inside the country, he was confronted by many serious problems, most of which he had inherited. This too was 1929, the year of the Great Depression, the consequences of which made his task even harder. Faced with a world economic recession, the peasants, his own supporters, were the first to suffer, and a hopeful nation that had turned to him when Vintila Bratianu resigned was becoming sadly disillusioned after only a year. Moreover, one of the three Regents, Buzdugan, died in October, leaving the country even more in need of leadership. If there were a governmental crisis, it would fall on an inexperienced young man and an elderly priest to try to resolve it, opening the door to the possibility of a military dictatorship.

There was some talk of replacing Buzdugan with Queen Marie, who was Carol's only possible rival as a person of stature. It would have been unusual to appoint a woman but her case was exceptional. She at least had authority, even if she had been associated with the Liberals, but, as she kept telling Carol, she was no longer young and was becoming tired. In any case it was not considered politic that both Marie and Nicolas should dominate the Regency Council. In the end one lawyer was replaced by another, the little known Saratzeanu, who may have owed his selection to the fact that he was related to Maniu's Minister of Finance, who was obliged to resign as the result of the ensuing criticism.

'The country has no leader,' Patriarch Miron Christea told Queen Marie. He obviously did not regard himself as such and he had no high opinion of his new colleague; and he held Prince Nicolas in a contempt that was reciprocated. What he said was the truth. Rou-mania had had no real figurehead since the death of King Ferdinand and no statesman with pretensions to run the country on his own since the death of Ion Bratianu. A child King and an ineffective Regency Council, together with a Prime Minister and government under economic siege, could neither command the respect of the country nor deal successfully with its massive problems.

In retrospect it could be seen that there had only been one answer since Ferdinand and Bratianu had died within weeks of each other. Despite all his faults, only Carol could pull the nation together. He was the only candidate to fill the vacuum that had been left by his father's death, if Roumania were to remain a monarchy.

Whether, if Maniu's political base had been more secure, he would finally have brought Carol back is an open question, but he was quick to realize that, in existing circumstances, this was the only way to secure his position. He had always maintained informal contact with Carol, but now he secretly opened more formal discussions to see if there were a basis on which Carol could be invited to return home.

Inside Roumania, references to Carol had been appearing with increasing frequency in the newspapers since Maniu had come to power and it was no longer forbidden to mention the name of the former Crown Prince. On 17 February 1930 the newspaper *Dimineata* reported on its front page that Carol had written to both his mother and brother that he wished to visit Bucharest for the marriage of his sister Ileana. In fact the wedding did not take place because it was discovered that her prospective husband was a notorious homosexual, but the newspaper significantly commented that Carol's letters were imprecise about his intention to leave Roumania after the ceremony. On 29 March the newspaper *Lupta* declared that Averescu, having originally opposed Carol, had now changed his mind. It went so far as to claim that General Conda, representing Averescu, had been 'received in audience by Prince Carol' in Paris, when he asked Carol to authorize Averescu to 'start proceedings' to bring him back to Roumania. Carol is alleged to have replied: 'I shall only return home when the country calls me. Until then I shall remain above party politics.' According to *Lupta*, Averescu was, however, entitled to regard this dignified response as a springboard for action.

Talks with Carol were conducted by various parties over a period of about six months, and Averescu actually met him in Switzerland on 25 April 1930. Although no great decision was taken at this meeting, the fact that it was reported in the Roumanian newspapers on 11 May was the clearest possible indication that the government was preparing the country for an announcement.

During this period, the attitude of Prince Nicolas was very ambiguous. In later years he came to dislike his elder brother, and more especially Magda Lupescu; he came to believe the worst, rather than the best, about Carol and he espoused causes and supported factions that were opposed to his brother. There may have been an element of jealousy. Even if he lacked the ambition or the desire to fill Carol's role, he could not understand how the country could still cling to a man who had behaved as Carol had done, especially by deserting the country for his mistress. This attitude was clearly revealed in his diaries, but since these were written in retrospect at a much later date, they cannot necessarily be taken as an accurate account of his sentiments at the time of his membership of the Regency Council.

'It is said,' he recorded, 'that once Maniu had decided to bring back Carol, he consulted the Regency Council. I never heard anything of the kind being mentioned at the Council and I was never consulted personally.' He admitted, however, that he was often away on military duty. 'Carol had not been idle,' he wrote. 'He had all along been in contact with Maniu and Averescu, always behind my back . . .'

Although Nicolas repeatedly insisted that he had been kept in the dark, many people, including Stirbey, were convinced that Carol and Nicolas were conspiring together. Even their mother believed that the two brothers were planning to meet in June 1930 outside the country. This may well have been true, for as early as 2 February of that year Carol's German cousin, Franz Joseph, had passed on a message to Carol from his brother, in a letter mainly about Ileana's unsuitable German fiancé, that Nicolas would 'make a tour through central Europe this summer with his car, and he will visit you and discuss all questions with you personally'. The same letter also contained the somewhat extraordinary sentence: 'Nicky told me to tell you that you should postpone your intention to travel to Roumania.' So, far from encouraging Carol's return, Nicolas may have been trying to delay it, or even frustrate it.

I believe that Nicolas did support his brother's return, thinking that he would probably join him on the Regency Council. It may be that he only did so when he saw no alternative or realized that that was where his own interest lay, but it seems impossible to accept that he was unaware of what was going on. One reason why Nicolas could have wanted Carol's return was that he was madly in love with a Roumanian woman, whom he wished to marry, although exactly the same objections were made to his marrying her as had been made when Carol wanted to marry Ioana Lambrino. Because the Constitution had been changed in 1923, after the marriage of Carol and Ioana, Nicolas needed royal consent. His letters to this woman, whom he did eventually wed in November 1931, show that she was more important to him than his position in Roumania and Nicolas may well have wanted Carol to return in order to be released from responsibility. There is, moreover, the evidence of Carol himself who, in his diary on 9 April 1937, referred retrospectively to Nicolas's 'act of help'.

Whatever Nicolas's position, the attitude of brother to brother is startlingly illustrated in a letter from Carol to Nicolas dated 16 November 1929. It is hardly the letter of a private citizen to the senior Regent of Roumania, but more that of an imperious monarch to someone who owes him a duty. 'I am taking advantage of the departure of a courier,' Carol wrote, 'to send you a few words, although your rebellious silence is becoming more and more stubborn ... In any case the fact that I am writing to you is a sign that I forgive you ..,' even if, he hastened to add, he had little confidence that his brother would mend his ways. He continued, in two brief paragraphs, to congratulate his brother about two minor domestic matters that had come to his attention, 'always by an indirect route'.

'The first part was to commend you, the second to reproach you,' Carol said. Why had Nicolas not sent him the list of modifications to the naval uniform, as promised? How could he have put his signature to the shameful decree appointing a certain person as Consul General in Vienna? He was, moreover, awaiting his brother's signature to a decree removing another individual from office and imprisoning him for embezzling public money. Why too had he failed to fulfil his promise to send him Roumanian cigarettes from time to time?

Carol went on to describe a pleasant day's shooting in Belgium when he had bagged twenty-three pheasants and nine small hares. 'I shot like a foot,' he said, it being his first time in four years. He then spoke in considerable detail about a new American car, the Cord, which he had tried out. He had not seen anything special at the Motor Show (presumably in Paris) but wrote about the cars that had caught his attention. Switching to the military, he enquired how the manoeuvres had gone.

There followed one of the few references in his letters to his son Michael. He was worried that the boy was receiving too much kingly education and not enough suitable for a child. 'Something must be done about this at all costs,' he declared, 'for I feel sick for this child when I see that he is overgrown, going around in long pants but with the appearance of a baby. In your position at this time, you not only have the right but also the duty to intervene in a forceful manner' – 'to put things right,' he added in English, the rest of the letter being in French, 'and you must do it.' 'I want to send the little boy a Christmas present,' Carol continued, 'but I do not know what things will make him happy.' The letter concluded in English: 'With best love, Carol.'

Carol's simultaneous preoccupation with matters serious and trivial was revealed here. Just as he would use an important letter to refer to his stamp collection, so his lack of Roumanian cigarettes was worth mentioning alongside the education of his son. What is noticeable is the interest he continued to take in even the most minor military matters and his vindictive attitude to those he disliked or who opposed him. Perhaps most obvious of all was the way in which he still felt able almost to command his brother.

The newspaper *Adevarul*, in an article on 12 May discussing the recent meeting of Carol and Averescu, referred to reciprocal commitments which had been made in Switzerland, the nature of which were, however, unknown. It speculated as to whether Averescu had the power to implement his side of the bargain, whatever it was. Discussing the role of Nicolas, it declared that he had come recently to display 'a cordial attitude' towards his brother. 'It is an open secret,' the newspaper reported, 'that, thanks to the personal intervention of Prince Nicolas, the pamphlet published by the Liberal Party against Prince Carol was not distributed.' The article further said that Nicolas had plans to take a holiday abroad after the end of the Parliamentary session and that it was very probable that he would meet his brother.

The meeting with Averescu on 25 April and its public revelation in Roumania on 11 May seriously alarmed the Liberals. On 25 May Vintila Bratianu made an important speech to his party congress, protesting against the government's overtures to the former Crown Prince. This was the first occasion on which any major politician had held the government itself responsible for contacts with Carol, although, as Minister of War, Averescu was unlikely to have visited Carol in a purely private capacity. Bratianu demanded that Maniu declare himself officially against Carol. A question was asked in Parliament about the government's attitude to the act of 4 January 1926 whereby Carol had been deprived of all rights following his renunciation. Vaida-Voevod, Minister of the Interior, confirmed that the government still respected the act.

The reality however was somewhat different.

15

For the Good of
the Country

Carol landed in Roumania on 6 June 1930. He had apparently driven from Paris, crossed into Germany and made his way to Munich, where he boarded the aeroplane that was to take him home. The exact circumstances of his return have been shrouded in mystery and many different versions have been published about it. Carol himself provides some evidence in his diaries, although sadly there is no contemporary account from him. As a young man he had kept a daily diary but, as he confided in a new diary started in 1937, these earlier 'notes of my youth were taken from me'. (Whether they were stolen or confiscated, they appear not to have survived.) 'In six years,' he declared in 1937, 'I have not written a line,' which he said was a mistake; and it is indeed a sad loss that, besides the disappearance of the early diaries, there are no notes for the first seven years following his return, perhaps the most important years of his life.

He did, however, keep a diary from 1937 until 1950, most of which has survived, and in an entry on 5 June 1940, he looked back on the tenth anniversary of his departure from Paris for Bucharest: 'My thoughts go back with great clarity,' he wrote, 'to the last ten years, from Strasbourg to Cologne to Munich, going through the mountains when the car radiator started to boil over, stopping at an inn run by a Protestant minister. I was anxious about crossing the border and worrying that someone might stop my plane, but all turned out well. It was a long journey that did not bother me and did not even tire me because, although I was so nervous and tense, I was secure in the belief that I would succeed.'

Most commentators have assumed that he flew from Paris to Munich, but from his own account he obviously motored there. It seems that the aircraft he boarded at Munich landed in Roumania at an air force base near Cluj in Transylvania, where he was greeted by army officers and where he changed into military uniform. He then flew to Baneasa, the military airport of Bucharest.

There are conflicting reports about the time of his landing in the capital, but Carol's diary establishes that it was at ten past ten in the evening. He wrote of a 'flight through the mountains and into unknown territory' and of the pilot's navigational problems before they spotted the casino and the Palace Hotel at Sinaia below them and knew that they were on the right flight path. Their late arrival led some people wrongly to think that the plane had been forced to land *en route*.

Carol was expected by the police and by units of the military, so his movements must have been known to the government; in the circumstances it is impossible to believe Nicolas's claim that he was taken unawares, except perhaps in terms of detail. He actually wrote that Carol had landed in the grounds of Cotroceni while he was at dinner: 'I was surprised by the music and troops,' he declared, 'so I went out on the terrace, and there, in front of me, was Carol. . . .' This conflicts with the many reports that Nicolas had actually met Carol's aircraft at Baneasa.

Admittedly Nicolas was remembering these events many years later when he had occasion to look back in bitterness, and perhaps his recollections had become distorted by the passage of time. In any case, it is very difficult to reconcile Nicolas's insistence that Carol returned without his knowledge with the quite widely held belief that he had helped to achieve his brother's return; and also to reconcile it with Carol's acknowledgement of Nicolas's 'act of help', which makes little sense unless his young brother had assisted in some way positively in connection with his return from exile.

Nicolas may not have been fully informed about his brother's return, or at least about all the events leading up to it, but he cannot have been ignorant of all the discussions about it, perhaps of its inevitability. He may at first have wanted to delay it as long as possible, even indefinitely, in the hope that he could make his own mark in the country and receive the popular support that was denied him; but more probably he came to think that it was not worth fighting any great battles when he had a chance of personal happiness with a woman he loved.

Whatever Nicolas's true position, Carol, at the age of thirty-six, returned home in 1930 after five years in exile. The news spread like wildfire throughout the country. Thereafter event followed upon event in rapid succession.

Maniu had undoubtedly made two conditions for Carol's return. The first was that he should assume the status of a Regent for his son Michael. The second was that he should abandon Magda Lupescu and, if possible, become reconciled with Michael's mother. Whatever Carol may have promised verbally, for there was nothing in writing, and whatever Maniu may have been led to expect, Carol had no intention of accepting either condition. It was obvious to him that he would not have been asked to return had he not been needed to pull the country together internally and help to secure financial support from the international community. Despite his peccadilloes, Roumania could not apparently do without him, so he was in a position to do almost as he liked. Being such a keen motorist, it cannot have escaped his attention that he was now in the driving seat and, especially when he realized that his return was a matter of great rejoicing in the country, he set about achieving his purpose. He rose to the occasion with a ruthlessness that was to serve him well in his enormous efforts to revive Roumania and that was to bring criticism on him for the way he treated both his family and those who had opposed him in the past.

Within hours of his return, he made it clear to Maniu that he not only considered himself King of Roumania but that he expected to be confirmed legally in that status as from the date of the death of his father. This put the Prime Minister in an impossible position. To have sought again to expel the man he himself had brought back would have made him a laughing-stock, even if he had the power to do so, which was very questionable in the light of the joy with which the armed forces and most of the people had received the famous exile. Maniu had been duped and there was nothing he could do about it unless he wanted to call his credibility further into account.

He had the grace to resign temporarily in favour of a member of his own party named Mironesco, on the grounds that he had already sworn allegiance to young King Michael. As early as 7 June, a council of political leaders met under Mironesco's chairmanship for three hours early in the morning. Overwhelmed by the astonishing public support, reflected in almost all the newspapers, for the returned hero, the decision was taken formally to recognize Carol as King. Maniu voted against, but this was the merest gesture. Averescu and all the other political leaders who made up the anti-Liberal alliance supported the proposition and only the Liberals were seriously opposed to the move.

Giving Carol the throne required the annulment of his renunciation in 1925 and the act of 4 January 1926 giving effect to it; and to preserve the fiction that Michael was not being dethroned, it became necessary also to date Carol's accession from his father's death, thereby fulfilling his wishes exactly. So Mr Carol Caraiman had been King all the time. It was again a case of 'The King will obtain whatever verdict pleases him', or, as Nicolas put it less kindly, 'given his mentality, anything could be done or undone'.

The National Assembly met the following day to debate and endorse these decisions. Jorga, who had once taught Carol, blamed Stirbey and the late Bratianu for having virtually forced King Ferdinand to disinherit his son when it had only been necessary to accept his renunciation of the throne, and he claimed that his advice, and that of Maniu and other opposition leaders at the time, had been ignored. He spoke of his old pupil as a victim of disgraceful intrigue. 'At last the day has come,' he declared, 'to rectify the wrong that was then done.' Maniu himself, despite his personal reservations, endorsed the measures on behalf of his party. He had to stand for some considerable time, unable to speak, because of a lengthy ovation by the Members of Parliament. Whether it was meant for him or for Carol, he was receiving the credit for having brought Carol back. The leader of every political party, except the Liberals, approved the measures in turn, ending their speeches with the declaration, 'Long live King Carol II'.

The Liberals perhaps wisely absented themselves from the proceedings, and a number of them cautiously vanished temporarily from the capital. This meant that they did not formally oppose the government action. Only one brave Liberal deputy, named Florescu, attended the debate, and but for his vote, the decisions would have been unanimous.

The session was interrupted while the temporary Prime Minister, Mironesco, went to Cotroceni, where Carol was staying with his brother, to inform him that he was now King of Roumania and to escort him personally to the National Assembly, where he was greeted with ecstatic cheering. Carol was noticeably moved by the occasion and by the obvious delight with which he was received. He had returned only two days earlier, hopeful but uncertain about his reception. Instead of playing himself in, he had gambled boldly on achieving his objectives in full; and despite some opposition from the very man responsible for his return, here he was, in less than no time, enthusiastically acclaimed King in Parliament and throughout Roumania.

Unable to restrain his tears, he made an emotional speech to the Assembly. The great demonstrations in the country, he declared, showed that 'certain persons whose words filled the heart of my father' had failed in the end to accomplish their purpose, but he bore no lasting grudge against them. 'I want,' he said, 'to bring together everyone able and willing to help advance the progress of Roumania.' He ended in suitably dramatic style: 'Now is the last wish of my dear father fulfilled.' (His dear mother was, more likely by chance than design, outside the country at the time.)

In accordance with custom, the Prime Minister tendered his resignation to the new King, who asked him to remain in office while a new government was formed. Carol's first thought was to select a neutral figure to head a coalition of national reconciliation. One name considered, on Jorga's recommendation, was General Prezan, but it quickly became clear that there was no way of involving the Liberals, and when Carol realized that only Maniu enjoyed the respect of most of the other political leaders, he reappointed the man who had resigned on a point of principle. Having defeated him once, Carol believed that he could always do so again, and he intended to keep careful control on him by insisting that the new government contain at least two ministers who had been personally very supportive of him.

Having so easily achieved his first and most important aim, the new King at once set about establishing his authority with his young son, who was given the important-sounding title of Grand Voevod of Alba Julia; 'a consolation prize', according to Jorga, more worthy of a Viennese operetta. Carol sent Nicolas to fetch the eight-year-old Michael to see his father, but Helen put her foot down. If the father wanted to see his son after such a long absence, he should do so at her home and in her presence, however difficult an encounter it might be for her. She had her way, and Carol visited her, looking, she said, just as he had done five years before.

This was a most awkward meeting. She reported that Carol came towards her, shook hands and simply said 'Hello'. 'The only thing for us to do is to be friends for Michael's sake,' she told him; and he replied, 'I quite agree, we will not talk of the past.' Helen went to fetch their son and Carol kissed him emotionally, borrowing him for an hour in order to appear with the child on the balcony at Cotroceni, where they were cheered by the crowd. Thereafter Michael was taken to visit his father for a short time each day.

It was easier for Carol to deal with a Prime Minister than with a former wife whom he had deserted. Where politics were concerned, he had no guilty feelings; but in private matters, although he could be ruthless, he was restrained to some extent by conscience. Helen feared that he would try to take her son away from her, but Carol's only concern was to offer himself to the nation as King with an heir apparent who would secure the dynasty. He loved the boy but did not, at that stage anyway, want to risk criticism by depriving his son of his mother's guidance.

This was particularly true because there was considerable discussion about the possibility of a reconciliation between Michael's parents, if only for form's sake. The details of their first meeting in five years were, surprisingly, reported in the newspapers, and it was openly stated that action was planned, either by legal process or by Act of Parliament, to annul the divorce.

Although she had been aware of the possibility of Carol's return, the actual event took Helen by surprise and left her in a dreadful state of uncertainty. When she asked Maniu why he had not alerted her, he replied that he had not wanted to compromise her or put her in a position where she might have tried to gather support against the move. She now found herself in an almost impossible position. The Roumanian people seemed to think that by waving a magic wand, the past could be erased, that Carol and Helen could be reconciled and live happily ever after.

It was never a serious prospect that they could resume an ordinary marital life, and if Carol had paid lip service to the idea of a reconciliation, it was no more than part of his ploy to return home. Although it appeared that he may have abandoned Magda Lupescu, he was still madly in love with her and not everybody accepted her declaration that 'on the day that his Royal Highness resumes his throne, I shall disappear forever'. Nicolas in particular did not believe this.

The news of Carol's impending return had been given to Helen on 5 June by Mihalache, who discussed with her the possibility of reconciliation. She asked him how anyone could expect her to accept a man who had mistreated her so badly. Telling her that it was an agreed condition that Carol should return alone, Mihalache added, 'The people expect Princess Helen to forget the past for the good of the country.' She was to receive many similar messages in the days to come.

She knew that to leave the country would mean losing her son whom she had brought up during all the time that his father was absent, but she did not relish the thought of remarrying Carol, even for the sake of appearance. No more did he wish to remarry her, although it would have been easier for him to accept a marriage in name only if it would secure his hold on the throne. He never had the slightest intention, however, of abandoning Lupescu. An annulment of the divorce, followed by a coronation ceremony at Alba Julia on 21 September with Queen Helen at his side, was always on the cards; but if this was to be avoided, he must clearly lay the blame at Helen's door. Who could criticize him for leading his own private life if Helen herself refused to accept the role he was seeming to offer her? Ironically the effect of the new legislation that made Carol King from the date of Ferdinand's death was that Helen had legally been Queen of Roumania, at least up to the time of the subsequent divorce.

Carol was probably banking on Helen refusing to annul their divorce, but when under pressure from the government and public opinion she showed signs of acquiescing – as the daughter of a King, such concepts as duty and sacrifice were not unknown to her – he realized that he had to take action if he were not to be caught in the remarriage trap. He did everything he could to persuade her to write a letter declaring that she did not want to annul the divorce; and he succeeded in his object except that the terms of the letter were not as explicit as he required.

An indication of how things were going, or perhaps not going, came on 24 June when it was reported in the newspapers that the September coronation ceremony had been cancelled for 'family reasons'. As the days went by, relations between Carol and Helen became less and less cordial and it was obvious that they would never get together. Neither wanted it, and Maniu, who had been outmanoeuvred by Carol about the monarchy, came to realize that the King had no will to bring about a reconciliation with his former wife.

Maniu might have been able to swallow his disappointments at the hands of the man he had brought home, particularly since Carol's return had proved so popular and in fact beneficial, but the one event he could not possibly accept was the return of Magda Lupescu. The country could survive and prosper under an unmarried King, but there was no way he could condone the return of the King's mistress.

Just when Lupescu returned secretly to Roumania is unclear. She may already have been in the country by the end of June. A German newspaper report to this effect, published on 4 July, was hurriedly denied by the government. Prince Nicolas said that it was on 12

August that Carol told him: 'I have a great surprise for you. Duduia is back.' Duduia was Carol's pet name for Lupescu; he rarely called her anything else. Helen heard the news later that month. Informed circles in the capital were beginning to hear about it soon afterwards, and by October Lupescu was seen openly in Bucharest. Realizing that he had been tricked, Maniu now resigned.

Paradoxically, his resignation strengthened Carol's position of authority. Nobody could stand up to him, not his former wife, not even the Prime Minister, and certainly not his family. He was in charge of Roumania. His mother summed up the situation admirably. 'Carol,' she said, 'is a great sinner, but he is a man. . . .' For Roumania, despite all his faults, he was the man of the moment.

16

A Dual Life

'I found it all quite natural,' Carol said about his new role. 'I became used to it almost at once. Possibly it was an atavistic instinct, something I carried in my blood.'

After standing in the wings and watching an understudy play his part, he was now the principal actor on the stage to which he had been born, and he rose immediately to the occasion. As King of Roumania, he at first wielded almost unbounded power in the country. The very circumstances of his return ensured this. After the uncertainties of the Regency, the people demanded a strong leader and were prepared to follow wherever he led them. The success and prestige of the nation were personified in the dignity of the new ruler.

Traditionally too a Roumanian monarch took an active part in the daily affairs of government, unlike a modern British monarch, and Carol found himself almost in the position of dictator, although his power was not of course absolute. It says a great deal for him that at all times during his difficult reign, he tried to act within the Parliamentary system, although he believed strongly that a young and vulnerable country required powerful, even autocratic, rule. He was concerned to act with due propriety, even if this meant that his adored mistress could not be at his side on State occasions.

Inevitably, he rewarded the friends who had remained loyal to him during his exile but, although many complaints have been made against him, examination of the facts fails to reveal any serious vindictive behaviour against his enemies, with the possible exception of Stirbey. No one lost his life or livelihood and the worst that can be alleged against him is that a few opponents went into exile, and that certain members of his family felt slighted by his treatment of them.

Much has been made of Carol's supposedly hostile attitude to his mother, but his mother's complaints against him, although important, relate to comparatively minor matters. Her official staff and her financial allowances were reduced, but was this much more than the inevitable reduction of her power? She had been so used to exercising authority that it was difficult for her to accept that she was no longer in her previous position. She believed that Carol was spying on her, and she saw a slight in everything.

One problem for Carol was that his mother supported Helen and also espoused the cause of her old friend Prince Stirbey, who left the country voluntarily, in Marie's 'best interests', as he told her. Stirbey was not formally forbidden to return to Roumania until four years later and after an attempt on his life had failed, which has never been laid at Carol's door, although there is no doubt that, of all Carol's opponents, Stirbey was the man who caused him the greatest offence and Carol did seek to cut off Stirbey's sources of income. His hatred for Stirbey has never been satisfactorily explained and it may well have had its deep-rooted origins in his mother's love affair. Not only had Stirbey usurped the place of Carol's father but he had influenced Carol's mother against her son and turned out to be the greatest stumbling block, apart from the deceased Bratianu, to Carol's return. His mother's alliance with his chief enemy and her continued attempts to contact and help him may go some way to explain Carol's attitude to her.

Marie undoubtedly complained to her children about her treatment at Carol's hands. Princess Ileana believed that Carol behaved badly to their mother and Prince Nicolas's diaries speak of 'a series of humiliations'. Nicolas gives as an example an occasion when Carol asked Marie to delay her return to Roumania for three weeks. She had been travelling in Europe with Ileana and there may have been a perfectly good reason for Carol's telegram to his mother, although it is just possible that he was punishing her for seeing Stirbey every day for two weeks in Paris while her friend was recovering from an operation after the attempt on his life.

What do all these charges against Carol amount to? Six years after he came to the throne, his mother wrote to him, listing her complaints. They were four in number: that she had been forced to economize, that she had been attacked for supporting Helen, that Carol had acquired too many personal honours and that she was now referred to as Queen Mother rather than as Queen. They hardly amount to a case against him.

Nor was it easy for Carol to help his mother when she constantly criticized him. In a letter to Nicolas dated 11 November 1931 she referred to 'the incredible misfortune Carol has brought over us', and even when she was declaring her love and support, as, for example, in a letter she wrote to Carol on 21 October 1936, she could not resist accusing him of persecuting Helen. When Carol sent the Prime Minister to complain to her about what she had said while on a visit to England in July 1936, she indignantly repudiated 'these accusations and calumnies' and accused him of causing her sorrow. Marie had always been a forceful personality and in her later years particularly, she was not an easy woman to handle. She saw everything from her own viewpoint and probably blackened Carol's reputation unfairly.

Carol himself referred to his mother in his diary as an energetic woman whose impulsive nature caused her to be unjust, especially to him. 'So many untrue stories have been spread about our relations,' he wrote. 'Latterly I have been accused incorrectly of having persecuted her. Any measures I was obliged to take were because she became a focal point for all discontented people.'

Carol's attitude to Helen may also have appeared more vindictive than in fact it was. His behaviour was motivated by the consideration that his son Michael would succeed him and by his love for Lupescu. He was determined to ensure that the boy should be brought up as he saw fit for his future role, and not unduly under the influence of a woman who might alienate him from his father. He also had no intention of remarrying Helen and wanted her as far out of the way as possible.

Carol hoped that Michael would come to like and accept Lupescu, and no doubt this possibility greatly troubled Helen and caused her to complain about her treatment at Carol's hands. The King may have been all-powerful in the land but he felt very vulnerable where Helen was concerned. As the mother of his son and heir to the throne, she could not easily be put aside. Had it been possible for her no longer to be on the scene, there might have been less animosity on both sides; as it was, the difficulties for Carol of Helen's presence and status made his behaviour appear in some ways petty and unjust.

Helen, like Marie, made a number of complaints against him. She was not allowed to meet Marie on her return to Roumania, but this was because Carol was greeting his mother and did not want to give support to the belief that he and Helen were about to reconcile. She was not supposed to make public appearances or have contact with politicians, and Carol did not want her referred to as Queen. He sought to suppress her name from public affairs and keep her in the background. She also protested that she was spied upon. These actions were more for political reasons than from any personal vindictiveness on Carol's part. He was not normally a man to bear grudges. On 7 July 1938, for example, his diary reveals that he invited Elisa Bratianu to lunch. 'It was my first meeting,' he wrote, 'with the widow of my great enemy since I returned to the country. . . . Elisa was very moved by this meeting and we talked most of the time about the Bratianu Foundation that she heads with unsurpassed energy and dedication. I promised one day to visit the Library.'

There were valid reasons for Carol's behaviour. As Maniu told Helen, 'Your Royal Highness must face the fact that it is the King's conviction that your presence prevents him from concentrating on the responsibilities of government; that it keeps division alive; that you are already becoming the centre of opposition to him.'

Carol saw no option but to encourage Helen to leave Roumania, the difficulty being her rightful position as Michael's mother. It was quite impossible for her to live a private life out of public view. She – and Magda Lupescu – inevitably found themselves at the centre of a personal court, surrounded by sympathetic or ambitious followers. There simply was not room for both Helen and Magda in Bucharest.

Whether deliberately or not, Helen attracted people whom Carol regarded with suspicion, notably those who were critical of his affair with Lupescu, and this of course influenced his behaviour towards her and towards his mother who espoused Helen's cause. In retrospect, once Carol had taken the decision not to abandon his mistress, what happened to his former wife was inevitable. In these circumstances his behaviour towards Helen was understandable and venial.

It was eventually arranged for her to live abroad. Generous financial settlements were made and it was agreed that Michael should be allowed to visit her for a month twice a year. She left the country on 17 July 1931 but was back again little more than three months later, for Michael's tenth birthday on 25 October. Carol, who thought that she had returned specifically for the occasion, was disconcerted when she made no early move to depart. Had she not been the mother of his son, he would undoubtedly have taken stronger action, but he was surprisingly lenient. She saw Michael every day, although she claimed that difficulties were put in her way and that she was closely supervised. This was understandable, given that her delayed return was a breach of the arrangement that had been made for her to leave Roumania, although some of the details had not been finalized, and given also that she was a source of possible friction where Michael was concerned.

How long she would have been allowed to remain in the country had fate not taken a hand is an open question. However, she had been in Bucharest little more than a month when she learnt that her mother was very ill in Germany, and she left for Frankfurt at once. Her mother died six weeks later, and Helen remained abroad.

Carol kept to the agreement whereby Michael was permitted to visit his mother twice yearly but he continued to be concerned that she should not influence the boy against him. His determination to dictate, down to the smallest detail, how his son would be brought up is illustrated by an incident in October 1932 while Michael was visiting his mother in London. Carol had given strict instructions that Michael should always wear short trousers, but Helen had a long-trousered suit specially made for him to go to tea with her at Buckingham Palace. She regarded this form of dress as more appropriate to the occasion, but the boy's aide-de-camp reported the breach to Bucharest and Michael was summoned home instantly, having spent only three days in London.

Carol's action may have appeared petty but there is little doubt that Helen took the opportunity deliberately to defy Carol in order to establish her rights as a mother. Although she claimed that it would have been discourteous for her son to visit the British royal family except in long trousers, protocol did not require a child to be so dressed, and in fact short trousers were usually worn in England by children of Michael's age at the time. She complained publicly about her treatment at Carol's hands, and articles to this effect in the London *Daily Mail* did little to endear her to her former husband.

Had Helen not provoked Carol, Michael would have remained with her throughout the month and would have celebrated his eleventh birthday in her company. Now, deprived of her son, she determined to break her arrangement with Carol by returning to Roumania for the birthday. Considering that Carol was being put under unusual pressure by both Helen and Marie, he acted with great restraint. When Helen defiantly returned home again, she was escorted off the train at Baneasa, just north of Bucharest, where the Foreign Minister greeted her with a bouquet of flowers. She claimed that she was then harassed all the time but she admitted that she was still able to see Michael daily, until he was sent to Sinaia. Learning that he was ill with influenza, she visited him there also.

For a woman who claimed to have been a virtual prisoner, she enjoyed considerable freedom of movement and if she was spied on as extensively as she believed, it is surprising that she managed to make her way to Sinaia, where, according to her, she was not allowed to go. Even Marie, while admiring her courage, told her that it was foolish of her to defy Carol. 'You are playing a losing game,' she said, '... this continual standing up against him only makes him worse.'

She became a thorn in Carol's side but he was nevertheless slow to react, perhaps being nervous that public opinion might support her if he appeared to be treating her badly. He was also anxious to avoid public comparisons between his ex-wife and his mistress which might favour the mother of his son and disfavour Lupescu. Helen may have relied on his vulnerability in this respect and also on his sense of guilt towards her, but she badly overplayed her hand and almost pushed him into a position where he had finally to get rid of her. He either became convinced that she was conspiring with his opponents – who admittedly were few in number at the time – or he seized on the excuse that she was receiving people whose interests were different from his. Her presence in Roumania made her a potential nucleus of opposition. The one thing he could not possibly tolerate was a pro-Michael faction organized by Helen.

Despite her protestations, Carol's decision to send her abroad, permanently this time as he hoped, was no more than giving effect again to the arrangement that had been made between them which provided for her financial security and allowed Michael to visit her twice a year. She was in the unfortunate position of many divorced women who had been deserted by their husbands for other women, but very few were as fortunate as she in terms of financial support. Her peculiar misfortune is that custody of her son, by virtue of his status as Crown Prince, was virtually in the hands of the father and for reasons of State, beyond those of divorce, she had restricted access to her child, although the loving relationship between herself and Michael continued.

The breakdown of the marriage caused unhappiness for both parties and Carol's position tends to be overlooked. His love for Lupescu, his adored Duduia, was real. It was certainly no passing fancy. His life might have been much easier if he had formed a different liaison but his passion for this woman must be understood if one is to understand him. Powerful as he was, he knew that he dared not marry her. This was the one action that could have rallied the public against him. He may not even have wanted to do so since he regarded himself as married in all but name, but legally married to her or not, she was the joy of his private life.

'A King must have a dual life, one royal, one personal,' he is quoted as saying. He believed that, although he was King, perhaps because he was King, how he conducted his private life was his own affair and should not be the concern of the nation. He would do his duty to the people but there were certain matters that pertained to him alone. If Lupescu could not share his royal or public life, she could certainly share his personal or private life.

He spent a fortune on her. A typical Antwerp jeweller's bill submitted in October 1931 listed six items purchased on 25 June – a necklace, three bracelets, a brooch and earrings – a further five on 30 September and an expensive headpiece on 19 October. Most, if not all these jewels, must have been for her. She was installed in a comfortable house in a fashionable district of Bucharest, with a direct telephone line from her bedroom to Carol's palace, although he saw her almost every evening.

She could not attend official functions in Roumania and it was not until 19 June 1938, when Carol was on a visit to Turkey, that she did so anywhere. Carol's delight when she joined him at dinner with the Turkish Prime Minister is recorded in his diary. It made him very happy, he wrote, that she was able to join his important guests. He described it as a major step forward.

Nor could she visit Carol openly, but most nights she would be driven unostentatiously to the palace and home again, either at the end of the evening or, when she stayed the night, very early the next morning. As she grew more confident, she organized soirées, sometimes attended by Carol, at which she entertained her family and particular friends, notably Nicolas Malaxa and Max Auschnitt, the biggest arms and steel manufacturers in Roumania. It has been rumoured that men such as these, whose business morality was often questioned, helped Carol not only to make money but also to deposit it in banks abroad, but there is little evidence for this. One of the cruellest things that his brother Nicolas ever alleged against him was that he had 'coffers filled with gold in North America', but this was totally untrue and part of a vicious plot by his enemies to discredit him.

Another frequent visitor was Barbu Ionescu, with whom Carol had stayed during his embarrassing visit to England in 1928. A number of Lupescu's friends were Jewish but she also entertained people of a notably Fascist tendency. It is a curious fact of life at the time that many Roumanians were anti-Semitic and yet cultivated their influential Jewish friends. Carol seemed to feel quite at home in her court – for that is what it was – perhaps for the very reason that it was such a contrast to his own. He wanted to separate his royal and his private functions.

In any case, he was besotted with his mistress. Somehow she fulfilled his needs as no other woman could. References to her are scattered throughout his diary. For instance, he recorded a visit to her on the evening before her birthday in 1937 when he took gifts and flowers. In his entry for the following day, when he had a fever, he declared: 'My heart and soul wish her so much happiness and any pain that I might cause her hurts me greatly.... She brings me everlasting joy.' Three months later he noted that she was happy that day, 'which is very important to me'. Her relationship with Michael, by then aged sixteen, was no longer frowned on, at least, he said, in the eyes of the court. 'All those cold beings,' he wrote, 'who see me only as the sovereign cannot understand what this fact means to me.' In a personal message at the end, 'Darling,' he declared, 'I love you and adore you.'

This was more than twelve years after they started their affair, when many real marriages might have cooled. Lupescu now referred to Carol and Michael as 'her boys'. On Michael's seventeenth birthday, the three of them 'celebrated with all our hearts and with all our love'. 'May she,' Carol said, 'live for a long time and through her happiness and pleasure make us happy too.' On her own birthday that year, he recorded that they had become even closer, if that were possible. 'I feel an absolute need for her,' he wrote. 'She is an integral part of my very being.' Almost a year later he was still writing in the same vein: 'My love for her is as deep as ever. I cannot imagine life without her.'

She must have been a very remarkable woman to have captured and held the affection of a man who had been considered a notorious womanizer, a man moreover who had no difficulty in finding female companionship. It would have been so much easier for him in his position to have abandoned her, as he had effectively abandoned Ioana Lambrino, but Lupescu had a strange hold over him and, of all women, it seems that he needed her. There is no doubt that he loved her, and as to her attitude towards him, who is to say that it was entirely calculated and without love? She brought Carol a great measure of personal happiness that doubtless helped him to face the enormous political problems that were to arise. It is all too easy to criticize Lupescu for her vulgarity and her pretensions but hers was a difficult role. It might have helped if she had been integrated gradually into the activities of the royal family rather than being left to her own resources, and it would certainly have improved relations between mother and son if Marie had made a gesture towards the woman who in all but legal name was her daughter-in-law, but there was never any prospect of such an accommodation. If she were not allowed to be respectable, it is little wonder that Lupescu was often forced to surround herself with more doubtful company. But at all times she aimed to please the King who adored her.

Carol kept in more or less friendly touch with all his family, but he had a peculiar and ironic problem with his brother Nicolas, who had fallen in love with, and wished to marry, a Roumanian divorcee, Joana Saveanu, who had resumed her maiden name of Dolete. This was a situation with which Carol was of course personally familiar, but he now found himself in the position of having to give or refuse his consent. It may seem extremely hypocritical of him even to have hesitated to agree, but he was under strong pressure from his mother. In a letter to Nicolas, already referred to briefly, Marie spoke of her 'incredible pain' that both her sons should, 'for the same reason', have been involved with unsuitable women. Had he not learnt from Carol's unfortunate experience? 'But you, like Carol,' she wrote, 'are destined to go down through women who suck your lifeblood and destroy your clean ideals. Between you both, you are ruining the work of two generations and neither of you open your eyes to see that you are dancing on the edge of a precipice.' Referring to Joana Dolete, his mother declared uncompromisingly that 'She does not love you, any more than Lupescu loved Carol,' and she warned him that he would be saddling himself with 'a woman who wants money, money, nothing but money. . . .'

Personally, Carol could not have cared less if his brother lived with, or married, the woman he loved, whether she were a Roumanian divorcee or a foreign princess. In fact if the public accepted Nicolas's choice, it might have made it easier for Carol to live openly with, and perhaps eventually marry, his own Roumanian divorcee. He was at first well disposed towards his brother and sent him in charge of two destroyers on an official visit to Malta in June 1931, and Nicolas certainly received the impression that Carol agreed to his marriage. Cynics have suggested that Carol kept open his options by encouraging Nicolas to proceed, but without giving his formal consent. If Nicolas presented him with a *fait accompli*, no blame could be attached to Carol, who could however react if necessary in accordance with resulting public opinion.

Nicolas and Joana were married in Tohani, a village far away from the prying eyes of Bucharest, and when the news reached the government, Carol felt obliged to deny that the wedding had his approval. Nicolas, in his diaries, categorically refuted reports that he was stripped of his military rank. He claimed to have been exiled but in fact Carol merely asked him to go abroad until the storm blew over. One suggestion was that he should go to Argentina for a time to study agriculture.

When Nicolas returned, unannounced and uninvited, the following spring, he was formally ordered to leave the country. Public opinion had not been sympathetic to his marriage and Carol obviously thought it sensible to keep him out of the way a little longer. There is no real evidence of any animosity on Carol's part and indeed there is no indication that he did more than acquiesce in what the government thought best in this matter at the time. That he continued to have affectionate feeling for his brother is clear from a study of Carol's diary.

In any event Nicolas was allowed to return home with his wife in 1935. Carol must have endorsed this decision, and may even have instigated it, but he found that his brother was a changed man, 'nasty and unkind about everybody', according to Marie. Carol appointed him a private counsellor on aviation matters and Nicolas worked closely with the Minister of Aviation, but he soon asked to be employed in a less onerous capacity. When invited to join the royal family's Christmas celebrations in 1936, Nicolas complained that he had not been given enough notice and in any case would not attend without his wife. Carol found his brother obstreperous, and he became exasperated by him.

What concerned him more, however, was Nicolas's new political affiliations. Carol could put up with quite a lot but his brother's link with his most dangerous enemies, the newly formed Iron Guard, was more than he could tolerate. It was finally decided that Nicolas must leave the country in 1937, but even thereafter Carol was concerned about his brother and there was nothing like a total rupture. For example, Nicolas sent a telegram from Venice to Carol in 1938, thanking the King for his kind birthday wishes, so obviously Carol kept in touch with the brother who had caused him so much trouble, perhaps at the behest of their mother. There is also an entry in Carol's diary, dated 23 June 1939, which showed his anxiety that his brother should be granted a dukedom and be entitled to call himself Most Serene Highness. This was hardly the gesture of a King determined to humiliate a member of his family.

On the contrary, it is abundantly evident from relevant correspondence that Carol was on reasonably good personal terms with his family. They were constantly exchanging presents and greetings. Where he appeared to behave badly, it was usually in the face of opposition to his plans and wishes. He saw Helen in particular as a challenge to his control of their son and as an impediment to the progress of his relationship with her successor, so she inevitably suffered, but he was not wilfully vindictive and she would have had little of which to complain had she felt able to withdraw earlier and more gracefully.

His great concern was to persuade Michael first to accept, and later love, Lupescu. In this he may to some extent have deluded himself but there is no doubt that young Michael was a sensible person who was able to establish a good relationship with his father's mistress while at no time being disloyal to his mother.

Carol's diary reveals that hunting had become a great interest for him. 'Many will criticize this passion of mine . . .' he wrote. 'They are wrong to do so. There is much health and life in the outdoors, even if just for a few hours. When I return, I feel like a new man, reborn, invigorated. . . .' He also liked indoor games, playing rummy with Michael, and other card games and backgammon with Lupescu. One of her great joys, which Carol shared, was to watch films in a room specially created for the purpose in the palace. He continued to read voraciously and Lupescu's house was full of French detective stories, which they probably both enjoyed. In these ways he tried to relax from his very troublesome affairs of State. He had plenty of them on his plate.

17

The Storms Ahead

The history of the 1930s in Europe is the story of the rise of Hitler in Germany. The world, perhaps anaesthetized to the evils of Hitler and his mob by the spectre of Communism, literally let the Nazis get away with murder. There was hardly an assassination in Europe, from that of King Alexander of Yugoslavia in France to the killings of two Roumanian Prime Ministers, Duca in 1933 and Calinescu in 1939, that could not be traced back to German influence and encouragement. Carol later significantly described Duca as 'the first victim of the Second World War'.

The Germans under the Nazis were masters at subverting other countries and securing support inside them, and Roumania was no exception. Of course it was easier for them to succeed in a country in economic trouble and among peoples who felt aggrieved or disadvantaged, and the Nazis may have regarded the Roumanian peasant, who to some extent was a second-class citizen in his own country, as a potential ally, especially if he could be made to oppose the wealthy bankers and influential industrialists, some of them Jewish, who seemed to enjoy all the benefits. The Communists too were looking for popular support but their fertile ground was among the industrial masses rather than the conservative peasantry.

When Carol came to the throne in 1930, the Communist menace was much more apparent than the Nazi menace. He could not have foreseen the rise of Hitler; and looking back, his efforts to build Roumania were thwarted by Hitler's ambitions. It hardly mattered what he achieved domestically if he could not maintain Roumania's independence.

Carol's plans for his country were laudable. He inherited grave economic problems and led the country towards material prosperity unequalled in its history. No sooner was he on the throne than it became easier for Roumania to borrow money abroad, and the stabilization of the currency, the cultural and educational developments during his reign, the reforms in land tenure and the country's industrial growth were a tribute to his energy and foresight. Unfortunately he was obliged by circumstances beyond his control to devote too much of his time to matters of foreign policy.

He had been much influenced by reading Bryce's *Modern Democracies* in 1927 in Paris. He was aware that Roumania was unlike the United States or Australia, for example, countries that were enabled by circumstances to make a fresh start in a new world. Democracy was an easy concept for them, whereas Roumania was part of an old world, in close proximity to two major powers, Germany and the Soviet Union – three if one counts Italy – that had opted, or were to opt, for a form of dictatorship. The vast influence of Nazi Germany and Communist Russia was mobilized against free institutions. No country, certainly not Roumania, was self-sufficient and Carol was very concerned at the possibility of some form of dictatorship finding favour in his own country.

If there were a dictator in Roumania, Carol was determined that it should be the King himself. He was not prepared to rule under the thumb of some local Mussolini. Although he did more than pay lip service to democracy and democratic institutions, he also knew that he could not afford to play the role of constitutional monarch in the manner, say, of George V in Britain. His intervention in the political arena was imperative.

He explained his position to British journalist A. L. Easterman. 'Democracy,' he said, 'cannot have the same connotation in Roumania as it has in England. Our civilization is younger. Your country has a Parliamentary tradition of long history. . . . The role of the sovereign in Roumania is not that of the monarch in other countries. The King in other countries must do what his ministers tell him. Here the ministers do what I tell them. . . . It is because of parties and politics in this country. The only element in the State which can maintain a strict line between them and so make for stability is the sovereign.'

Only those closely familiar with Roumanian politics of the period can fully appreciate the truth of Carol's observations. Apart from the fallen Liberals, and the recently formed anti-Liberal alliance around the National Peasant Party, the country was a mass of small political parties jockeying for position. Their behaviour was frequently unpredictable and their alliances opportunist and surprising. They often made strange bedfellows indeed, and to some extent this was true of Roumanian society as a whole. An anti-Semite, for instance, might befriend a Jew if it seemed to be to his advantage or perhaps because he liked him. Hypocritical as this might appear to an outsider, it was all part of the Roumanian game, explicable perhaps by a long tradition of making the best of difficult circumstances under the yoke of the Ottoman Empire and others who had control over Roumanian lives.

Carol could not readily rely therefore on a strong government to help him. In fact he suffered a succession of weak governments. Apart from his two Prime Ministers who were assassinated, two lasted for less than a week and another two for no more than two months. Only Jorga, Tatarescu and Miron Christea survived for longer than a year! Although there were Parliamentary elections to which Carol naturally had regard, the choice of Prime Minister was entirely a matter for the sovereign, but Carol could only choose from among the available candidates. He did not deliberately select second-rate people. Since the death of the elder Bratianu, nobody had arisen who could command wide popular support in the country.

Before considering Carol's foreign policy, it is worth looking briefly at what he achieved on the domestic front. There is no question that he left Roumania more prosperous than it was when he arrived back in 1930. He paid particular attention to the country's oilfields, which because of their increasing output were to play an important part in events to come. Indeed by 1936 oil represented over forty per cent of Roumania's export revenue, outstripping the country's traditionally largest export, cereals, which accounted for just over thirty per cent. Roumania was at the time the fourth largest producer of oil in the world. This was a period also of rapid manufacturing developments.

Carol took a personal interest in improvements in the army, although there was some criticism that he was more concerned with uniforms than with efficiency, and he encouraged the development of both military and civilian aviation. By 1935 there were already six internal air services linking Bucharest with other parts of the country.

He also founded a Social Institute to help the peasants, but it can be argued that he did not do enough for them. Ironically, King Ferdinand's break-up of the big estates had served only to throw the peasant farmers into the arms of bankers and money-lenders. The peasants were potential fodder for agitators against the existing order, especially as their importance in the economy was dwindling as manufacturing industry increased, and whereas Carol was aware of the nature of their problems he did not appear to realize its gravity. After all, four-fifths of the working population were still engaged in agriculture, which meant that the great mass of the country was disadvantaged.

Where Carol cannot be faulted was in his determination to encourage a native Roumanian culture. Roumania was a country of minorities, and many journals were published in German, Hungarian, Russian and even Yiddish, but Carol was eager to foster a specifically Roumanian identity. He did this generally by setting up royal foundations to foster the arts and he was diligent in supporting them. In 1933 a new Foundation for Literature and Fine Arts was established, which was one of several organizations that gave annual prizes for literature. In 1935 a new branch of the existing Carol I Foundation was set up specifically to publish books of social and historical interest. Carol took a delight in opening art exhibitions and his speeches on such occasions were both intelligent and enthusiastic. His interest in music continued and was acknowledged by Roumania's leading composer, Georges Enesco, in a letter to Carol of 8 November 1932, thanking the King for receiving him recently and for the royal promise to help a colleague who was in trouble.

Carol was also concerned to assist scientific studies. The Institute of Scientific Research was opened within months of his return to Roumania and in 1934 it assumed responsibility for the work of the Physical Astronomy Observatory in Bessarabia.

When Carol came to the throne he was regarded as the saviour of the country and had he been able to modernize Roumania and improve the condition of its people in his own good time, he would have been acknowledged as an outstanding ruler. Most of his ideas were good and all his intentions were excellent, even when his policies were misguided. Unfortunately, there was nobody in his entourage, and virtually nobody in government, sufficiently strong to guide him. The result was that he was inclined to react inconsistently to events.

He was a classic victim of bad timing, not on his own part but at the hands of fate. Even before Hitler gained power in Germany, a new movement was afoot in Roumania known as the Fascist Legion of the Archangel Michael, which developed into the notorious Iron Guard. It was one of several similar organizations set up in Europe to oppose the Communist menace, but whereas some of them faded into obscurity, this one thrived, partly because of Roumania's troubled condition and partly because of the charisma and personality of its leader, the film-star handsome Corneliu Codreanu. Fiercely nationalistic and supportive of the Orthodox Church, the movement was avowedly anti-Semitic, misleadingly emphasizing the alleged connections between Jews and Communists. It also cleverly espoused the cause of the peasants, who were inclined to regard all bankers and money-lenders as Jewish. It is not impossible to imagine that an impressionable peasant thought he was actually seeing the Archangel Michael himself when the good-looking Codreanu, clad in white peasant costume and carrying a sword in one hand and a religious icon in the other, rode into his village on a white horse.

Codreanu's party first won seats in Parliament in 1931 and by 1937 it had sixty-six seats. All the time it grew in power, numbers and daring, and its green-shirted members became as boisterous and dangerous as Hitler's Brownshirts in Germany. While pretending loyalty to the Crown and all established institutions, it painted Carol as a weak and foolish man under the evil spell of a Jewish whore and adventuress. She was blamed for every problem in Roumania and the Iron Guard vowed to destroy her, along with all the Jews in the country.

The movement might have died an early death or expired for lack of support had the Nazis not come to power in Germany and seized on it as a means to subvert Roumania. The Iron Guard presented Germany with a ready-made Trojan horse in the country, and the Nazis skilfully kept it alive and helped to nourish it with massive financing and bribery. In fact the stability of a country could be tested by the ease with which the Nazis could organize pro-German support and influence, particularly among ethnic minorities. Like the Communists, they became adept at the art of infiltration and nowhere was their task simpler than in a comparatively unstable country like Roumania. Hitler was a master mole who burrowed beneath the surface to destabilize countries that he planned to control and if necessary to occupy.

Part of the Nazi plan was to expand Germany's economic mission to Bucharest, demanding closer trade links between the two nations. The aim was to make Roumania increasingly dependent on Germany and incidentally to secure for Germany the bulk of Roumania's strategic output, particularly oil. Britain and France were curiously blind or unconcerned about this. It infuriated Carol that his country was in danger of falling into the Nazi trap. He soon recognized Hitler's will to dominate Europe but found it surprisingly difficult to create closer ties with the apparently complacent British and French.

Perhaps the British had not forgiven him for trying earlier to take advantage of their hospitality. It was said that old George V did not like him.

Anybody can be excused for not realizing the full dangerous potential of Hitler and the Nazis in the very early days, and even as late as April 1937 Carol himself had no real inkling of the extent to which Germany was financing the Iron Guard. He would not otherwise have told the editor of the London *News Chronicle* that the right-wing organizations in the country were not financed from abroad but were the expression of Roumanian nationalism. He had, however, received an ominous warning of things to come when his Prime Minister, Jean Duca, was murdered on 29 December 1933.

Duca, an old friend of Queen Marie and Prince Stirbey, had become the leader of the Liberal Party, and Carol's selection of him as Prime Minister in November 1933 took most people by surprise. Why would the King bring to power a representative of the party who had opposed him all along the line? Among the many explanations that have been offered, the only one that makes sense is that he wanted to put a stop to the activities of the Iron Guard and Duca seemed the person best able, and most willing, to do so.

Although Carol did not formally give his consent, he was entirely behind the Prime Minister's brave decision to dissolve the Iron Guard. Duca not only proscribed the organization but arrested huge numbers of its members in a sudden move on 9 December. Somehow Codreanu himself escaped the net and, less than three weeks later, took his revenge. After a meeting with the King at Castle Peles, where the royal family were spending the Christmas holiday, Duca was waiting at Sinaia railway station for a train back to Bucharest, when he was shot and killed by members of the Guard in circumstances that suggested disgraceful inefficiency, some even alleged complicity, on behalf of the police, although three assassins were arrested.

Codreanu later surfaced and was acquitted of complicity in the crime, largely through lack of evidence of direct connection. Amazingly it was rumoured that he had hidden in a house belonging to a cousin of Lupescu. The outlawing of the Iron Guard effectively died with Duca and the movement increased in influence throughout the country, although almost four years were to pass before Carol was faced with another internal crisis of such magnitude.

Carol was at least well served during this time by two politicians, Prime Minister George Tatarescu, who assumed office in January

1934 and who introduced martial law into the country, and Foreign Minister Nicolas Titulescu, who was the one Roumanian statesman widely respected outside the country, having twice been elected President of the League of Nations. Tatarescu, who had been Duca's Minister of Industry, was selected by Carol in preference to Constantine (Dino) Bratianu, the other brother of Ion and Vintila, who was President of the Liberal Party largely because of his family connection. This split the Liberals into two factions and weakened them permanently as a political force. Whether this was Carol's intention is uncertain but it is interesting that he looked again to a Liberal as the best means to combat the Iron Guard. He doubtless reckoned also that his new Prime Minister's experience in the industrial field would serve the country well. Tatarescu succeeded to some extent in cooling passions internally and had the distinction of being Carol's longest-serving Prime Minister.

Titulescu helped Carol formulate an intelligent foreign policy. It would be wrong to compare Titulescu too closely with Churchill but he did recognize the German menace earlier than most people and he believed that the way to combat it was to forge more secure links with countries opposed to, or threatened by, Germany. This involved first a closer relationship and increased trading with Britain and France, although unfortunately there seemed less interest on the part of the British and the French. The next step was to improve relations with neighbouring states, particularly those that stood physically between Germany and Roumania. An alliance had existed since 1920 between Czechoslovakia, Roumania and Yugoslavia, and further steps were taken to reinforce this Little Entente, as it was known, notably soon after Carol's return to Roumania in 1930 and again in 1933. One result of the new friendship was that Czechoslovakia provided financial and practical assistance in enabling Roumania to expand its armaments industry very significantly. In February 1934, Roumania and Yugoslavia joined with Greece and Turkey to form a Balkan Pact, and better relations with Poland were also pursued vigorously by Roumania.

In this way Carol and Titulescu hoped to make it unattractive for Germany to threaten Roumania. There was never any hope of alliance with Hungary or Bulgaria, which were traditionally opposed to Roumania, but alliances or arrangements with other adjacent countries were achieved with the intention of improving the nation's security. Roumania's biggest neighbour was the Soviet Union and there were two entirely different views about the value of an alliance with the Communist monster. Much of the support for Germany and for right-wing movements of all sorts was based on a detestation and fear of Communism, which Hitler exploited to the full. An American across the ocean, or even a Briton on an island separated from the Continent, might have been able to avoid taking sides, but that was almost impossible in a country like Roumania, menaced by Germany from the west and the Soviet Union from the east. Queen Marie was typical of many Roumanians. Although she wrote to her son from abroad, warning him of the Nazi menace, she was quite unable to accept that one way to combat the danger was to seek the protection of a regime that had killed so many members of her Russian family.

Carol's attitude to the Soviet Union was revealed in his diary. 'Our relationship with them must be one of correct and good friendship,' he said, 'even polite, but not loving. The USSR is a neighbour with whom we cannot be hostile, but the permanent interests of Roumania demand that we should not be friendly either.'

When one realizes that even four or five years later statesmen like Chamberlain appeared still to have doubts about Hitler's intentions, it says a great deal for Carol's perspicuity, and that of course of Titulescu, that as early as 1934 he recognized the German threat for what it was by bravely pursuing an accord with the Soviet Union, which finally recognized the incorporation of Bessarabia into Roumania when diplomatic relations were restored between the two countries.

The more one looks at Roumanian foreign policy during Carol's reign, the more obvious it is that he was seeking to ally the country with Germany's future enemies, and the failure of Britain and France, as well as the United States, to respond to his friendly overtures is difficult to understand, since their negative attitude could well have thrown Roumania into the arms of the Nazis. Whatever the world may have thought of the Russian accord, its implications were certainly not lost on Hitler. If for any reason Germany were to invade Roumania – which admittedly would mean first occupying at least one neighbouring country – there was now the possibility that the Soviet Union would intervene. The Germans did everything they could to destabilize those who opposed them and when his brother-in-law Alexander was killed in Marseilles by a terrorist from Macedonia, shortly after the murder of the Austrian Chancellor Dollfuss, Carol may well have asked himself whose hand was really on the trigger. And if the King of Yugoslavia could be disposed of so readily, how safe was the King of Roumania? Prince Nicolas revealed in his diary that Carol was highly nervous about the possibility of assassination.

One royal death that could not possibly be blamed on the Nazis was that of King George V in Britain in 1936. A fortuitous consequence of this sad event was that Carol was able to return to the country that he dearly wished to cultivate and from which he had been expelled in 1928. Now he was received with full honours as Head of State at the British King's funeral. The offence he had caused George V was of far less concern to George VI, who became King when his brother Edward abdicated at the end of the year to marry Wallis Simpson – 'she, like Lupescu, will remain in history,' wrote Queen Marie, drawing the obvious comparison. It was this friendlier personal relationship with the British monarchy that made it possible to make a State visit to Britain two years later.

First, however, Carol made a State visit to Poland in 1937 as part of the plan to cultivate neighbouring countries. Accompanied by Prince Michael, he spent six days there. 'Despite the fact that the political results of this visit have been unsensational,' he wrote in his diary, 'much has been gained through personal contacts. . . .' One potential embarrassment was saved by the tact of the Vatican, which arranged for Carol to be received by a special Papal Nuncio when the Cardinal Archbishop of Cracow 'was seized by certain religious scruples' and refused to receive him, one reason being Carol's divorced status.

Meanwhile political conditions were not improving inside Roumania, although the country was becoming more prosperous. It was in such conditions that Carol made what looked like a serious error of judgement. Tatarescu, who had been in power since the beginning of 1934, faced a General Election in November 1937 and had every expectation of success. He had brought a measure of stability to the country, despite the continued agitation from right-wing and minority groups, and hoped to gain support from the remarkable progress that had been made in the oilfields, in heavy industry and in the field of textiles, as well as from excellent harvests in the countryside. It was difficult for the party in power to lose an election in a system, created in an attempt to secure strong government, that ensured that whoever polled forty per cent of the votes received seventy per cent of the seats in the House of Representatives.

Ironically Carol's choice of Tatarescu in preference to Dino Bratianu now came home to roost because instead of presenting a united front that would presumably have secured forty per cent of the votes, Tatarescu was able to gather only thirty per cent. Although his was the largest share, it was insufficient to secure him a Parliamentary majority. It seemed a clear case therefore for a coalition government.

For historical, religious and racial reasons, modern Roumania had never managed to create a natural governing class. Philip Whitwell Wilson made this point very well in 1935 when he explained that Roumania no longer had a landed aristocracy, that its industry was too young to have thrown up more than a handful of powerful industrial employers or trade union leaders and that the professions were too limited in influence. 'It is this weakness,' he observed astutely, 'that the monarchy is expected to correct.'

This explains the almost dictatorial power of the King in Roumania and further helps to explain why Carol was summoned back in 1930 to fill what many regarded as a vacuum. Even Carol, however, was not expected utterly to flaunt the wishes of the people as expressed in a General Election.

In November 1937, however, the voice of the nation was unprecedentedly indecisive, so what would Carol do? He had returned from an interesting visit to Czechoslovakia early in November where he had discussed the vexed Sudeten question with President Benes. The Nazis were using the issue of a German minority in what had become Czechoslovakia to provoke trouble, and the two Heads of State discussed messages from the British urging a peaceful solution, in other words an appeasement of the Germans. Carol also visited the armament factories that were producing guns for his army. He described them in his diary as 'quite admirable' and said they would 'give a new sense of worth to our infantry', pointing out also that the machine-guns would soon be manufactured in Roumania.

'Benes,' he wrote, 'believes in the Little Entente and the Balkan Pact . . . he considers them to be our best guarantee of peace. We find ourselves in perfect agreement on this point. . . . Our only divergence of opinion concerns help from the West in the event of danger. He believes in it much more than I do.'

On his return home, Carol considered the internal political situation and the forthcoming General Election. 'I have been very pleased,' he recorded, 'with Tatarescu's term of office, in which much progress has been made.' He said that if there had to be a new Prime Minister after the elections, 'experiences from the past' would not encourage him to select Maniu, but it would be quite impossible to choose Codreanu, whose selection would mean 'a complete

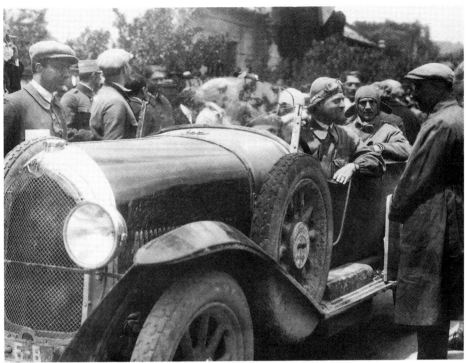

[27] Carol driving his racing car at Cluj, 1925

[28] *below left* Prince Nicolas on his motorbike

[29] *below right* Queen Marie, in white mourning for her husband, in 1928

[30] *left* King Carol greets General MacArthur on the American soldier's honorary visit to Bucharest in 1932

[31] *below* King Carol and Crown Prince Michael review Boy Scouts in national costume

[32] *opposite above* King Carol's passport, dated July 1938

[33] *opposite below* King Carol with King George VI on his State visit to England, November 1938

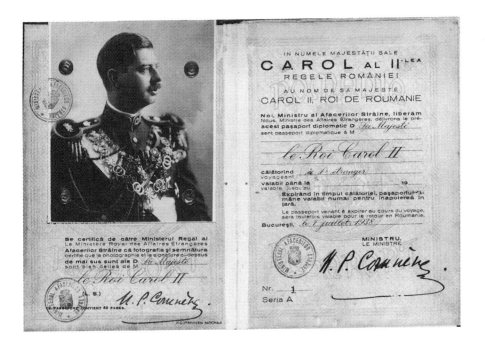

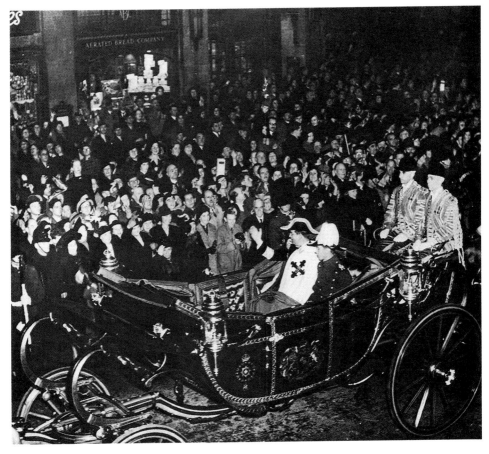

[34] King Carol with Hitler and Ribbentrop at Berchtesgaden, November 1938

[35] King Carol and Crown Prince Michael at a military ceremony, 1939

[36] *far left* Marie as Queen Mother, 1935

[37] *left* Mignon, Carol's sister, who became Queen Marie of Yugoslavia, 1939

[38] *centre* Queen Marie's funeral, July 1938: King Carol (left) heads the procession, followed by his brother Nicolas, his three sisters and his son Michael

[39] *bottom* The cathedral at Curtea de Arges, where Queen Marie's body was buried alongside other members of the Roumanian royal family

[40] *left* King Michael with his mother, Queen Helen

[41] *below* King Michael at a military ceremony with Antonescu; Helen, the Queen Mother, is on the left

[42] *opposite above* The striking resemblance of father and son: the profile of Carol Mircea (left), Carol's son by his marriage to Ioana Lambrino, and that of King Carol II on a Roumanian postage stamp

[43] *opposite centre* Prince Friedrich of Hohenzollern, 'Friedel', who remained Carol's friend from childhood through to his final exile

[44] *opposite below* Carol and Magda Lupescu – Princess Elena – in exile in Lisbon with King Umberto of Italy and the Count and Countess of Barcelona

[45] *above* Carol with
the stamp collection
that was his lifelong
hobby

[46] *above right* Carol
and Princess Elena in
Estoril

[47] *right* Princess
Elena scatters earth
over King Carol's
coffin at his funeral in
April 1953

overthrow of social order and of our traditional foreign policy'. Carol was also suspicious of an alleged electoral pact between Maniu and Codreanu which, although vehemently denied by Maniu, was widely believed to have been agreed.

It came as a severe blow to Carol therefore when Tatarescu failed to get his majority. The National Peasant Party polled second and the Iron Guard came in third with over fifteen per cent of the votes. Carol's eventual decision to call upon Octavian Goga, who secured only nine per cent of the votes, seems so bizarre and attracted such criticism internationally at the time that it must be put down as a bad mistake. Many theories have been advanced about Carol's motives but we now have his own version of the facts as recorded in his diary.

He regarded the Liberals as having been rejected by the electorate, although they had secured most votes, and, 'following the Constitution', as he put it, he invited a leader of the second party in the voting to form a government, perhaps in coalition with supporters of Vaida-Voevod, who represented a strongly nationalist element. His reasoning was that some representation for the right-wing was necessary, if only to pull the rug from under the Iron Guard extremists, but Mihalache, representing the National Peasants, refused even to talk with Vaida-Voevod.

Carol's next option would normally have been to call on the leader of the third party, but there was no way he would consider Codreanu as a suitable Prime Minister. 'For me,' he declared, 'this was a complete and absolute impossibility. The terrorist methods he had adopted, his violent anti-Semitism, his obviously fixed foreign policies, the resultant upturning of our alliances, his unnatural inclination to favour only Germany, generally all his radical and anti-social methods' ruled him out of consideration.

Carol's explanation for his eventual choice of Goga is as follows: 'There was only one constitutional option left to me, that of calling upon the National Christians of Goga and Cuza. It was obviously a bad solution but the least of the bad choices. I am perfectly aware that a government with these quite decidedly anti-Semitic elements would be of short duration, and afterwards I would be free to take other stronger measures that would free me and likewise the country from the unpatriotic tyranny arising from the malevolent interests of the political parties.'

In other words Carol from the start saw Goga as merely a stop-gap solution and he imposed on him the condition of including four National Peasant members in his Cabinet, including the vital posts of

Foreign Minister, Minister of Justice, Minister of Agriculture and Minister of the Interior – 'a guarantee for me', to use Carol's words.

Goga's Cabinet also included a man who was destined to play a major part in Roumania's future, the notorious General Ion Antonescu. Even at the time Carol referred to Goga's Minister of War as 'this unstable man of ambition'.

To object to Codreanu but not to Goga may seem extraordinary, for it was a question of who was the more extreme. Goga's followers were a collection of racists, religious zealots and extreme nationalists with the same ruthless, anti-Semitic stance as the Iron Guard. The appointment could hardly be believed outside Roumania and only the Nazis in Germany and the Fascists in Italy had cause to rejoice.

Carol admitted to another motive in selecting Goga. The National Christians were deadly enemies of the Iron Guard and 'ready to take any step to get rid of them'. He failed, however, to take into account the repercussions of the appointment outside the country, where it was seen as an anti-Semitic, pro-Nazi move. There was serious consideration in the West of economic measures against Roumania.

Carol was not anti-Semitic or pro-German; one has only to read his comments about Codreanu and the Iron Guard to realize that his sympathies lay in an entirely different direction. But whatever his reasoning, his choice of Goga was naive and ill-conceived. He knew this almost as soon as he made his decision. 'While waiting for the new year,' he wrote in his last diary entry for 1937, 'I spent a few days after Christmas at Sinaia with Duduia and Michael. It was a physical and moral rest before the inevitable storms ahead.'

18

Unbounded Power

Goga did not last long. The uproar abroad was too strong and Carol was forced to dismiss him after less than two months in office. 'Israel has triumphed,' was Goga's verdict. With no politician commanding popular support and with the impossibility of replacing Goga with another right-wing leader, Carol decided that he had virtually to act both as King and government. Perhaps he had this in mind all along when he appointed Goga to what we know from his diary he regarded as a stop-gap position.

In February 1938 Carol called into being the National Rebirth Front, which was intended to act as a party of national unity, a coalition of all political elements opposed to extremism. Declaring himself Royal Dictator, he appointed the old Regent, Patriarch Miron Christea, to head a Cabinet that included other religious leaders, army officers and politicians of many persuasions, including members of the National Peasant and Liberal Parties. Maniu was the one prominent figure deliberately excluded.

As if to show the world that his choice of Goga had not been intended to support terrorism, he now set about suppressing the Iron Guard. Ever since George V's funeral, Carol had been angling for an official invitation to Britain. He desired British support above all else and saw a British alliance as a final safeguard against German encroachment. In particular, he wanted to conclude a trade deal to supply oil to Britain, instead of pouring it into Hitler's thirsty war machine, in exchange for arms with which to protect Roumania. Following the Goga episode, British Foreign Secretary Anthony Eden had expressed the view that Carol was no longer a suitable person to be invited to London on a State visit, which had been planned for March 1938. Carol hoped, correctly as it turned out, that he would restore his prestige in Britain if he could eliminate the German-backed Iron Guard.

He set about this with a will, arresting Codreanu and hundreds of his supporters. The Iron Guard leader and thirteen of his principal supporters were tried for treason and, although the evidence produced was inconclusive, they were sentenced to ten years' imprisonment. Evidence was produced in secret session at the trial of the vast amounts of money paid to Codreanu by the German Legation in Bucharest, although Carol himself may not have known the details.

At least he was able to give the impression that, in the words of the London *Evening Standard*, he had saved Roumania 'from the dangers of extremist rule by Mr Codreanu's Fascists'. His rehabilitation in British eyes was confirmed by the renewal of an official invitation to visit London in November 1938. This was a critical time in European affairs, with the Nazis carrying all before them. Carol agreed with his friend Benes, who had declared that the only way to beat the dictators was by firmness. 'If the Western democracies are strong,' Benes said, 'there will be peace. If they show a weak front, there will be war.' This was so obvious to Carol, and yet Chamberlain was to return from Munich in September still with an apparent, or perhaps well-disguised, disregard of the real nature of the Nazi beast.

On 6 July of that year Carol had commented in his diary about the blindness of the Western nations. In view of their attitude, it required immense patience 'not to surrender and jump immediately into Hitler's camp'. 'I remain faithful to my old decision,' he wrote, 'to keep our political and economic independence, but to achieve this we need assistance, at least in small ways, from our friends in the West.' He made clear his reliance on Great Britain to help Roumania to avoid the German clutch. As soon therefore as he heard from the British Chargé d'Affaires in Bucharest on 8 July that he could expect an invitation from London, planning for the forthcoming State visit became his priority.

On the very day that he received the good news, he also received a letter from his mother in Germany dated 5 July. Although he was aware that she was being treated in a clinic in Dresden, he almost certainly did not realize just how ill she was. She now announced her intended return home to Sinaia on the 14th or 15th of the month. It was a sad letter from an obviously dispirited woman, almost entirely taken up with her wish to change her doctor and her choice of a replacement aide-de-camp. 'I may not have many more years when you, my son, will have the occasion to be kind to your mother,' she wrote, and begged him to use his 'unbounded power' to meet her wishes. It was to be the last letter she ever wrote to him.

In view of some extraordinary allegations that have been made about Carol's behaviour to his mother at this time, including one that he refused to allow her to return by plane because of the cost, we should perhaps let his diary put the record straight. He had obviously been monitoring Marie's health, without suspecting the worst, because he was aware of her intention to return even before he received her letter. He had met Dr Mamulea, the man she wanted to replace, on 7 July, when they discussed the dangers of a long train journey, and he had already arranged a meeting the following day, before Marie's letter arrived, with the administrator of the Crown estates, General Ballif, and the country's leading surgeon, Dr Hortolomei.

Carol heard for the first time at this meeting, attended also by Mamulea, that his mother's condition was incurable and that it was dangerous for her to travel in any circumstances. It was decided to send Ballif and Hortolomei to Dresden, armed with a letter from the Patriarch, to urge her not to risk the journey. Dr Mamulea was entrusted with the task of informing Carol's sisters Elisabetha and Mignon of the situation. Ballif expressed the opinion that nothing would stop Marie from returning home. Carol agreed. 'My feeling,' he wrote, 'is that Mother believes she cannot recover and, knowing she will die, she prefers to come home so as not to be at that time among foreigners.'

His diary for 14 July records Marie's firm decision to return to Roumania. Ballif had reported that no amount of persuasion could stop her. Carol therefore motored to Sinaia the following evening – beating his record because the roads were free of traffic – to receive his mother on the 16th. The train, however, was held up because Marie had started haemorrhaging again during the journey, confirming the doctors' fears about the danger of travelling. It does not appear that it was at any time suggested that Marie should have flown home. She doubtless thought that she would be more comfortable in a train, which for her was a normal and familiar method of moving from place to place.

Marie finally reached Sinaia on Sunday the 17th. Elisabetha had travelled with her, along with Hortolomei and Ballif and the head of the Dresden clinic. Carol, accompanied by Michael, met the train. He was pleased to find his mother more lively than he had expected, and she said how happy she was to be back home. That evening he took Michael to visit her. She was sitting up in bed, looking lovingly at her scrapbooks, but she was very weak and, after an hour, said she felt tired and asked them to return the following day. 'She told me,' Carol wrote, 'that she had so many things to tell me.'

Carol was informed in the morning that his mother had bled again in the night. He knew her condition was hopeless and had perhaps been aggravated by the journey. He went to her at once and was met by Elisabetha who told him that the doctors had forbidden anyone to enter Marie's room. 'However, I went in and saw her,' he wrote. 'I could not speak to her. She was much too weak, but she smiled at me.'

Carol and Elisabetha immediately telephoned Nicolas, Mignon and Ileana, and sent telegrams to other close relations. Carol also summoned the Patriarch and the Ministers of the Interior and of Justice. At 2.30 that afternoon, having left his mother for a short while, he was told by the doctors that she was slipping fast. He rushed to her side with young Michael. Elisabetha had remained with Marie. 'When I kissed Mother's hand,' Carol recorded, 'she opened her eyes and smiled at me, for the last time. From that moment until the end I remained almost all the time in Mother's room.'

The Patriarch arrived at 4.30 and at five o'clock said prayers for her. The doctors then insisted that everyone else leave the room. Carol stood in the corridor, talking to the Patriarch. At 5.38 Dr Hortolomei came out of Marie's room and signalled to Carol that his mother was dead.

According to Hannah Pakula, Marie had suffered from dilating blood vessels resulting from a rare form of cirrhosis of the liver. Carol simply reported that she died from loss of blood. He took comfort from the fact that she did not appear to be in pain. That evening, in an interesting footnote, Carol recorded that Michael had telephoned his mother with the news. Carol also spoke to Helen, on the advice, he said, of Magda Lupescu. He also noted the fact that Marie had died almost eleven years to the day after her husband.

Members of the family and foreign dignitaries began to pour into Bucharest for the funeral. In view of his impending visit to England, Carol was very pleased to receive the Duke and Duchess of Kent to represent the British Crown. Ileana, Marie's favourite child, who received forty per cent of her mother's estate whereas the other children had fifteen per cent each, arrived on the 20th, as did Nicolas. Carol told them that, with their mother's death, he was now the focal point of the family and that they must all rally around him; that he was, however, not only a brother but also the King and that sometimes he had to undertake unpleasant measures. He asked them to remain united forever and good friends.

So Missy, as she had been known to her family, was dead at the age of sixty-two, and in some symbolic way her eldest son was now more than ever on his own. His relationship with his extraordinary mother had never been easy but it had always been loving, as his diaries fully confirm, and give ample refutation of some of the more ludicrous allegations that have been made against him.

The death of Queen Marie gained some sympathy for Carol and Roumania, especially in Britain, France and the United States, where she was much loved. On 23 August George VI wrote a letter in his own hand to Carol from Balmoral Castle: 'My dear Carol,' it read, 'I was so glad that it was possible for George (Duke of Kent) to represent me at Cousin Missy's funeral, as I so well remember all her kindness to me when I was in Roumania for your father's coronation at Alba Julia. I am happy to think that there is nothing to prevent your paying your postponed State Visit to my country after the end of your Court Mourning in October, and it gives me great pleasure to invite you and your son Michael to stay at Buckingham Palace from Tuesday November 15th until Friday November 18th. Elizabeth and I hope that these dates will suit you, and we much look forward to seeing you then.' The letter was signed 'Your affectionate cousin, Bertie.'

Carol set high hopes on his visit to Britain and gathered together some of his ablest diplomats and economists to put his country's case to the West.

19

Up for Sale

In the spring of 1938 the Germans had finally occupied neighbouring Austria, and by the time Carol arrived in England they had effectively killed the Little Entente by seizing part of Czechoslovakia on the ridiculous pretext that the Sudeten minority were being oppressed. The world had barely raised a voice to protest, let alone a finger to stop the Nazi progress. British Prime Minister Chamberlain had recently returned from Munich with a hollow claim to 'peace in our time' which even he could not have believed.

Unfortunately, Carol's diary is missing for the period 23 August 1938 to 13 March 1939, which covers the State visit to Britain and his subsequent meeting with Hitler, but the events of those critical months have been fairly well recorded elsewhere. Carol arrived with his son Michael and a team of diplomats and economists. He was very warmly received, understandably since he was virtually asking Britain and her allies to save Roumania from falling under German hegemony. The pressures and the threats from Berlin were relentless. Hitler had done everything he could to upset Roumania, both by internal subversion and by seeking to weaken the system of alliances on which the country's security depended. Equally important, he had tried ruthlessly to involve Roumania in exclusive trade arrangements that would have made the country economically dependent on Germany.

Carol came to England in the hope that there was an alternative. He could deal with the Iron Guard at home and protect the Transylvanian frontier from possible German-inspired aggression by the Hungarians, but he needed a bigger Western market for Roumania's produce, notably its valuable oil, if it was not all to land up in Hitler's hands.

The astute *New Statesman and Nation*, one of Britain's leading political journals, saw the point of Carol's visit very clearly. 'It would perhaps be too cynical,' it declared, 'to say that he is putting Roumania up for sale by auction, but he certainly wants to learn whether Britain is prepared to make a bid. . . .'

The Roumanians offered to send almost all their oil, their wheat and other agricultural produce to Britain, and were surprised at the lack of interest. They were told that oil from Mexico was cheaper and of better quality, seemingly ignoring as of no consequence that only Hitler could benefit from a British rejection. There was no battle for Roumania's soul; the British were prepared to let it go by default to the Germans. The British could not have been more polite but, although negotiations were opened that in due course produced some financial support for Roumania, albeit not on the scale suggested by Carol's delegation, he was virtually sent away with a flea in his ear. As the *Scotsman* put it, 'King Carol may well return to Roumania with the highest opinion of British goodwill and a less exalted estimate of British good sense.'

It was almost as if the British did not want to offend the Germans so soon after Chamberlain's return from Munich, or perhaps they thought that they had enough on their plates without involving themselves at that stage in further responsibilities, and that Roumania was unreliable. Carol found exactly the same attitude among the French when he went to Paris for similar discussions following his British visit, stopping *en route* for a private visit to Belgium where he was splendidly received by King Leopold, who sent the royal train to collect him at Calais. The British and French must have put their heads together to reject him, although they received him with great pomp and circumstance.

The Nazis had done all they could to dissuade Carol from going to London. Aware of his ties to the British royal family, they had reminded him of his connections with Germany, using his cousin Prince Friedrich, who was now head of the Hohenzollern-Sigmaringen dynasty, for this purpose. When it became clear that Carol was not to be put off, it was suggested to him that he should meet Hitler at Berchtesgaden on his way back home. He agreed, partly because he did not wish to appear to be adopting an anti-German stance by visiting Britain and France, but also in the hope that some advantage might come of such a meeting. He had hoped to talk to the Fuehrer from a position of strength but the failure of his visits to London and Paris to secure much more than some personal acclaim left him in a position of weakness.

It was the first occasion on which Hitler had been visited by a ruling monarch and he was determined to make the most of it. After the usual nonsense of the Fuehrer being photographed two steps above his taller visitor, Carol and Michael had tea with Hitler and Goering. Hitler spoke at great length about the Communist menace. 'Only I,' he declared, 'can protect mankind against the march of Moscow,' and assured Carol of Germany's peaceful intentions. 'He even told me at Berchtesgaden,' Carol confided to his diary the following June, 'that he did not want to wage war. Can one believe him?'

This was only a preliminary, however, to Hitler's specific references to Roumania. He argued the value of a German alliance to protect the country from Soviet claims to Bessarabia and Hungarian claims to Transylvania, and in case Carol thought – as he had good reason to do – that Germany was behind Hungary, he told the King that he did not like the Hungarians and would not support their 'border pretensions'. Hitler also stressed the benefits of economic co-operation between the two countries, without perhaps realizing that Roumania had little alternative following the apparent lack of interest in London and Paris.

It was towards the end of the meeting that Hitler asked Carol to release Codreanu from prison. The Iron Guard, he argued, was a loyal organization and in no way subversive. Codreanu and his followers had been too harshly treated. They were patriots who were merely expressing their opposition to what they regarded as matters harmful to Roumania. Carol could hardly have had better confirmation of Germany's support for the Iron Guard and their terrorist activities. He was frankly outraged by this plea or demand, but for which Hitler might have regarded the meeting as something of a success. Carol had no illusions about Codreanu and the other Guardist leaders. They were dangerous men whose aim was to subvert the country, and he now knew for certain that they were working for a foreign power against Roumania's interests. They were particularly active in Transylvania where, as recently as the day he had set out from Paris to Germany, they had murdered the Chancellor of the University of Cluj.

Neville Chamberlain may or may not have been fooled by Hitler, but King Carol was certainly not. He came away from Berchtesgaden fully aware of the sort of man he was up against. It took great courage on his part but he was determined, despite the lack of concrete results from his journey to London and Paris, to stand up to Hitler. His was the sort of action which, had it been pursued earlier by more powerful countries, might have stopped the Nazis in their stride. Moreover, he acted swiftly and decisively.

Carol's answer to Hitler was loud and clear. He arrived back in Bucharest on 28 November to reports of widespread disturbances, including arson and bomb-throwing, which he rightly believed were provoked from Berlin, although he had good reason to think that Codreanu was still able to issue instructions to his followers from gaol. There was also talk of unrest in certain sections of the army. The following day General Antonescu, the former Minister of War in Goga's short-lived government, was relieved of his military command. The old aristocrat Prince Alexander Cantacuzene, who had lent his support to the Iron Guard and who had escaped from custody the previous June, was re-arrested; Carol had described him in his diary as 'that demented man with an aristocratic name' and said that he was the most dangerous of all Guardists, 'capable of anything'. On the very next day Codreanu and thirteen of his closest associates were killed, allegedly while trying to escape from prison. They included the three men who had assassinated Prime Minister Duca. With Goga already dead from natural causes, most of Roumania's principal Fascist leaders were no longer alive. Carol may have lived to regret that he merely dismissed Antonescu from his command.

The news about Codreanu was sensational, coming within less than a week of Hitler's request for his release. The official version was that the prisoners were being moved secretly to another gaol when, at about five o'clock in the morning, the lorries transporting them were stopped by firing from woods on either side of the road about twenty-five miles north of the capital. Taking advantage of the situation, the prisoners tried to escape and, ignoring warnings from the guards, were shot by them in fulfilment of their legal duty.

This story was not widely believed, although it is not entirely improbable that news of the secret movement of prisoners may have leaked to their friends through well-bribed prison officers, and there may in such circumstances have been an attempt to rescue them. The fact, however, that every single prisoner was shot dead rather than just wounded obviously suggest that the killings were a deliberate act of policy. It would be easy to accept this conclusion if the instigator were Hitler or Stalin or one of their henchmen; it is more difficult to believe that Carol would deliberately have concurred in such tactics.

Nobody has openly accused Carol personally of deliberately killing the Iron Guard prisoners but the suspicion has always existed that the government was behind the affair. The only previously unpublished reference to this subject is what Carol wrote in 1945 in 'Orbit of Satan', a manuscript in which he discussed the causes of the Second World War and dealt at length with Hitler's pressures on Roumania. In this, he simply confirmed that Codreanu had been shot while trying to escape.

Carol is on record as indicating in another matter that desperate circumstances require desperate action, and there is no doubt that conditions in Roumania were desperate. Nazi-inspired Fascist agitation was threatening to destabilize the country and throw it into the German camp. Carol was on the side of the Western democracies, even if they rejected him, and almost anything was preferable to allowing Roumania to become a German satellite. The interests of the country required him to quash all subversive opposition and to build up its defences against the dangers ahead. It should perhaps also be pointed out that Roumania in 1938 was not Nazi Germany or Stalinist Russia, but neither was it the United States of Franklin Roosevelt or Great Britain ruled by a Parliament with a constitutional monarch. An event must be looked at in the light of its surrounding circumstances.

The most eloquent evidence of conditions in Roumania was provided by a special order issued to the police force on the day of the shooting of Codreanu and the other Iron Guard prisoners. 'Political terrorists are to be attacked immediately,' it read, 'without need to comply with existing regulations about warning before opening fire. No mercy should be shown in matters designed to maintain order and authority at any price.'

The Germans were in no doubt about the meaning of Carol's immediate actions on his return home. As far as they were concerned, he was now a marked man. The sad fact is that the Western democracies did not seem to want to come to his aid.

20

Worse Days
to Come

Carol's efforts to woo the Western democracies were not entirely unrewarded. The following April, for what it was worth, Britain and France formally guaranteed Roumania against aggression, but this was after Hitler had annexed Czechoslovakia and Mussolini had conquered Albania without any effective opposition. Britain also provided some modest credit in July to assist Roumania's defence budget, but the money was barely a quarter of what Carol had requested.

Carol noted the conquest of little Albania as 'an inelegant deed carried out by a Catholic country on Good Friday'. He remarked on 'a lack of reaction on everybody's part', fully aware that if the dictators could get away with such gross behaviour, they would assume that there was nothing to stop them doing whatever they wished. Albania was uncomfortably near Roumania but worse was the annexation of Czechoslovakia, with which Roumania was allied. This brought twenty-five German divisions into the newly created Republic of Slovakia, which had a common frontier with Roumania for a few miles in the Carpathian mountain area.

Poland had earlier received a guarantee also, but did it have any meaning? How in any case would Britain and France be able to implement their guarantee to Roumania if the country were attacked, and did it apply no matter whence the attack originated? Had the guarantors even considered the possibility of an attack from the east? The Roumanian guarantee was obviously intended as a warning shot across the German bow, but as Carol wrote in his diary, 'Germany considers the Anglo-French guarantee to be a bluff.'

This was a very uneasy time for the whole of Europe. Roumania did what it could to resist Hitler's economic grip but was forced into new trade agreements that were favourable to Germany. Meanwhile Carol did what he could to strengthen the country's defences, building what became known as Carol's Dyke along the borders, notably with Hungary and the Soviet Union, for Carol was under no illusions that he was threatened from both west and east. The democracies had woken up too late to the Nazi threat, which was already more than they could cope with; despite their hatred of Communism, they barely recognized the threat from the Soviet Union.

Carol's rebuff of his efforts to side with Britain and France was probably irrelevant in the historical context. Looking back now on events, it is clear that Roumania was not naturally involved in the struggle between the Western democracies and Hitler but in that between Nazism and Communism. It might have been better if Carol had been able to take sides since the fate of his country was not, as it turned out, in the hands of the democracies but in that of the dictators. The balance of power had changed in the world, and with the Americans not yet committed to intervention in Europe, the destiny of Roumania was in the hands of Germany and the Soviet Union. Roumania was unable to seek the protection of either country, and when eventually Hitler and Stalin signed their notorious non-aggression pact and divided Poland, Estonia, Latvia and Lithuania between them, Carol must have realized that his country was doomed, perhaps to suffer the same fate, and that he personally could not win. The 'concubinage', as he described it, between Nazism and Communism did not altogether surprise him, and all he dared hope was that the dictators would allow his country to remain neutral in their power struggle.

Nevertheless, despite their unpreparedness, he believed that the Western democracies would defeat Germany in the event of war, and incidentally he forecast in August that war would be fought largely in the air. That the British and the French would be the eventual victors was for him 'almost axiomatic', he confided in his diary on 14 April, a month after German troops had occupied Prague, but perhaps this was wishful thinking based on his sympathies. He hated Hitler and his cronies, as perhaps befitted a man who believed himself to be at the head of Hitler's blacklist for the Balkans, together with Prince Paul of Yugoslavia. His diary recalls a Hitler joke that was current in 1938: What is the difference between a misfortune and a catastrophe? If the Fuehrer went for a walk and a brick fell on his head, that would be a misfortune. If the brick did not fall on his head, that would be a catastrophe. 'Goering,' he recorded on 26 August, 'wants to come hunting here on October 1. These people are incredible!'

The Nazi leader had requested a royal invitation and Carol was delighted to fall back on protocol which made it impossible for him personally to invite anyone but a Head of State.

Goering and his friends were, however, already hunting in Roumania in a different way, and on 21 September, within three weeks of the outbreak of the new World War, Prime Minister Calinescu suffered the fate of Duca. He was murdered in the centre of Bucharest. If Carol thought that the Iron Guard was finished when it lost its leaders, he was quickly to realize how wrong he was. This was their first effective reply to the death of Codreanu ten months earlier. It was later alleged that the plan for the assassination was drawn up in Germany and executed in accordance with techniques taught at one of Himmler's special training camps.

Armand Calinescu had been Prime Minister since the death of Miron Christea in March, and had been a tower of strength to Carol at a most difficult time. 'I could find no one in the country better able to perform the task he was given,' Carol wrote. 'For me personally it is an irreplaceable loss. I could be relaxed with him. He was very capable with a clear and far-seeing political acumen, and he took measures befitting all situations.'

Carol's own version of the murder was that a cart pulled up unexpectedly, but presumably deliberately, in front of Calinescu's car, which was forced to stop. The Prime Minister and his bodyguard got out to see what was happening and were shot at by people in another vehicle close behind that had been following. Ten minutes later a transmission of waltz music on the radio was interrupted by cries of 'They are killing us – a band of Guardists' and an announcement made that the death sentence on the Prime Minister had been executed!

Seven men had apparently rushed into the radio station and overpowered the announcer. The murder plan may have been executed skilfully but its success must have gone to the men's heads because they were all arrested before they could escape. They not only confessed to the murder but implicated two others, one of whom committed suicide while the second was seized.

Some light on Carol's attitude to the death of Codreanu is thrown by his diary entry concerning the fate of Calinescu's murderers:

'The eight assassins were executed at the scene of the crime, the two or three Iron Guard leaders first. It was a ghastly step, strictly outside the law, but justified in the interests of the country's equilibrium after what happened today. We cannot play around or jeopardize the future when such acute danger exists both internally and from outside.

'I went to bed but could not sleep, thoughts flying around. I cannot come to terms with the fact that this good and trustworthy public servant is no longer alive, and in my soul there is not just pain but a horrifying emptiness. It is not only a crime but an act of high treason in these times. The aggression at the radio station shows the true colour of their characters, their hopes of causing unrest and of provoking revolution.'

'His replacement,' Carol wrote of Calinescu, 'will be a problem of the most difficult and delicate nature,' and indeed he was right. His first two choices lasted one week and eight weeks respectively, and it was not until November that he called back Tatarescu, who had served him so well and for so comparatively long until failing to secure sufficient votes. Tatarescu, like Calinescu, was a good man to have at hand in difficult times.

Britain and France, among other countries, had declared war on Germany when Hitler ignored the guarantee to Poland at the beginning of September. The guarantee, however, had done nothing to save Poland in the short term and no practical help could be expected from the West if Roumania were similarly attacked by the Germans or their satellites. All Roumania could do for the time being was to declare neutrality and hope that its position would be respected.

In this uneasy situation, virtually sandwiched between Nazi Germany and the Soviet Union, Roumania dared not put a foot wrong. For fear of seeming partisan, Carol had even refused to accept Poland's gold for safe keeping. He was concerned about internal subversion. As he recorded on 11 December, the Iron Guard 'far from being dead, is alive and well' and was 'conducting terrorist activities from outside our borders'. His own life was not safe. 'Unfortunately I could not go hunting,' he wrote on 15 October, 'because of fears of attempts on my life.' The whole country was in a state of uncertainty. Even Lupescu was having trouble with provisions. 'I helped her get some linen,' he recorded on 12 September. 'Everybody is hoarding things for worse days to come.'

The last words were prophetic.

21

The Nation's Agony

The only really bright light in Carol's life at the beginning of 1940 was his love for Magda Lupescu. This remarkable woman had certainly tamed the womanizer. Their relationship, he declared, 'was created by God's hand'. 'Fifteen years have passed,' he wrote, 'since we came together, never again to separate, to face together all the vicissitudes of life, both the hardships of fate and the real joys. Our love has stood like a rock . . . and has been for me the essence of life, a divine talisman and a supreme refuge in the most difficult times. This love is such that I cannot conceive life without it.'

Carol's diary for the early part of the year, in which he again declared his love for his mistress, shows him relaxing by shooting and fishing, playing poker and backgammon, reading and watching films, and attending to his stamp collection. If his love was solid as a rock, everything else around him seemed to be crumbling.

In many ways the situation in Roumania in 1940 was similar to that in 1916, except that there was now far greater unrest internally. The dictators were carrying all before them. Every German success, whether in Norway, the Low Countries or in France, was recorded in Carol's diary as bad news. 'Nobody is secure,' he wrote, noting that 'in facing the brutal strength of Germany, moves that could be interpreted as aggressive must be avoided,' and on 17 May, as France was being overrun, 'Oh God,' he declared, 'what does the future hold for us?'

How could Roumania hope to defend itself with Carol's Dyke when the supposedly invincible Maginot Line had proved so utterly ineffective against the Germans? By the middle of the year Hitler was virtually the master of Europe. Of his major enemies in the West, only Britain remained outside his control, having rescued its troops from the Continent by the skin of its teeth, and there were not many people who would have laid long odds against Hitler being in

London before the end of the year. As for the Soviet Union, having subdued the courageous Finns, it was now looking to develop other countries on its borders as buffer states against further German expansion eastwards. Roumania was a sandwich in the middle. To be squeezed between Hitler and Stalin was a fate not to be envied.

There was no one to come to Roumania's aid. The United States had not yet entered the war and it was all Britain could do to defend itself. On the tenth anniversary of his return home as King, Carol received telegrams of congratulation from London. 'I have watched with respect and admiration the efforts which Your Majesty and the Roumanian government are making to preserve the independence and neutrality of Roumania and I wish you continued success in these efforts.' This was the message from his 'affectionate cousin', King George VI. 'It is my earnest hope,' it went on, 'that Roumania will be spared the horrors of war, and thus will be able to continue uninterrupted the achievement of the progress and development which have been so remarkable under Your Majesty's enlightened rule.' The British monarch also approved the growing collaboration between the Balkan countries and 'their increasing determination to resist aggression from whatever quarter it may come,' but, as if to tell them that they were on their own, he pointed out that his own country was already 'bearing a very heavy burden in our fight for the liberties of mankind'.

Carol expressed himself as 'very moved' by this message, although he was precluded by the international situation from publishing it. It was intended as a personal encouragement to mark the anniversary of his accession and it meant more to him than most of the gifts he received, except perhaps the Lincoln-Zephyr car from Magda Lupescu. The official presents included a painting by El Greco and a portrait of Tsar Nicholas I. There was also 'an endless collection of gold pieces of very great value', including a 'massive gold plaque' from the National Bank of Roumania.

All these details were recorded carefully in Carol's diaries, in which he also looked back at 'ten years of hard work, effort and endless worry'. 'I have a clear conscience,' he wrote, 'that I have done everything in my power' for the country's good.

There was also a telegram from the new British Prime Minister, Winston Churchill. 'Recent events,' he declared, 'have shown that at any moment neutral States, however careful they have been to observe their neutrality, may be engulfed without warning and without pity. Against such a fate, the first and most essential line of defence is the firm determination of the remaining neutral countries of Europe to combine together and to maintain a resolute front in the face of all threats and attempts at intimidation. If I venture to put these considerations to Your Majesty, it is because the British and French governments have together given a guarantee to Roumania.'

In other words, please do what you can to protect yourself by making common cause with such of your neighbours as may be neutral.

Roumania was bordered by traditionally unfriendly Bulgaria, by Yugoslavia, pro-German Hungary, German-occupied Czechoslovakia, Poland, now in possession of the Germans and the Soviets, and the Soviet Union itself. Churchill could only therefore have had in mind the sort of Balkan alliance that Carol himself had sought to foster, between Greece and Yugoslavia for certain and Bulgaria and Turkey if possible. He knew that he was clutching at straws, especially with Italy in control of the other Balkan nation, Albania, but it was the best advice that he could offer.

Carol himself had no illusions about the effectiveness of the Balkan Pact. A month before receiving Churchill's message, he had referred in his diary to Yugoslavia as being 'insecure'; 'nor can we count on Greece,' he added. 'The only country that might be of value is Turkey.' Churchill's reference to the guarantee reinforced Britain's commitment but what could she deliver in practice if Roumania were invaded? In the short term at least, the answer was nothing. As for the French guarantee, it was worthless, the Germans having overwhelmed the guarantor.

In his diary Carol completely ignored the personal letter he had received from Goering, offering him good wishes for the future. Good wishes from Britain were another matter and far more welcome, but he knew that they amounted to no more than wishes. Another country made different and more effective representations within three weeks of the messages from London. Carol was awakened by Urdarianu at two o'clock in the morning of 27 June with a message from the Roumanian Ambassador in Moscow that Molotov had delivered an ultimatum. Ernest Urdarianu was the man who had been closest to Carol since soon after his return to Roumania in 1930. As Lord Chamberlain, he was head of the royal household and the King's closest confidant and adviser, a very powerful figure in the land. The nature of the ultimatum became clearer at 7 a.m. The Soviet Union demanded the return of

Bessarabia and the northern part of Bukovina, and allowed twenty-four hours for a reply.

'Whatever the risk,' was Carol's immediate reaction, 'my opinion is that we must resist and stick to what we have said so many times, that if we are attacked we will defend ourselves.'

A meeting at nine o'clock with Urdarianu, Prime Minister Tatarescu and the pro-German politician Ion Gigurtu received the news that Molotov required Roumania to cede the territories within four days; Soviet troops would then move in at noon on the fifth day. Carol again expressed the view that the move should be resisted but Gigurtu was not sure that this was feasible and Tatarescu hesitated, 'tilting towards surrender', as Carol described the Prime Minister's position.

It was decided to inform the Axis countries, Germany and Italy, and to consult the members of the Little Entente, and it was clear within hours that Roumania was on its own. Even had Roumania wanted to call on Hitler to come to its aid, it was made obvious that no help could be expected from that source; Germany would act against the Soviet Union in its own good time but not at the behest of Bucharest. As for Roumania's friends, Yugoslavia, either for itself or for other members of the Little Entente, advised submission to Moscow.

In these circumstances Carol summoned a Crown Council at which the army Chief of Staff explained the military situation. His advice was to keep the armed forces intact to face possible troubles on other fronts in the days ahead; in other words, to surrender to the Soviets in order presumably to retain sufficient strength to protect Transylvania if it were attacked from the west. 'From the beginning, the tendency to yield was obvious,' Carol wrote, and added that he was unhappy. In the event, no firm decision was taken at that particular meeting except to mobilize the army, and even that sensible step was opposed by Ballif. Ten members of the Council voted to accept Moscow's ultimatum and eleven, led by Jorga, voted against; but since four members opted to postpone a decision pending further information and another chose to abstain, there was no majority in the Council for any course of action.

Carol left the meeting determined to force government changes that very day and to summon an enlarged Crown Council, to include representatives of the threatened provinces. He wanted to press his opinions, although he suspected that he was in a minority. He persuaded Alexander Vaida-Voevod to act as President of the

Council but could not convince him to accept the Premiership, so Carol had to be content with a reshuffled government under Tatarescu in which Vaida-Voevod agreed to serve.

The new Council finally decided by twenty votes to six to accede to Moscow's demands. Carol listed the six people who had supported him: Nicolas Jorga, Victor Iamandi, Silviu Dragomir, Traian Popp, Stefan Ciobanu and Ernest Urdarianu. 'Their names should be carved in letters of gold,' he wrote, 'in the annals of Roumanian dignity.' It will be noted that neither the Prime Minister nor the man whom Carol had wanted to replace him was in favour of resistance.

Carol closed the meeting with a speech in which he deplored the decision as a 'great mistake'. He felt 'embittered and disgusted', and refused to shake anybody's hand. Somewhat dramatically, he recorded that he spent the night with Magda Lupescu, 'crying bitterly'.

What might have ensued had Roumania resisted the Soviets, we can never know for sure, but that at least was Carol's wish and the decision to surrender precipitated other demands on Roumanian territory from other quarters. Carol described 27 June 1940 in his diary as 'a day of national shame'.

Roumania was of course no more than a pawn in the as yet undeclared war between Germany and the Soviet Union. The Soviets were setting limits as to how far they would allow the Germans to go in their eastward march. The Nazis were naturally furious that the Communists had advanced their frontier from the Dniester to the Prut, although they had been unwilling to prevent it by force of arms, and decided that their best response would be to seize Transylvania through the agency of the Hungarians.

Taking advantage of Roumania's weakness and embarrassment, the Bulgarians sought the return of part of Dobruja. Roumania could doubtless have resisted this claim but decided that this territory was not of the very greatest strategic importance and that a gesture to their southern neighbour might help to foster friendship among the Balkan nations and perhaps Turkey. Roumania had no other possible support at hand and in these circumstances eventually yielded to Bulgaria's demand.

The Hungarians tried to use the fact that Roumania had acceded to Soviet representations to advance their own claim to Transylvania on ethnic and historical grounds, and throughout the month of August the two countries were in constant negotiation. Just as it would have been difficult for Roumania to call on Germany to protect it against the Soviet Union in connection with Bessarabia, so it was unthinkable to call on the Soviet Union to protect it against Germany and Hungary in connection with Transylvania. The Roumanian government knew that it had to sacrifice more of its territory and the negotiations became an exercise in damage limitation. The Germans soon lost patience and decided to impose a solution. By what became known as the Vienna Diktat, Germany forced Roumania into yielding the larger part of Transylvania under threat that German troops would otherwise occupy the entire province, in which case the Soviets would probably have occupied the rest of the country, as had happened in Poland.

In little more than two short months, neutral Roumania, despite any Balkan alliances and the British guarantee, was reduced to the size it had been when Carol was born forty-six years earlier.

What could he have done? Roumanians would never willingly have tolerated the protection of the Communists against the Nazis. There were enough pro-Germans among them to have perhaps made it possible to sell the country a policy of inviting the protection of the Nazis in return for a guarantee that Roumania would remain inviolate, but that might well have provoked worse Soviet intervention and turned Roumania into a battlefield; and in any case the Germans had shown that they were unwilling to become involved except on their own terms and in their own time. It was one of those situations where it was impossible to win, and Carol was forced to walk a tightrope without benefit of a safety net. He personally had the courage to stand up to the Soviets but could hardly have forced his will in such a vital matter in the face of very powerful opposition.

His domestic policies were a reaction to events outside the country and he received wildly conflicting advice. Those who believed that Roumania's best course was to appease the conquering Germans advocated reconciliation with the Iron Guard. Although this was anathema to Carol, it seemed worth making a gesture if the Guard could be neutralized, and German-inspired talks to this end, instituted as early as February, resulted in a virtual amnesty for the movement in March in return for a pledge of loyalty to the Crown. It was a pledge, however, that no one wanted to put to the test. The Nazis had shown on many occasions that they were not to be trusted, and the same applied to their followers. Every concession was correctly regarded as a weakness, of which they immediately took advantage.

Germany's code of conduct under the Nazis was not that of a

civilized nation. Carol's old friend and great supporter, Foreign Minister Manoilescu, a declared admirer of Mussolini, could not believe for example how he had been tricked by his German counterpart Ribbentrop over the fate of Transylvania, and actually suffered a series of heart attacks as a result of his devastating experience. In his naivety he did not realize that he was dealing with a ruthless gangster to whom the niceties of diplomatic procedure meant nothing. In the same way the Roumanian politicians were sadly deceived in thinking that it was possible to tame the fanatical Iron Guard.

Carol found himself in an altogether impossible situation in which he was compelled to twist and turn. Having been persuaded to make concessions to the Iron Guard, he found himself under pressure from the Nazis actually to include terrorist representatives in the government, which alone may have provoked, and even perhaps justified, Soviet intervention. At one point he agreed to accept Codreanu's successor, Horia Sima, into the Cabinet. He disliked and mistrusted the man, but thought perhaps that it was better to have him under his eye rather than leave him loose in the country. Sima, however, resigned very quickly, intent perhaps on gaining power in other ways and seeing his own position as inhibiting his freedom of action.

The Russian occupation of Bessarabia and part of Bukovina was the final straw. The outcry in the country was such that Tatarescu had to resign, a sacrificial lamb to events, and there was little alternative but to replace him with, if not a pro-German Prime Minister, at least an anti-Soviet one. There was virtually no difference and Carol may even have thought that by selecting an alleged friend of Goering he would be securing German support for his regime at this critical time, and perhaps saving Transylvania for Roumania. This was yet another miscalculation in how to deal with the Nazis, for although the new Prime Minister, Ion Gigurtu, immediately adopted a pro-German position, visiting both Hitler and Mussolini at the end of July and securing in return what he thought was their support for Roumania over the Transylvanian question, he was as shocked as Manoilescu at German betrayal.

The one thing that can be said for Carol and those who were advising him at the time is that they were not alone in misunderstanding the Nazis. Despite all the evidence of treacherous behaviour by Hitler and his followers, there were even then people who treated them as if they could be trusted to keep their word.

Roumanians as a whole desired their independence, but Carol and his ministers found no way to maintain it. Every friendly inch they gave resulted in a mile being taken, whether by Germany or Russia. How could Roumania have held on to Bessarabia? How could it have saved Transylvania? As the cards lay, these losses were unavoidable. The first surrender was humiliating enough to provoke widespread anger but the second resulted in fury and despair. Inevitably Carol was blamed, although he had been among the least willing to surrender to the Soviet Union. He might have survived if the country had been relatively calm but its stability had been undermined by agitation and worse from abroad.

In all these matters the attitude of Antonescu is of special interest. Although he had fallen foul of Carol, whom he somewhat despised, he was not a member of the Iron Guard, who might have welcomed German occupation of the country as a means of seizing power for themselves. He was a man whose political sympathies were in tune with those of the Nazis but who preferred to set up a Fascist regime independent of the Germans. Neither of these options was of course possible for Carol. Needless to say, Antonescu had nothing good to say for the Communists.

He persisted in presenting his views to Carol by letter, and on 1 July, following the enforced concessions to the Soviet Union, he wrote to the King once again. He referred to 'the nation's agony'. 'The people and the army,' he declared, 'having surrendered without even a fight, are demoralized and have lost faith in their government. Their hatred is directed towards the leadership. The Crown Council convinced you to capitulate, and this decision has created a revolutionary situation that can only bring anarchy in its wake ... the country is stunned and panicked.' Unlike the average Roumanian, Antonescu was fully aware of the circumstances in which Carol had been forced to agree to the cession of Bessarabia and part of Bukovina.

Antonescu admitted that he himself had 'contributed considerably to the catastrophic events that have occurred internally in the country,' but said that 'we have a duty to hold together' to try to achieve the impossible. It seems clear that Antonescu was seeking to isolate the King from his incompetent advisers and putting himself forward as the candidate to save the country. The task ahead 'must not be undertaken', he said, 'by those who may have been the cause of all the troubles ... if Your Majesty does not listen and act on the wish of the people, total collapse will follow, with sinister results and the destruction of the country. . . .

'I gave warning two years ago,' Antonescu continued, 'verbally and in writing to the government and the military leaders, but also to Your Majesty, that catastrophe was imminent. . . . I was laughed at and ridiculed, but in face of the present crisis I am prepared to forgive and help with honesty, but in return I expect honesty. I shall not complain or avenge myself if attacked by anyone. I will try only to save what is possible for the Crown by restoring order and our frontiers.'

Exactly how he thought he might recapture the territory lost to the Soviet Union was left unsaid. What he was offering were his honest services to work with Carol in an almost impossible situation to bring back some order and dignity to the nation. 'Listen to me, your Majesty,' he pleaded, 'at this time. I have never been your Majesty's enemy. I have been a fanatical servant of this country. I have been surrounded by calumny and intrigues by those who have brought the country to its present abyss, and by occult forces. I beg your Majesty to close your ears to them.'

Antonescu's admission of past errors and the strength and purpose of his appeal may well have attracted Carol in the existing circumstances, especially since Antonescu was proposing to uphold the Crown, although he might have paused at such words as 'fanatical' and, more so, 'occult', a sort of codeword among certain Fascists for Jews, gypsies, Freemasons, Communists and others whom they were not prepared to understand or tolerate. It must have been a very strange man indeed who saw his opposition as evilly possessed people. Nevertheless he had a certain drive and undoubted authority and, whatever his personal motivation, was a patriot.

'This is my last appeal and warning of danger,' Antonescu concluded, and Carol may well have wondered what these words were intended to mean. In any case he took no immediate steps to respond and chose Gigurtu to replace Tatarescu following the country's humiliation at the hands of the Soviets. Gigurtu, however, could not survive the Transylvanian debacle, particularly since he had relied on his friendship with the Germans, and their promises, to secure continued Roumanian sovereignty over the province.

The Nazis had shown their contempt for Roumania by their actions. If even a pro-German policy could not protect the country's territory, what was the point of further appeasing Hitler? Perhaps the sensible course was to appoint a strong man whom the Nazis might respect because of his military background and total opposition to Communism. Like Gigurtu, Antonescu was ideologically acceptable to Germany, but unlike Gigurtu, he had some influence. At least that was the way Carol assessed the situation when he reluctantly asked Antonescu to assume the office of Prime Minister on 4 September 1940. The appointment was a last desperate attempt to keep what was left of Roumania intact.

Whatever the true intentions of Antonescu when he wrote to Carol on 1 July, virtually seeking power in order to protect the Crown, no sooner did he take office than he cheated his King in exactly the way that Hitler and Ribbentrop had cheated Gigurtu and Manoilescu. He was a product of the same school, in which promises were a worthless means to an end. Either from choice or because he realized that he was dependent on the support of the Iron Guard to maintain his new position of power, and certainly under German influence, he immediately reneged on the implied offer to work with Carol. He demanded dictatorial powers, allowing him if necessary to take decisions without reference to the monarch. As Carol revealed in his diary, Antonescu agreed to accept office only 'on condition that he is in total charge and has full powers, becoming thereby full master of the country. In fact I would become a sort of figurehead with only decorative powers.'

It is interesting to compare the ruthlessness of Antonescu in getting rid of Carol with Carol's own ruthlessness when he returned home in 1930 to seize the throne. 'If it is for the good of the country,' Carol now wrote, 'any personal sacrifice is welcome,' but he was furious. It soon became clear, however, that Antonescu wanted even more, after visiting the German Ambassador and virtually taking his instructions. Carol was faced with hastily arranged, and carefully orchestrated and unprecedented anti-royalist demonstrations, and a demand that he should abdicate. A 'fatal document', as he put it, was delivered on behalf of Antonescu, requiring him to 'renounce the throne so as to restore order in the country'. This was, he was told, 'the wish of the man in the street, of the army and of the politicians'. He realized that, to save their own reputations, the politicians were ganging up on him, trying to make him the sole scapegoat for the country's disasters.

Carol naturally discussed the situation with Urdarianu and was disappointed to find his friend in pessimistic mood. Urdarianu expressed the view that it might be sensible to withdraw before being forced to do so. Other advice that Carol sought among members of the royal household was surprisingly equivocal and unhelpful. He next saw Generals Mihail and Theodorescu, who alone among his supporters said that it might be possible successfully to resist Antonescu. Manoilescu did not want Carol to leave but was terrified of the Germans. 'He seemed to realize how erroneous his pro-German policy had been,' Carol wrote, 'and it made me sorry for him.' Manoilescu incidentally revealed that he had been questioned as to where Carol might want to go if he left the country; there was some thought that he might join his family in Germany, although it can never have been acceptable to Hitler that the King's Jewish mistress could be allowed to live in the Reich.

'Then began for me,' Carol wrote, 'a search of my soul and conscience to determine what my duty was.' It was a terrible dilemma. He had sworn allegiance to the country but was it better to stand up to the 'horde of madmen' or surrender? 'If I remain,' he said, 'there will be resistance, bloodshed, disturbance, even more important, intervention from unfriendly foreign powers.' He came therefore to the conclusion that no viable alternative was available to him and he was forced to negotiate an arrangement that, while conferring extraordinary powers on his Prime Minister, protected the position of the Crown.

'I finally decided to concede,' Carol revealed in his diary, 'and not wanting to reply to Antonescu, who did not have the courage to face me' – he had delivered the 'fatal document' through an intermediary – 'I wrote a proclamation transferring power to Michael and asking the country to support him so that it could come out of its difficulties.' On the advice of Urdarianu, who was against a formal abdication, Carol made this announcement 'as an act of delegation', to use his exact words. The document dated 6 September and published in Roumania on the 7th, deliberately avoided any specific use of the word 'abdication'. Instead Carol referred to 'passing the burden of the Crown to my son'. Antonescu was not interested in the niceties of the document. He had got rid of Carol within twenty-four hours. It would not be as difficult for him to deal with young King Michael and in any case he would stand in better stead in the country if he remained loyal to the concept of the Crown and if the nation still had a figurehead. One of his first actions was to recall Michael's mother to provide even more solidity for the monarchy.

What might have happened had Carol stood up to Antonescu is a matter of speculation. His failure to do so was yet another example of appeasement of a dictator, or in this case a would-be dictator, but in Carol's favour, he was barely in a position to bargain and he was merely playing for time. Roumania, without fighting and now supposedly a neutral country, had been reduced to a rump by its Communist and Nazi neighbours and weakened internally by agitation, largely inspired from abroad. The reality of the Transylvanian loss was that Roumania had been defeated by the Germans just as surely as if the two countries had gone to war, and Antonescu, despite his patriotism, was to all intents and purposes Germany's representative in Bucharest. Carol was King of a defeated nation and was hardly in a position to make his own terms. If ever a man were a victim of circumstances, it was he.

Within a day of selecting a man who had vowed to protect the Crown, Carol saw this man betray him. Antonescu had obviously intended to get rid of the King from the moment he was offered office, and with the King, of course, the King's mistress, who was poison to his anti-Semitic mind. Carol may have considered that his departure was the only means to save his life and that of Lupescu.

Short of involving an already battered Roumania in civil war by calling on the army to support him against one of its own generals, Carol was virtually in Antonescu's hands. He saw that passing over the throne to Prince Michael, now just over a month away from his nineteenth birthday, was the safest way of protecting the dynasty. This was a determining factor in his mind. Although he hesitated to leave his young son in the hands of Antonescu, only in this way could the monarchy be saved. 'In this whole dramatic situation,' he wrote, 'the most pathetic figure is Michael. He must remain alone, a victim of circumstances, inexperienced and perhaps unable to cope amid a pack of wolves and jackals.' He revealed that Michael did not want to accept the situation and that Lupescu had 'used all her talents of persuasion to make him understand that his sacrifice is a duty to Roumania and that if he leaves too, everything will collapse'. Carol reported that his son asked how he could be expected to succeed where his father had failed. 'I spoke to him myself,' he wrote, 'and explained that as a Prince he has a duty that overrides personal unhappiness and inconvenience. He has to remain dignified in his role, which is that of standard-bearer of the nation.'

Cynics may wonder why Carol had not always applied the same sentiments to himself, but it is far easier to give advice to others, and in any case the advice was given in a highly emotional climate. 'I have jotted down this chain of events,' Carol declared, 'that has given such pain to myself, such a crisis of conscience and such bitter desolation.

Today, 5 September 1940, something broke in my heart. . . .' He went on to accuse Antonescu of treason. Even if his action was for the good of the country, he said, he would be unable to wipe away its moral stain.

Carol was also concerned with safe conduct for himself and Lupescu, and his close friends who chose to leave the country, and also with suitable financial provisions. Fortunately, Antonescu was prepared to promise almost anything to get rid of him.

Antonescu was offered the Premiership on 4 September. Carol finally acquiesced to his demands late on 5 September and on 6 September Michael became King. Two days later Carol left Roumania with Magda Lupescu and Ernest Urdarianu, accompanied by four military aides, a number of servants, three poodles, the late Queen Marie's two pekingese, and a vast quantity of luggage in which they had packed almost all their portable possessions.

Whatever Antonescu may have promised, an attempt was made on Carol's life before he left the country. Whether Antonescu was behind this is open to question. He had originally announced his intention to accompany Carol to the border but at the last minute pleaded illness as an excuse. In his diary Carol wrote that 'both Duduia and I were suspicious that something fishy was afoot. . . .' When the train stopped briefly at Lugoj, Carol learnt that the Iron Guard had intended to stop the train earlier at Turnu Severin to prevent him leaving and, having failed to do so, were now planning to stop it at Timisoara, the last big town before the Yugoslav border, and to kidnap Magda Lupescu. It could well be that Antonescu, who definitely wanted to see the back of Carol, had been forced to compromise as regards Lupescu, but the truth probably is that the situation in that area was largely outside his control at that particular time.

Carol ordered that the train should not stop either at Timisoara or at Jimbolia on the actual frontier, and guards were posted at the train windows with machine-guns, which indicates that Antonescu's soldiers were still willing to take orders from their former King. Later, according to his diary, Carol sensed that the train was slowing down as it entered the station at Timisoara and he heard shots, which he claimed to identify by their 'dry sound' as the German weapons used by the Guardists. As the train started to pick up speed, the firing increased and his own guards fired back. They had already barricaded the windows of the royal compartment, and Carol and Lupescu lay side by side on the floor. The train survived with only a few broken windows and the royal carriage was unscathed.

The last stretch of the journey was completed in considerable anxiety in case there was another attempt by the Iron Guard at Jimbolia, and when the train came to a stop forty-five minutes later, Carol was greatly relieved when the door opened and it was Ernest Urdarianu. 'We are at Viliki Kikinda, which is in Yugoslav territory,' he announced.

Prince Paul, the Regent of Yugoslavia, sent General Petrovici to meet the train at Zenica to accompany Carol to the Italian border. It transpired that some Iron Guardists had followed the train beyond Jimbolia and actually attempted to cross into Yugoslavia, where there had been an exchange of fire with the border guards. The loyal guards who had protected Carol on the train were allowed to remain in Yugoslavia when Carol suggested that they might be shot if they were to return to Roumania.

In such a fashion King Carol II and his entourage were hustled and harried out of Roumania.

22

A Disappointing Answer

The fate of Roumania since King Carol II was forced to leave the country in 1940 does not make happy reading, but that was in no way the fault of his son King Michael I, who was as much a victim of Stalin as Carol was of Hitler. By the end of January 1941 Antonescu, with German support, had been able to crush the unruly Iron Guard; several hundred were killed, and Antonescu was now in full control as a military dictator. It is ironic that Antonescu should have suppressed the very people who had helped him to power, and with a ruthlessness that Carol had never been able to employ; and further that Hitler, who needed a strong man in a puppet Roumania to support the invasion of the Soviet Union, should likewise have been willing to suppress his natural adherents.

On 22 June 1941, after Hitler had launched his massive attack on the Soviet Union, Antonescu issued a proclamation to the Roumanian people declaring a 'Holy War' against Russia, 'for the preservation of the civilized world' – and to recover Bessarabia and northern Bukovina. It had popular support throughout the country. Most Roumanians, however, wanted the army to stop after it had recovered the lost provinces, but Antonescu continued into Soviet territory, actually capturing Odessa in October with the help of the Germans and proclaiming that part of the Ukraine a Roumanian province. This provoked Britain to declare war on Roumania, after Antonescu ignored an ultimatum to cease military operations inside the Soviet Union. Ironically, Britain declared war on 7 December, the day on which the Japanese attacked Pearl Harbor.

It was not until August 1944 that Michael was in a position to arrest the dictator Antonescu and break the German connection. His bravery was ill rewarded, however, by the Soviets, who occupied Roumania and manipulated it into the Communist fold, and by Britain and her allies, now of course joined by the United States, who let them do so. Roumania was literally sacrificed by the Western Powers and almost awarded to the Soviet Union as a spoil of war by the Yalta agreement. The events forced King Michael to abdicate at the very end of 1947.

These facts, while not immediately relevant to Carol's story, form the background to his life in exile. Carol decided to get as far away from Hitler and Antonescu as possible. He went first to Lugano in Switzerland, *en route* for the south of France, now under control of the puppet Vichy government, and thence to Spain on 12 September, reaching Barcelona on the 14th. Spain was a neutral country but its dictator Franco had been supported during the Spanish Civil War by both Hitler and Mussolini, and it was by no means certain that Carol and Lupescu would be safe there if the Germans chose to hound them. Carol had reason, however, to expect fair treatment at the hands of Serrano Suñer, Franco's Foreign Secretary and brother-in-law; and indeed Franco was to prove a surprisingly independent ruler who more than once refused to support German plans.

It was not Hitler, but Antonescu, who proved vindictive, alleging that Carol had stolen money that belonged to the State and demanding his expulsion from Spain and return to Roumania for trial. Although Carol did not realize this, Antonescu's move was designed to appease the Iron Guard and other extreme factions. He would have been horrified had the former King returned when he had just succeeded in his aim to get rid of him. By alleging, however, that Carol had made off with money that was not his, Antonescu was seeking to gain support even from royalists who might have been angered at the way in which he had acted towards the former King.

What is the truth about Carol's money? For years stories have circulated about millions in foreign banks, El Greco paintings and cash in suitcases. Prince Nicolas in his diary mentioned a figure of $30 million, but he had confused this sum with the $50 million of Roumanian funds which had been frozen by the United States in October 1940 to avoid it falling into the hands of the Germans. It is true that Carol later laid claim to certain funds in the Chase Manhattan Bank, which he had difficulty in collecting, presumably because his personal title to these monies was in question, and it was largely through the intervention of the American State Department that he eventually received part of the funds five years later and not before the end of the war. They were not, however, of the order suggested by his enemies and he had very little ready money at his immediate disposal when he left Roumania. Why else would he have written to the Spanish Foreign Minister on 10 December, pleading with him to help him leave for Portugal, giving as one reason that he could barely afford the high cost of living in Seville? It is known too that he later sold a château in Nice bequeathed to him by Queen Marie and that in 1950 he obtained $56,000 for part of his stamp collection. Such sales, which he must have been loath to make, would have been unnecessary had he absconded with millions or had huge funds been hidden away in foreign banks. Moreover he was seeking his son's help in 1947 to obtain a sum of some $5,000 through the agency of the Brazilian Ambassador to Moscow; the letter requesting this was to be given to King Michael by hand, but he never received it.

Carol decided that he would be safer in Portugal, a country slightly less vulnerable than Spain to German influence. Doubtless he remembered also that his father was the son of Princess Antonia, daughter of Portugal's Queen Maria and King Ferdinand. In practice, although he may not have known it, as long as he did nothing openly political, he was perfectly safe in Spain and was able to move around the country. He stayed for example for a short time in Sitges near Barcelona before arriving in Seville. He may have been under the impression that he needed permission to move but Franco wanted only to keep an eye on him so that he should not embarrass the Spanish government, and there is no reason to think that, provided he kept the authorities advised of his intentions, he could not have gone where he wanted inside the country.

It seems, however, that he was not allowed to leave Spain, perhaps because Franco had agreed to keep an eye on his activities, though why else the Spanish should have wanted to keep him is a mystery. He would have been far less of a problem to them in Portugal. Carol was firmly under the impression, as he wrote to the Papal Nuncio in Madrid, seeking Papal support for his transfer to Lisbon, that 'I am kept by force in Spain'. Earlier he had written to Prince Paul of Yugoslavia, claiming that he was a prisoner of the Spanish government at the instigation of Antonescu. In a second letter to Paul, saying that 'royal families should stick together', he repeated his belief that he was not allowed to leave Spain for Portugal and he sought Paul's help in the matter. He asked him moreover to solicit the support of his son Michael and his former wife Helen. He wrote direct to Suñer on 10 December to protest, not for the first time, at his 'detention on Spanish soil'.

The Spanish would probably have been pleased to see the back of him, and they made no difficulty about allowing Urdarianu to visit

Lisbon to get permission and make tentative arrangements for Carol and Magda Lupescu to enter Portugal. Urdarianu actually obtained visas for them. In deference, however, to German and possibly Roumanian wishes that Carol should remain in Spain where his activities could be closely monitored and he could cause them no trouble, the Spanish did not wish to be seen to be encouraging him to leave. When he did so therefore, it was in deadly secret, although one wonders whether the Spanish authorities were altogether ignorant of the cloak-and-dagger arrangements for his departure and whether they turned a blind eye to them. Carol left Spain within six months of his arrival there and the circumstances of his leaving were at least such that the Spanish government was able to say that it had not given permission for him to go abroad.

Urdarianu had already been in Portugal for four months when Carol made his extraordinary escape from Spain. The original plan was postponed slightly following a hurricane of quite exceptional ferocity that took Portugal by surprise, destroying hundreds of trees and causing immense damage. Carol and Magda Lupescu finally set off early in the morning of 3 March 1941. His diary recorded the involvement of a colourful assortment of characters, including Colonel Jurawscki, who is believed to have been a member of the Polish secret service, and a habitual smuggler named Rente, who was very familiar with the problems of crossing from Spain into Portugal and back again. He was also assisted by a man called Joly.

At least one Spanish policeman was assigned at all times to watch Carol, and although this was intended for his protection as well as for surveillance, it was one of the reasons that Carol considered himself a prisoner. He was obliged to inform the officer of his movements but there was never any attempt to restrict him, and the police were obviously used to his somewhat eccentric royal behaviour. When therefore he told the policeman on duty at 3.30 a.m. that he and Magda Lupescu were driving to Llerena, about halfway between Seville and the border town of Badajoz, he was allowed to proceed on his way. We do not know when the matter was reported to the authorities.

The reason for leaving at such an early hour was that it was planned to cross into Portugal before seven o'clock, at which time the border guards were brought up to full strength. The escape route and timetable, prepared by Jurawscki, was written on a small piece of paper, which Lupescu clutched in her hand for the early part of the journey. The trip was supposed to take two and a half hours.

Carol wrote that he and Lupescu prayed to God before they

embarked on their little adventure. He had hidden a purseful of money beneath his trenchcoat and she had secreted two bags, presumably containing more money or valuables, under her fur coat. Their car was so stuffed with belongings, which had been carefully placed so as not to attract the attention of anyone who might cursorily have examined the vehicle, that Carol had difficulty in climbing into the driving seat.

It does not say much for the police surveillance if nobody spotted the car being loaded, which lends further credence to the possibility that the authorities knew about the escape plans and were happy for them to proceed. It is significant too that during the whole journey, they never saw a police car, although Magda Lupescu was charged with the task of looking out through the rear window from her seat in the back in case anyone was following them.

Carol, with his long experience of fast driving, crossed the Sierra Morena at a speed rarely achieved on such twisting and mountainous roads, arriving ahead of schedule at his first stopping point, where he was met by Joly and his chauffeur. The chauffeur took charge of Carol's car and its valuable contents and set off with it to Badajoz, where he was to leave it at a petrol station for later collection and delivery to Carol in Portugal. Carol and Lupescu then left in Joly's car, with Joly at the wheel, for their next rendezvous, just outside Badajoz, with Rente. This somewhat elaborate scheme had been designed to confuse the police in case they were looking for the original car.

This time Magda Lupescu sat in front with Joly while Carol lay in the back, covered by a rug. They reached their destination at 5.20, ahead of time, and had to go in search of Rente. When they found him, the escaping couple transferred to his car and Joly drove off.

Rente's car, 'an old banger' to use Carol's description, was nevertheless unique. A special space had been created beneath the back seat, no doubt to smuggle goods across the frontier, although on this occasion the goods were nothing less than the former King of Roumania and his mistress. The couple found themselves in a sort of large box, big enough for them both to lie at full length, but very hot and stuffy. 'It was not very comfortable,' Carol wrote, 'but such was our plight that we did not bother about that.'

It was also a very bumpy ride, for they could feel every undulation in the road. After a time the car stopped and their hearts thumped as they could hear people talking. It later transpired that Rente, who had earlier crossed into Spain to take his wife to the dentist, had agreed to pick up a Portuguese border guard and a friend on his way back into Portugal. Rente was a frequent traveller across the border and his illicit activities were probably helped by his friendly relations with the men who guarded the frontier. It is an amusing thought that one such officer may well have been sitting on the seat that hid the escapees. There were two further stops, first at the Spanish and then at the Portuguese customs, and it may well be that the deliberate involvement of a Portuguese guard avoided any sort of inspection or enquiry, though Rente was the sort of man who was almost able to come and go as he pleased across the frontier.

Shortly afterwards, Carol sensed that they had moved on to an open road. Rente's Portuguese passengers had presumably left the car on their side of the border, and Carol suddenly felt a sense of relief. All his suppressed emotions burst out, as he said, and inside their box he and Magda embraced and thanked God for their escape. It is a story both funny and touching.

After driving a few miles, Rente stopped the car, opened up the back seat and spoke one word: 'Portugal'. 'This word seemed magic to our ears,' Carol recorded. 'It was the word of salvation.'

At a crossroads just outside the town of Elvas, they met Urdarianu. Both Carol and Magda Lupescu were very moved to see their good friend again. They then went to Rente's farm, where they waited for Joly to take them to his home in Lisbon. Rente, who had obviously been well paid for his assistance, still had one further task: it was his job to collect Carol's own car, stuffed with valuables, from the petrol station in Spain and deliver it to him in the Portuguese capital.

Carol announced his arrival to the Portuguese authorities on 5 March, but having gone to such great lengths to enter the country, he remained there barely two months. It is clear now that he never intended to stay, first because he felt that he and his beloved Duduia would be safer outside Europe and second because the Portuguese government insisted that he should engage in no political activity, whereas he wanted freedom to adopt a political role. He set sail for Cuba at the beginning of May, stopping on the way at St Thomas in the American Virgin Islands and in Bermuda. By August he had arrived in Mexico, which was to be his home for three years and where he rented a furnished house in fashionable Coyoacan, on the outskirts of the capital.

Carol was not by any means the first former King to live in exile and he shared the experience of the small band of like people who found themselves in his situation. His position was similar to that of the Duke of Windsor, the former King Edward VIII who had been forced to give up the British throne for a woman regarded as unsuitable, with the difference that Carol was not married to Lupescu. In these circumstances the ex-King sought to maintain his dignity, to be respected and to keep in touch with as many influential people as could help his cause.

Carol played the royal game by organizing his household on a formal basis, with Urdarianu continuing to act as Lord Chamberlain, sometimes called Great Chamberlain; and he and Lupescu were able to live a fairly relaxed and happy private life among the friendly Mexicans. At first he found the climate excellent after the sultry heat in Havana, and he was not worried by the altitude. He was treated by the authorities as a special case and allowed for example to sport diplomatic licence plates on his cars. What he really wanted, however, was continued influence and he never gave up the thought that one day he might be recalled home to Roumania.

He lost no opportunity to remind the world of his existence. He wrote to Franklin Roosevelt from Havana in July, saying what a warm welcome he had received in St Thomas, and congratulated the President for his courageous protection of world freedom. He wrote to him again in August, asking for what Roosevelt in his reply described as 'assistance in assuring the well-being of your son'. Earlier, during his stop-off in Bermuda, he had given a lobster and steak dinner at a local golf club for the island's Governor and distinguished guests. It was when he was settled in Mexico however that he really got to work.

On 1 September he wrote to the United States Ambassador to Cuba, with whom he had established a good relationship while in Havana. Apart from asking him to obtain news about King Michael 'because my son cannot write openly', he reported that he had already met the American Ambassador to Mexico, George Messersmith, and several of the local United States diplomatic staff at the wedding of the Mexican Foreign Secretary's daughter, and he made the comment that the Allies were not doing enough in Central America to counter Axis propaganda. He made much the same point in a letter of the same date to Lord Halifax, Chamberlain's Foreign Secretary whom Churchill had appointed to the important post of British Ambassador in Washington. 'Nazi propaganda,' he wrote, 'has been very clever and insinuating here.' He found no love for the Nazis but equally 'a certain indifference to the cause of the Allies and their victory'. The efforts of Britain's friends in Mexico were not adequately supported by official British representatives on the spot. 'The enemy is active,' he declared, 'and you are not.'

His main idea at the time was to set up a Free Roumania movement now that Antonescu had aligned the country with the Germans. Although by no means an original idea, it was certainly worthy of consideration. Carol first broached the subject towards the end of August and on 24 September he wrote to King George VI, asking why Great Britain was so long in responding. As the German grip on his country grew tighter, he said, so did the cry grow stronger of those Roumanians 'who want to see my country express through an official organization its true feelings and hopes for the future'. He was receiving more and more news about discontent back home, but nothing could be done internally without help from outside. 'It is not only my country's interest,' he stated, 'but also the common interest' that should encourage Britain to support 'the fighters for Roumania's freedom'. He also expressed his 'admiration for the wonderful courage and energy of the British nation' and announced that 'every news of progress on the road of victory fills my heart with joy and hope'.

Carol's official proposal, requesting the support of both the British and the Americans, declared that Roumania's alignment with Germany was contrary to the wishes and interests of the Roumanian people. King Michael could not be held responsible for this new situation since he was a prisoner of the effective ruler of the country and of the Germans who were now the real masters of Roumania. Having regard to Roumania's vital interest in an Allied victory, and in response to many appeals, it was Carol's duty to raise the flag of Free Roumania on the side of the Allies. He proposed the setting up of a National Council of Free Roumania with the aims eventually of liberating the country and returning King Michael to his rightful dignity.

Carol formally presented his plan to the British and United States governments, and separately wrote a number of letters to important people whom he hoped might influence a favourable response. There were further letters, for example, to George VI and Lord Halifax, and Carol must have been encouraged by the latter's reply: 'I have good reason to believe – though I should be grateful if Your Majesty would treat this as confidential – that the British Government are now prepared to give favourable consideration to the possibility of taking action at an early date in the sense which Your Majesty suggested.' This letter from the British Embassy in Washington DC was dated 9 October, and in response to a further letter from Carol, Lord Halifax told him on 7 November that 'I have no doubt that His Britannic Majesty's Government will give [your proposals] full and sympathetic consideration'.

Carol had heard nothing further when he wrote to his former brother-in-law, King George II of Greece, on the 24th, saying how much he admired his country's epic struggle. 'You and your country had more chance than me and mine,' he said. 'You had an outlet which enabled you to put up a resistance to the Nazi invasion. . . . I did not have that luck, being surrounded by enemies on all sides and stabbed in the back by the traitors inside the country . . . the way they have enslaved Roumania as an absolute vassal to Nazism is heart-rending. . . .' He went on to say that they had got rid of him because he believed firmly in an eventual Allied victory and that now he was trying to raise the flag of Free Roumania so that the 'real Roumania should also fight for the same ideals at your side'. The letter incidentally mentioned that both Michael and Helen sent him telegrams and an occasional letter. 'I think that anyhow you will be pleased to have this news about your sister. My great sorrow is being separated from Michael. My longing for him is immense.'

The reply to Carol's plan for a National Council of Free Roumania came eventually in the form of a letter from Buckingham Palace, dated 22 December 1941:

'Dear Carol, I am grateful for your letter of October 22nd, and I heartily sympathize with you in your anxiety about your country and your son.

'As regards the setting up of a National Council of Free Roumania, my Government have most carefully considered your proposals. We all have much sympathy with your desire to help Roumania to free herself from the toils of her German masters. At the same time my Government hold the view that the liberation of Roumania can never be achieved by any movement which does not emanate from forces operating within Roumania. For this reason it would, I am afraid, be impossible for them to support your plan in present circumstances.

'I am sorry to have to give you such a disappointing answer, but I feel sure that you will appreciate our difficulties here. I remain your affectionate cousin Bertie.'

King George may or may not have known but the British government had been keeping open communications with opponents of the Antonescu regime. Their main contact was Juliu Maniu, who had been attempting since the beginning of 1942 to work out an agreement with the British whereby Roumania would change sides, which would involve organizing a coup against Antonescu with Michael's help.

Receipt of King George's letter cannot have made the prospect for 1942 very enticing for Carol, although there was one great ray of hope. On 7 December the Japanese had attacked Pearl Harbor and the United States was now in the war. From Carol's point of view, however, his country was in the hands of the enemy; his son was their virtual prisoner; now his great scheme had been turned down by the British and he felt personally rejected. Perhaps however Franklin Roosevelt would now respond favourably. Within hours of the Japanese assault Carol had written to the President, deploring the attack 'by an acolyte of Nazism' and reminding him of the sad plight of the Roumanian people, already embroiled in the struggle. He sat down at the end of the year and sent new year greetings to the crowned heads of Great Britain, Greece, the Netherlands, Norway and Yugoslavia; and to Benes, Churchill, De Gaulle, Halifax and Sikorski among others, and of course also to Roosevelt.

Early in the new year he received a letter dated 5 January 1942 from the White House. 'My good friend,' the President wrote, 'Your letter of December 8, written immediately after the wanton and ruthless attack of Japan on the United States was symbolic of the revulsion the world must feel against this new act of the aggressor powers. I thank you sincerely for this message.'

Carol must have cherished a small hope that Roosevelt would respond favourably to his plan and perhaps persuade the British to change their minds, but the official United States response to his scheme for a Free Roumania came two days later. The Department of State declared 'that it would not be in a position to extend to an organization with which King Carol may become associated such expressions of support or collaboration as have been withheld from other similar groups'.

Carol had been rejected again and his 'good friend' had turned out to be not quite such a good friend after all.

23

Forced Inactivity

Carol's life after this disappointment was in the nature of a postscript to an exciting and romantic past that had been packed with almost incredible incident. He did not at first allow his rejection at the hands of Britain and the United States to deter him from seeking to foster the idea of a Free Roumania, and he set up small organizations in many different countries. He briefly canvassed the possibility of making Canada the base from which to operate, but his efforts were still-born once Britain and America refused him. He had the support of the United States Ambassador to Mexico, but the American State Department found him an embarrassment. Perhaps like the British, they took the view that he was unreliable.

He never complained publicly but he was badly treated by Washington. Although they were at all times extremely polite and helpful in small matters – and actually financially supportive – they would not even allow him to visit the States when he received an invitation from the Romanian Orthodox Episcopate of America to attend their annual Independence Day celebration in Grass Lake, Michigan. The State Department was concerned that Carol's presence would turn a patriotic and religious festivity into the wrong sort of political occasion and it was conveyed to him that such a visit would be inappropriate at that time.

Carol must have been desperately disappointed once again but he put a brave face on the matter and on 4 July, when he had hoped to be among the American people, he had to satisfy himself with a letter to his friend, their Ambassador to Mexico, in which he referred to the United States as the supreme hope for the civilized world.

As he sent out his new year messages at the end of 1942 – this time including a telegram to President General Carmona of Portugal – Carol realized that his own personal cause had not prospered during the year but that at least the dictators no longer had everything their own way. The democracies were fighting back, even without the help of a National Council of Free Roumania. As he wrote to George of Greece, 'Although far away, I continually follow with the greatest of interest all the events that are going on over there, and you can very well understand how much I suffer not to be able to take part actively. . . .' To King George of Great Britain he wrote: 'Although Mexico is agreeable to live in, one is too far from the happenings and my forced inactivity makes it very hard for me who has only one wish, that of being actively useful to the cause of the United Nations and to the future of my country.' In both letters he noted happily the Allied progress, particularly in North Africa; as he told his British cousin, 'The events on all battlefronts seem to be happy omens for the coming year.'

Carol's world role was declining all the time, and although it was by now practically non-existent, he still clung to the fond hope that he might be restored to some sort of power following an Allied victory. He continued therefore to maintain contact with world leaders, using every opportunity, every anniversary, to send messages of support and congratulation. In August and September 1943, for example, he wrote to Paul of Yugoslavia and to Bojidar Pauritch, the Prime Minister of the Royal Yugoslav Government in exile in London, urging them to establish diplomatic relations with Mexico. He always received polite, often grateful replies to his messages, which must have bolstered his morale a little.

1944 was an important year for both Roumania and King Michael. Antonescu's support for Germany in the war against the Soviet Union had cost Roumania heavily in lives; thirty army divisions had taken part in the disastrous siege of Stalingrad in 1942, when Roumania suffered some 300,000 casualties. By the spring of 1944 the Soviets had turned the tide and re-entered Bessarabia. German-occupied Roumania was now about to be attacked, or perhaps liberated, from the east. Its oilfields at Ploesti were also a major target for Allied bombers. It was in these circumstances that, towards the end of August, King Michael and his political colleagues decided to act. King Carol had been informed by Pangal, the Roumanian Consul in Portugal, of negotiations by Maniu and the Roumanian opposition with King Michael, and that Prince Stirbey was going to Cairo to discuss possible armistice terms with the Allies. Antonescu was aware of these talks, since the opposition had tried unsuccessfully to persuade him to change sides and agree to an armistice. The talks were conducted while the German and Roumanian armies were in heavy combat with the Red army and both Antonescu and the opposition were playing for time and a better position from which to negotiate.

It was on Antonescu's return from Germany, where he had been summoned by Hitler to renew his pledge of support, that King Michael took action. After failing to convince Antonescu one last time to change course, and knowing that Antonescu was leaving for the front earlier than scheduled, Michael ordered his guards to arrest him. Thus ended four years of military dictatorship tied to the Nazi cause. It was a brave and risky move that took the Germans by surprise and although they retaliated by bombing the capital, they were soon forced into retreat before the Roumanian divisions joined by the Soviet army. King Michael hastily formed a new coalition government of National Peasant Party members, Liberals, Socialists and Communists, under General Constantin Santanescu, and he broadcast over the radio the cessation of hostilities against the Allies. Sixteen army divisions were kept mobilized to liberate the rest of Roumania's territory and to help the Allies drive the Germans out of Hungary and Czechoslovakia. In these final stages of the war, there were some further 170,000 Roumanian casualties. Roumania was no longer a German vassal but sadly, as Michael and his advisers were shortly to realize, it was soon to become part of an even less independent Soviet empire.

The arrest of Antonescu effectively put a stop to negotiations that Carol had been conducting, largely through Urdarianu, with a representative of the Soviet Union in Mexico. As early as February, when Soviet troops reached the former Roumanian border in the east, Carol had been urged to sound out the intentions of the Communists towards the monarchy in Roumania. Urdarianu first contacted the Soviet Embassy in Mexico City on 6 May and found Ambassador Constantin Oumansky a cautious but interested listener to the former King's plans, with Soviet help, to detach Roumania from the Nazi alliance and to allow him perhaps to return home as Prince Regent. He sought guarantees from Moscow of Roumania's territorial integrity and democracy, and their help to recover Transylvania. On 10 June Urdarianu was notified that 'the Soviet government does not consider collaboration with King Carol impossible', showing that Carol had perhaps been right to maintain his optimism about his future place in world affairs. A definite answer was promised not later than the beginning of July. In fact Carol never got his answer and when, very soon afterwards, Antonescu was deposed,

Stalin no longer needed Carol. They could manipulate his son just as well.

1944 was also the year in which Carol finally left Mexico for Brazil. It was almost as if symbolically the former King, realizing that he was not after all to achieve his aim of returning to Roumania to assist his son, was further distancing himself from events at home, although in fact Rio de Janeiro is slightly closer to Bucharest than Mexico City. The departure of Carol, Lupescu and Urdarianu, with his new bride, was very sudden but it was not prompted by the Mexican government. Carol had made a point of informing them about his conversations with Oumansky and they had never objected to his political activities.

The reason for leaving Mexico was that Lupescu needed to live at a lower altitude for her health. Ideally they would probably have liked finally to settle in the United States, but this was never on the cards. For reasons that have never been satisfactorily explained, the American authorities seemed not to like Carol's politics or his morals, although politically he had always supported the United States and he had lived with the same woman for over nineteen years, which might not have gone unremarked in the land of divorce. Yet when the couple arrived in New Orleans on a cruise ship on 17 October, they were not even allowed to land. It cannot surely have been their dogs to which Attorney General Francis Biddle objected or the fact that they arrived with no less than 115 trunks and suitcases! Urdarianu insisted that the State Department had indicated that the party would be allowed to go ashore while the ship was in dock for five days, but the Attorney General amazingly categorized the former King as 'undesirable'. What must he have thought if he had seen President Roosevelt's letters to his 'good friend'?

Carol was angered and humiliated, and he wrote in protest the following day to George Messersmith, the American Ambassador to Mexico. Messersmith was away from his Embassy and did not receive the letter until 5 November, but he wrote to Carol on the 7th in his new home in Rio, saying how surprised he was at Carol's sudden departure from Mexico and how sorry he was not to have been there at the time. Referring to the embarrassing business in New Orleans, 'It seems incredible,' he said, 'that the immigration authorities of my government should have taken the action which they did. . . . The attitude of the Department of State was entirely correct, as I was sure it would be since my conversation with the President in January of this year. How it was possible for the Department of Justice and the Immigration Service to carry through this unnecessary and arbitrary action is beyond me, but it shows to what extraordinary degree in these troubled times agencies of government which have nothing to do with foreign relations can interfere with them.' He went on to say that Carol was 'entirely justified' in his anger, and could only add that he hoped 'that you will hold no resentment against my country for these acts, for I have every confidence that more considered and understanding attitudes will be found'.

Such has sometimes been the fate of kings. One minute they are rulers of all they survey; the next they are denied permission to do what is usually open to anyone. The American Justice Department obviously had it in for Carol. On 8 January 1945, two inoffensive Roumanian Orthodox priests and the editor of a small Roumanian newspaper in Michigan received remarkably harsh sentences – one got five years and was fined – for failing to register with the State Department as agents of a foreign power – the power in question being the former King Carol. They were alleged to have tried to gain entrance for him to the United States. Such action was inexcusably vindictive and a kick in the teeth from people whom Carol had every right to expect to be friendly. It is almost incomprehensible in the light of the extremely helpful attitude of the State Department at much this time in respect of releasing funds for Carol in Brazil.

Carol referred to the unfortunate priests in a letter to Messersmith, his most regular correspondent. He denied that the men were his agents except perhaps in the most technical sense. 'Those who have been condemned,' he wrote, 'were working for a noble cause, not for a bad one. They wanted to work for the United States, not against them.'

Meanwhile Carol and Lupescu watched the changing world from their hotel in Rio de Janeiro, and particularly the events in Roumania. It was in Brazil also that Carol started to write 'Orbit of Satan', his history of Europe since the Treaty of Versailles. It revealed him as being far more astute and politically aware than many people might have expected. He was certainly in no doubt about the nature of Nazism or Stalinism.

24

'A Nice Mess
of Things'

Carol was remote from the momentous events in Europe, but he observed them meticulously. Being detached physically, he perhaps saw them less subjectively than he might have done had he still been, like his son, in their midst. He was saddened by the death of Franklin Roosevelt and sent telegrams both to the widow and to the United States government. He had a very different reaction to the deaths of Mussolini and Hitler, and to the Allied triumph in Europe in 1945. Unfortunately his elation was qualified by his suspicion of Soviet plans for his country. On a more personal note, it amused him to hear that the Germans, who had been occupying one of his French châteaux, had been replaced by Americans. Lupescu expressed the hope that the newcomers had first disinfected the place and Carol noted the irony that whereas he was not allowed to enter the United States, American officers were his guests in France.

As was his fashion, he sent telegrams to all and sundry to celebrate the Allied victory, which of course also reminded everybody of his existence. 'On this great day of victory,' he addressed King George VI, 'I think with deep emotion of you and your people.' To Winston Churchill he said: 'To you who fought with such courage and persistence for victory, I send from all my heart my best wishes on this great day for the free and civilized world.' General De Gaulle, whom he much admired as the leader of a free government in exile, a model for his own would-be role, was told, 'In this great day of victory I think with emotion of glorious and eternal France.'

Perhaps the telegram he was most pleased to send was to King Michael in Bucharest. 'On this great day of victory, my dear son,' it read, 'all my most loving thoughts.' Sadly, he knew as he wrote it that Michael's future as King was hanging by a thread.

Doubtless he would have liked to return home immediately, but this was impossible. The only circumstance in which he could realistically have gone back was as a Soviet puppet King to replace his son. Moscow had kept open the possibility of Carol's return in case it suited their purposes, but with the war in Europe over and with the Germans out of the way, they did not need him. They had already made themselves masters of Roumania. It was part of their plan to colonize the country, along with Bulgaria, Czechoslovakia, Hungary, Poland and other countries, or at least to imprison them inside a Soviet bloc. Although one can appreciate their anxiety for security after their quite horrendous losses at German hands, it is difficult to excuse the ruthless and deceitful methods by which they operated to bring unwilling peoples under Stalinist rule.

At first unrecognized by the Western world, which was understandably willing to reward the Soviets for their massive efforts in defeating Hitler, Stalin adopted policies in Roumania that he used equally successfully elsewhere. With the right wing discredited by the Nazi defeat, the left-wing parties naturally came into their own, but it is doubtful if ten per cent of Roumanians were Communist. However, the Communists were more ruthless than the somewhat naive Liberal and Socialist politicians who were eager to share power with them, and they had many pliant and ambitious supporters in the working-class movement. Most important of all, they had the active support of the Soviet Union.

The activities of the small Communist Party in Roumania were regulated by three people sent from Moscow, including the notorious Anna Pauker. The first triumph for the Communists was the inclusion of one of their members in the key position of Minister of Justice in the government. When Prime Minister Constantin Santanescu, Antonescu's successor, balked at appointing another Communist to the even more important post of Minister of the Interior, no less a person than Andrei Vishinsky arrived in Bucharest to press the Soviet case. Santanescu could take no more and resigned.

Fully realizing that the more one gave way to the Communists, the more they demanded, King Michael refused to appoint their candidate Petru Groza as Prime Minister and instead chose a man of impeccably anti-Nazi qualifications, General Nicolas Radescu. This did not please the Soviets and less than two months later, on 27 February 1945, Vishinsky was sent again to Bucharest to demand his dismissal. On 3 March, Michael gave way and appointed his grandmother's old friend, Prince Stirbey, who had returned home after Carol's departure, but this was not at all what Vishinsky had in mind.

The decision had been taken in Moscow that Petru Groza was to be their puppet Prime Minister of Roumania.

Even had Michael wanted to acquiesce in the appointment of this inexperienced farmer, he knew that very few of the country's professional politicians would be willing to serve under him and that Groza could only fill his Cabinet with Communists or sympathizers. The Soviet pressure on Michael was intense, and it was made clear to him that they would take what they were not given.

Michael clung to one last hope, that the United States and Britain would save him, but all he got was sympathy, which was perhaps all he could have expected while the Western democracies and the Soviet Union were acting together in the last stages of the war against Hitler.

On 6 March 1945, barely six months after Soviet troops had entered Bucharest, what was virtually a Communist government took over in Roumania. Over forty years later, the Communists still run the country.

Carol's high hopes for an Allied victory did not thus result in freedom for the nation he had served as King. It was a bitterly disappointing outcome for him, for his son, and of course for the monarchy. Thereafter his connection with Roumania grew even more remote. A birthday or Christmas greeting from Michael was his main contact with Bucharest and when his sister Mignon heard a rumour that he was thinking of returning home in 1947, she wrote to him from London, begging him not to do so. It would only cause more problems, she said, for Michael, whose situation was difficult enough already. 'Let us leave it to the younger ones to do better than we did,' she wrote. 'In some cases we made a nice mess of things. . . .'

What Mignon may not have known is that Carol had actually obtained visas for himself, Lupescu and the Urdarianus to enter Portugal in August 1945, but these were cancelled on the representation of the United States and British governments, who did not want him to interfere in Roumanian affairs. It may be that his only motive was that he was extremely restless in Brazil. The Mexican climate had not suited Magda Lupescu, and the Brazilian had proved little better. In particular the summers were much too hot for her. In August 1946 Carol had made enquiries about the possibility of moving to Argentina, but was advised that the summers were equally hot there. Lupescu's health had suffered in Mexico and had deteriorated in Brazil. Carol explained the matter to George Messersmith by saying that 'six months of bad treatment in Spain' and 'three and a half years of Mexican altitude', together with the extraordinary emotional strain under which they had been living, had been more than she could stand. 'There are good doctors here,' he wrote from Rio, 'but they do not seem to be able to do much.' It was not clear what was wrong with Lupescu. The indications were not serious but she was weak and run down.

In the early part of 1947 she kept to her bed for much of the time and her condition was eventually diagnosed as pernicious anaemia. Carol was advised, somewhat surprisingly, that there was no known cure, which may have been the basis for rumours that began to circulate that Lupescu was dying. Her illness soon became a matter of concern to her friends all over the world. 'Sweet and lovely friend,' Barbara Hutton cabled, 'am so distressed to learn of your illness and want you to know that all my heart, thoughts and prayers are with you.'

On 5 July, having lived together as man and wife for over twenty-two years, the couple were married in a small private ceremony in their hotel bedroom. Carol, concerned that his mistress might be dying, decided that it was right and proper to legitimize their relationship, especially as marriage now was unlikely to make any difference to his situation in Roumania. This was his last gesture of love towards her, or so he thought. In fact, perhaps reanimated by the knowledge that she was the wife of a King and now known as Her Royal Highness Princess Elena of Roumania, she made a quite remarkable recovery and outlived her husband by many years.

Cynics have gathered from this that she had been faking illness in order to trap Carol into marriage but nothing could be further from the truth. There may have been a depressive element to her illness, but her anaemia was genuine and she was fortunate to discover a Hungarian doctor, a refugee in Rio, who helped her with blood transfusions. She of course enjoyed the new status she had always wanted but knew she was unlikely to achieve while Carol ruled Roumania or while there was the remotest chance of his recall; but marriage, particularly after so long a time, was not vital to her and it is absurd to suggest that she engineered it.

Despite her recovery, the doctor advised that she should move to a place with a more temperate climate and, the war now over in the Far East also, Carol decided finally to return to Europe. He had deliberately maintained close relations with the Portuguese authorities and on this occasion, through his friendship with President Salazar, quickly obtained permission to reside in his paternal grandmother's country, promising that he would eschew politics. He had also applied to resume residence in France but French procrastination made him decide to opt for Portugal.

It was from Brazil, however, that he watched the last struggles of his son to hold on to his position in Roumania. All decisions of the Communist government were made in the Kremlin, which was determined to crush all opposition. The gaols and prison camps were full of people considered enemies of the new regime, and in July the country's oldest and most distinguished statesman, following the recent death of Stirbey, Juliu Maniu, was among those arrested and sentenced to life imprisonment on ridiculous charges. Their only offence was their passionate dislike of what Maniu had called 'a government of murderers, the most odious government Roumania has ever possessed'.

The Soviets were very quick to approve King Michael's visit to Britain for the wedding of Princess Elizabeth to Prince Philip of Greece. They hoped that he and his mother would not return, and indeed Michael was urged by anxious friends in London not to do so, having regard to the Soviet record where royalty was concerned. It happened too that Michael fell in love, while in England, with Princess Anne of Bourbon-Parma and he informed his father by telegram on 15 December of his intention to marry her. Carol at once sent a message of congratulation and was delighted to receive an acknowledgement on the 18th which also thanked Magda Lupescu. Many young men in Michael's position, knowing how precarious was his hold on the throne, might have decided to cut and run for personal happiness. Michael however regarded it as his duty to return home.

It was one thing for the Soviet Union to accept the return of Michael as a figurehead King, but quite another for him to return as a popular hero who would attract support to himself and the monarchy by a royal marriage. His days as King were numbered anyway but his wish to marry brought the issue to an abrupt head. He returned home just before Christmas, which he spent in Sinaia, from where both he and his mother were summoned by the Prime Minister to the capital on 29 December to discuss a family matter, which he naturally assumed to be his marriage. Instead he was confronted by Groza and George Gheorghiu-Dej, a railway worker who had become Secretary General of the Communist Party, who demanded his abdication. They promised that he could retain his money and property in Roumania in return for his consent, and presented him with an act of abdication which they had prepared for him and insisted that he sign on the spot.

There were many indications that the Communists meant business. There was no practical way for Michael to appeal to the people, and even had he been able to do so, what could the people have done to save him? The country was in an iron grip and there was no point in fighting a losing battle. He was literally forced to give way.

The act of abdication was published on 30 December 1947 and on 3 January 1948 Michael left Roumania forever, as his father had done over seven years earlier. The document he signed renounced the throne, not only for himself but also for his descendants. Carol may well have noted that he had not himself abdicated formally and so might still have a legal right to the title of King of Roumania, but the reality was that the only King of Roumania resided in the Soviet Union and was called Josef Stalin.

Ironically the document that Michael had been compelled to sign ended with the words: 'I leave to the Roumanian people the freedom to choose the new Constitution.' Can any statement ever have been less true?

Whatever Michael may have thought of events, his father was horrified. 'The Roumanian Democratic Popular Republic has been declared,' he recorded in his diary and expressed the view that it would have been better if his son had not returned home rather than have signed away his birthright. 'I cannot bear the thought,' he wrote somewhat piously, 'that my son as Sovereign should have put his signature to such a document.' He made the interesting point that a King was a better safeguard of democracy than a President, who was a party political figure. Michael, his father believed, had given authority to the establishment of a republic that would effectively kill Roumania.

25

A Bad Shock

Carol bought a villa in Estoril in Portugal, where he made friends with another deposed King, Umberto of Italy, with the Count and Countess of Barcelona, and the Comte de Paris, among other exiles. He set up a court with the faithful Urdarianu still acting as Lord Chamberlain and head of his household.

He and Princess Elena became familiar figures in Estoril. They lunched every Sunday in the same hotel, were occasionally to be seen in the casino and were such frequent patrons of the local cinemas that the managers reserved the same seats for them. Carol particularly enjoyed listening to music and was as absorbed as ever with his stamps. When in 1950 he sold part of the valuable collection to help meet his heavy expenses, he was in close contact with the Royal Philatelic Society in London, and even the Sultan of Johore, obviously aware of his interest, sent him some new issues.

His most frequent correspondent at this time was Friedel, his German cousin Prince Friedrich, who kept him fully informed of the affairs of the Hohenzollerns, but Carol continued to keep in touch with world personalities, although increasingly they were royal figures rather than statesmen. Haakon from Norway, Leopold from Belgium, Gustaf Adolf from Sweden, Juliana from the Netherlands, Paul from Greece, Elizabeth and Philip from Britain – these were the signatures on telegrams he received, usually in reply to a greeting from him. One message that especially delighted him was a telegram in 1949, signed Michael and Anne, announcing the birth of a daughter. He may not perhaps have realized that he was already a grandfather, for the author of this book had been born to his son by Ioana Lambrino, one year before! Also to be found among his private papers is a personal letter dated 25 February 1952 from the present British monarch, in her own handwriting, thanking Carol for his letter of condolence upon the death of her father, King George VI.

There were suggestions in 1949 that Carol and his beloved Duduia were going to divorce, which had no real basis, although he may have been concerned at her extravagance at a time when he was temporarily in slightly straitened circumstances. To confound these rumours and to declare their love for each other publicly, the couple arranged a religious marriage ceremony in August of that year in their villa. Father Martinian Ivanovitch, head of the Roumanian Church in Paris, was brought from France specially for the occasion, in case there was any doubt in Orthodox eyes about the validity of the Brazilian marriage. The bride, only one month short of her fiftieth birthday, looked at least fifteen years younger. She was married in white and looked dazzlingly lovely with her red hair and full red lips beneath a veil of Alençon lace, which fell to the ground behind a beautifully made and obviously expensive satin dress with lace bodice. Standing beside her in a morning suit with white tie, Carol looked serious and somewhat drawn in comparison.

It may be that, already in 1949, he was not a well man, but there was no indication of any health problem until early 1953. According to Monique Urdarianu, he complained of chest pains early in March of that year and visited a Lisbon clinic for a cardiography examination. The medical report, dated 15 March, gave him a clean bill of health.

Less than three weeks later, on Good Friday, 3 April, Carol complained of a sudden pain in his left side and arm. A doctor was called who found the patient seemingly well. 'Don't worry about me,' Carol is supposed to have said, 'look after the Princess who has had a bad shock.' She was to have an even worse one, for while the doctor was still in the room, Carol suddenly died.

On 10 March my father had sent Carol a telegram to say that his mother, Carol's first wife Ioana, was dying, but he never received a reply. The message was found in a drawer after Carol's death. There is no way of knowing whether Carol actually saw it or whether, perhaps because he was unwell at the time, it was deliberately kept from him. By an irony of fate, Ioana Lambrino, whom he had never forgiven for suing him in Paris, died exactly one week before him. Is it too fanciful to ask whether news of her death could have brought on his own heart attack?

Carol was only fifty-nine when he died. His last and greatest love, who was then fifty-three, survived him by twenty-five years. They had been together for twenty-eight years and he had been willing to sacrifice almost everything for her. His funeral was her last great occasion. There being no Orthodox Church in the country, the Portuguese government, in view of Carol's relationship with their royal family, allowed his body to rest in the Royal Pantheon at the São Vicente monastery, besides those of the Kings of Portugal.

President Salazar also provided a full military escort for the funeral, which took place on 7 April. It was well attended by close friends and members of the diplomatic corps, but only Prince Nicolas of Carol's immediate family was present. He came, he said, out of duty. Elisabetha, who herself died three years later, may not have been well enough to travel. Mignon, who said she was too distressed to go to Lisbon herself, sent her son, Prince Andrew of Yugoslavia. It was not easy for Ileana to make the journey in time from America and Michael excused himself by saying that he could not leave his wife while she was expecting a baby.

King Carol's widow was a very different woman from the one who less than four years earlier had made such a glamorous impression in her white wedding dress. Now she wore no make-up and was shrouded from head to foot in black. She was in tears throughout the funeral and had to be supported out of the monastery at the end of the ceremony. Whatever terrible things had been said about her, or still remained to be said, one fact is incontestable: she had a remarkable power over one man in particular and he happened to be a King.

He was a King whose life was in many ways stranger than fiction, who found himself squeezed between Hitler and Stalin, but who ironically will probably be remembered not for his political struggles but for the women in his life. However one assesses Carol, as man or King, one fact stands out clearly and speaks strongly in his favour: while he was around, the Roumanian profile was high throughout the world and Roumania meant something on the international scene.

Select Bibliography

Benger, G., *Rumania in 1900* (Asher & Co, London 1900)

Bocca, Geoffrey, *Kings without Thrones* (Weidenfeld & Nicolson, London 1959)

Bolitho, Hector, *Roumania under King Carol* (Eyre & Spottiswode, London 1939)

Callimachi, Princess Anne-Marie, *Yesterday was Mine* (Falcon Press, London 1952)

Cars, Guy des, *Les Rois de Coeur* (Laffont, Paris 1965)

Cartland, Barbara, *The Scandalous Life of King Carol* (Muller, London 1957)

Daggett, Mabel Potter, *Marie of Roumania* (George Doran, New York 1926)

Dillon, E J., *The Inside Story of the Peace Conference* (Harper, New York 1920)

Dimancescu, D.D., *King Carol II and the British Press* (E.T. Heron, London 1939)

Easterman, A. L., *King Carol, Hitler and Lupescu* (Gollancz, London 1942)

Elsberry, Terence, *Marie of Romania* (Cassell, London; St Martin's Press, New York 1972)

Ferris, Paul, *The House of Northcliffe* (Weidenfeld & Nicolson, London 1971)

Fischer-Galati, Stephen, *Romania* (Prager, New York 1956)

Hill, Captain George A., *Go Spy the Land* (Cassell, London 1932)

Hoven, Baroness Helena von der, *King Carol of Roumania* (Hutchinson, London 1940)

Lambrino, Jeanne, *Mon Mari le Roi Carol* (Calmann-Levy, Paris 1950)

Lee, Arthur Gould, *Helen: Queen Mother of Roumania* (Faber, London 1956)

Marghiloman, Alexandru, *Note Politice 1897–1924* (Bucharest 1927)

Marie, Queen of Roumania, *The Story of my Life* (3 vols) (Cassell, London 1934–5; published under the title *Ordeal*, Scribner's, New York)

Moats, Alice-Leone, *Lupescu* (Holt, New York 1955)

Pakula, Hannah, *The Last Romantic* (Simon & Schuster, New York; Weidenfeld & Nicolson, London 1984)

Pridham, Sir Francis, *Close of a Dynasty* (Wingate, London 1956)

Rommenhoeller, C. G., *La Grand Roumanie* (Nijhoff, The Hague 1926)

Seton-Watson, R. W., *A History of the Roumanians* (Cambridge University Press 1934)

Sitwell, Sacheverell, *Roumanian Journey* (Batsford, London 1938)

Spector, Sherman David, *Rumania at the Paris Peace Conference* (Bookman Associates, New York 1962)

Index